T0369077

# Man on the Move

## *The Pete Friesen Story*

PETER ROWLANDS

iUniverse, Inc.
New York   Bloomington

Copyright © 2009 by Peter Rowlands

All rights reserved. No part of this book may be used or reproduced by any means, graphic, electronic, or mechanical, including photocopying, recording, taping or by any information storage retrieval system without the written permission of the publisher except in the case of brief quotations embodied in critical articles and reviews.

iUniverse books may be ordered through booksellers or by contacting:

iUniverse
1663 Liberty Drive
Bloomington, IN 47403
www.iuniverse.com
1-800-Authors (1-800-288-4677)

Because of the dynamic nature of the Internet, any Web addresses or links contained in this book may have changed since publication and may no longer be valid. The views expressed in this work are solely those of the author and do not necessarily reflect the views of the publisher, and the publisher hereby disclaims any responsibility for them.

ISBN: 978-1-4401-5955-8 (sc)
ISBN: 978-1-4401-5957-2 (hc)
ISBN: 978-1-4401-5956-5 (ebook)

Printed in the United States of America

iUniverse rev. date: 10/01/2009

Library of Congress Control Number: 2009932774

*for our fathers*

Forgive your parents and believe in yourself.
Pursue your God-given talents and never, never give up.

Peter D. Friesen

# Contents

Introduction                                    xi

1.  Born to Move                                1

2.  On the Move                                 17

3.  The Inventor                                31

4.  The Builder                                 47

5.  Highland Park                               61

6.  Joliet                                      77

7.  Chicago                                     91

8.  Minneapolis                                 105

9.  The Unlucky Fifties                         119

10. San Antonio                                 131

11. The Association                             147

12. The Consultant                             161

13. Block Island                                175

14. Cape Cod                                    193

15. Detroit                                     213

16. Minneapolis Encore                          229

17. Hatteras                                    249

18. Newark                                      277

19. Lynden                                      295

Epilogue                                        315

Acknowledgments                                 317

# Introduction

Subsequent to completion of his motion picture, entitled *Pete: Moving Man Made Mountains,* Pete Friesen pursued the idea of a written story about his lifetime—a human journey filled with enormous challenges on the way to awe-inspiring success. Building on a skeleton of technical material compiled by Pete's friend and colleague, Carl Tuxill, and enthusiastically promoted by Pete's personal assistant, Cheri McKay, the story was developed over a two-year period with the able assistance of the writer's encouraging editor and companion, Susan. With the exception of those credited otherwise, all photographs herein are courtesy of Peter D. Friesen.

Pete Friesen survived an oppressed childhood by understanding and by forgiving. He also learned to think laterally, decades before many of us knew what that term meant. Then, with little formal education, he became an inventor and innovator in the business of relocating very large buildings. During his busy lifetime of breaking trail and exploring new territory, Pete ignored the critics behind him and overcame the obstacles before him; he acquired faith in his own being and he enjoyed the freedom to think for himself. Although he has seen the depths of despair and suffered heartbreaking personal loss, Pete Friesen has never, never given up.

Following this story's concluding chapter, a dedicated section attempts to acknowledge scores of people across North America who generously contributed to the project. Most often reached by unsolicited query, many authors, engineers, architects, historians, and librarians freely provided scads of vital information; so too did representatives of heritage and cultural preservation societies in the largest cities and in the smallest of communities. Of course, this story would not be possible without the participation of Pete's many contacts within the structural-moving industry, the vast majority of whom were more than eager to help Pete's legendary story into print. As stated by several of them, "Pete Friesen has already forgotten more than most of us will ever know."

Far from being a how-to book for would-be house movers, this story explains structural-moving technique in everyday language, and it is hoped that uninitiated readers will enjoy the description of the process as it gradually unfolds with ever-increasing complexity. It is also hoped that experienced structural movers will happily abide pages of attempted technical description while enjoying further insight into a very human being who helped shape their industry. Being neither a comprehensive personal biography nor a complete vocational record, this book endeavors to convey Pete's message of hope and inspiration by presenting an overview of his fascinating life in context with his string of amazing achievements.

The terms *think it through*, *visualize*, and *derch denche* (from Pete's childhood German tongue) all have the same meaning; they are included within the text on a recurring basis to remain connected with the origins of Pete's journey and to encourage formation of visual imagery from the written words. Pete's presence and personality are often seen through one of his favorite expressions: "Lo and behold!"

# 1

## Born to Move

Dietrich heard his dogs begin to bark and knew trouble was coming his way. With a tender and knowing squeeze of his wife's arm, he slipped out of bed and hurried down the back stairs and out a kitchen window. Running through darkness on the familiar route to his barn, he could hear horses approaching the front of his home. After crawling deep into the bowels of a corner hay-pile, he heard loud voices coming from the house—obviously shouts. It was the bandits all right, and they were looking for him again. Dietrich dug in deeper.

Within minutes he heard the scuffling of boots on the barn floor and heard the murmurs of angry men who began shouting his name, ordering him to come out, making sure he knew they meant business, serious business. Dietrich fought to control his breathing while his heart raced to the sounds of a pitchfork and, probably, rifle barrels probing his cover. "Be still, my son," Dietrich prayed to himself. "They won't harm the women and children … it's you they want." After a quarter hour that seemed like four, he heard the small mob of interlopers shuffle from his barn. Relative quiet seeped in with a returning sense of calm. Dietrich swallowed hard and gave thanks.

Crack! Crack! The sharp sound of gunshots filled his body with fear. His relaxing heart rate reversed its trend and, like a spring-loaded switch, his entire being snapped back to a state of high tension. He had to fight his impulses and remain quiet. He had no choice. "Stay where you are," Dietrich cautioned himself. "It's probably a ruse; they want to see you. They probably want to kill you."

Long after hearing horses and men retreat through his front gate, Dietrich crept cautiously toward the rear of the house and peered in. There were no bandits to be seen, but his life was irrevocably altered by what he saw. His beautiful wife, covered in a veil of blood, lay cradled in the arms of a house servant while his two sons wept in misery. Aganetha was dead; so too was the child she carried. While Dietrich Friesen had survived another close encounter with rebellious Russian bandits, his life was robbed of its most precious element. Overwhelmed with grief and remorse, he was on the edge of hysteria. Though running on a full tank of red-hot anger, he stayed reasonably calm while adjusting to the new reality. Obviously, women and children were no longer immune from the brutality of would-be revolutionary bandits. To survive in a country falling toward anarchy, Dietrich still had to think about his two sons and himself.

While this was one of many such tragedies in a country being consumed by bloodshed and chaos, the murder of Aganetha Friesen in May 1918 signaled the end of a prosperous and civilized era for the Mennonite people living in Ukraine. Originating in northern Europe, where they had broken away from the Catholic church in the 1600s, Mennonites were known for their close-knit farming communities and for their pacifist beliefs. In 1789, promising religious freedom in exchange for their successful agricultural methods, Catherine the Great invited a large number of these devoutly religious people to settle the recently acquired Ukrainian territory. Encouraged by low taxes and exemption from military service, several generations of Mennonite farmers enjoyed bountiful success on the good soil, using the machinery they invented and cheap labor. Both born in the 1880s and married in 1909, Aganetha (*née* Heinrichs) and Dietrich Friesen were two such Mennonites. Employing as many as thirty servants and fieldworkers on their large estate, they were raising two healthy young sons in their very comfortable home when World War I erupted in Europe, shortly followed by the Bolshevik Revolution. Up until then, Dietrich Friesen seemed to have it all.

War and revolution devastated the Russian people and their economy. While the countryside was being scoured for available men and food for the front lines, major cities were immobilized by striking workers and confused leadership. The social order was disintegrating and food grew scarce. In desperation, those in charge threw open many jailhouse doors and released hundreds of prisoners back into the chaos. Soon, the prisoners formed small armies of "revolutionary" bandits, who swept through the countryside, raping and pillaging villages and enclaves. Often joined by former servants and peasant workers, these anarchist bandits began taking revenge on aristocratic landowners while taking control of their farms and industries. By early 1918, marauding gangs of horsemen were on the loose in the Ukraine region, plundering the remains of a once-rich agricultural area. Notable among these bandits was a cruel leader named Machnov, who left few Mennonite farmers untouched.

Immediately following his wife's murder, Dietrich Friesen and his two sons, Jakob and Kornelius, began sleeping outside their home in fear of the bandits' return. Soon giving up their home as lost, Dietrich and his boys became aristocratic vagabonds, staying with friends and relatives. Food was scarce and violence was escalating. Almost a year after giving up their estate, Dietrich and his sons were in hiding at the home of Dietrich's mother and aunt a few miles away. On a black night in May 1919, Machnov and his gang rode up to the senior Friesens' home and barged in. After forcing everyone present into the basement at gunpoint, the bandits opened fire and killed them all. Dietrich's mother, one of his brothers, two of his sisters, and his youngest son, Kornelius, were all murdered. Dietrich and his eldest son, Jakob, who had been sleeping in the barn, escaped the slaughter undetected and fled into the forest.

In this rural community, near the village of Ekaterinoslav, lived a young Mennonite woman named Anna Unger. As a young girl, Anna had seen her mother die of typhoid. By age fourteen, she was taking care of two younger sisters and seven brothers. Having taught herself to sew and cook, young Anna worked as a seamstress and threshing-crew cook on Dietrich Friesen's estate, where she was always eager to take care of young Jakob while—as she confessed to a friend—being somewhat attracted to Dietrich. Having been overwhelmed by the Bolshevik rampage, Mennonite society was in disarray. By 1919, Anna had lost her father, one brother, and a brother-in-law to the bloody swirl of revolutionary violence. Although the war in Europe had ended, rebellion in Russia went on, transforming into a decade of general anarchy and social disarray. Along with the Friesen property, many other estates and business opportunities had been abandoned. Having fled from Machnov and his anarchist bandits, many Mennonites were now living together with friends, family, and former servants; frequently, they were crowded ten or more people to a room. After living in such circumstances for more than a year, Anna Unger and Dietrich Friesen were married in May 1921. Although living conditions remained cramped and fear-ridden, Anna and Dietrich happily embarked on their new life together. They welcomed their son Peter into the world on March 31, 1922.

The violence continued. With Russia transitioning into a communist state, crime was rampant while political and military leaders fought for control. Fearing for their lives, Anna, Dietrich, Jakob, and Peter departed their homeland in July 1923. By foot and by *leiter-wagen*—a horse-drawn cart without any suspension—they traveled five hundred miles to Moscow. Invited onboard for the long exodus was Cornelius Heinrichs, a teenaged nephew of Dietrich's first wife, Aganetha. Having recently deserted his military duties, Cornelius traveled as the Friesens' eldest child. Once in Moscow, the blended family joined a multitude of other refugees on the eight-hundred-mile train journey to the Baltic seaport of Riga.

Although not as physically exhausting as their wagon journey, the train ride out of Russia was almost as difficult and even more stressful. All too often, officials of dubious affiliation examined travel documents and interrogated travelers while other uniformed officials of dubious intent demanded money or precious possessions in exchange for safe passage. Affluent modern air travelers who bounce comfortably between continents with minimum restrictions can only imagine such a journey. Most of us cannot imagine the emotional pain felt by people who are forced to abandon their homes and communities. The trauma caused by unwilling forfeiture of property and lifestyle can only be truly known by those who are dispossessed. Of course, Anna and Dietrich Friesen were also living with an additional fear: if Cornelius's desertion was found out, the whole family would be denied passage or perhaps sentenced to something more terminal. When that particular train to Riga finally chugged across Russia's western border, the emigrant voices onboard, Mennonite and otherwise, erupted into hymns of praise and gratitude.

From Riga, the Friesen family traveled by steamship to Southampton, England, and then across the stormy North Atlantic to the city of Quebec in eastern Canada. After immigration proceedings and a required period of quarantine, they boarded a train for another long ride. This one carried them almost three thousand miles through seemingly endless forest and across an ocean of grassland to the western province of Alberta. Here, on the high-elevation Canadian prairie, Dietrich Friesen found work helping farmers with their fall grain harvest. Soon, with assistance from other Mennonites, the Friesens were able to occupy the Blair farm, seven miles outside the town of Provost, where a large and comfortable house on 480 acres of reasonably fertile soil provided a fresh beginning. By this time, brother Cornelius was properly known as cousin Cornelius. With help from the cowboy vernacular, Jakob transformed into "Jake," and baby Peter grew into little "Pete." In 1925, Anna gave birth to a daughter, Frieda, who was eventually joined by three more sons—Bill, Walter, and John. Anna and Dietrich had survived cataclysmic social change before abandoning their homeland to begin a new life in a strange new country. Whatever else might be said of Dietrich Friesen, it is important to recognize his dedication to family and to appreciate the strength of his will. It was not easy letting go of his homeland, and it was not an easy task to safely escort his young family almost halfway around the globe. Some men would not have even tried.

However, Dietrich was not a happy man. The raw and windswept prairie farm was a poor substitute for the lush refinement of his Ukrainian estate. He was finding little fun in leading ornery horses through deep snow and mud while remembering his full-time, uniformed carriage driver and all that shiny brass and well-oiled leather he had once owned. Without thirty servants to command, harvesting grain and shoveling manure became painful chores. Of course, he was also haunted by the loss of Aganetha—the love he could not forget.

Dietrich, perhaps unconsciously, took out much of his anger on young Pete. For example, on the family's very first Sunday at the Blair farm, Dietrich entered the house and saw three-year-old Pete on his mother's lap, listening to her stories about Jesus and heaven. Erupting in anger, Dietrich forbade Anna to ever take Pete on her lap again unless she did the same for Jake. Being a large lad of twelve, Jake probably enjoyed very little time on Anna's lap, and therefore his younger brother also spent little time there. In fact, while known for his ability to recall events from his earliest years later in life, Pete could not remember receiving childhood hugs from either of his parents. He did remember, however, that his father always seemed to treat him more harshly than he treated Jake. Not only was Pete forced to do the most menial farm chores from a very early age, but he was also subject to regular, sometimes daily, beatings at the hands of an irate father. On one occasion, triggered by his four-year-old son's quick tongue, Dietrich knocked Pete unconscious with a piece of firewood. When Pete came to and asked why, his mother could only caution him to respect his elders.

Fortunately, a caring aunt took Pete on her knee and explained the family situation: Dietrich had never forgotten his love for Jake's aristocratic mother, Aganetha. Pete's mother, Anna, was a servant, and therefore Pete was a servant's son; Pete was regarded as a servant and was treated as such. Although such thinking is unacceptable today, Dietrich was a child of an earlier time; his approach to family affairs and workplace management was learned at home from a very early age. Although extremely harsh on young Pete, Dietrich cannot be painted entirely black: he and Anna raised five healthy children, all of whom became highly educated and highly successful in their chosen fields. Also, as Bill, Walter, and John would later attest, Dietrich did mellow with age; their father was not in the habit of beating them. However, during his early years on the Canadian prairie, Dietrich Friesen was still hooked to his past and unable to shake his upbringing as an aristocratic Mennonite. This man, who once had the best of everything in Russia, was now a dirt-poor Canadian dirt farmer trying to support his family on a windswept farm with a windmill that constantly broke down.

Whenever the windmill was out of service, young Pete was given the chore of pumping water by hand. To do this, the little guy had to reach above his head and pull down the large pump handle before hauling his small frame up and across it, leveraging his full body weight for each downward stroke. This awkward activity could go on for many hours before the windmill was back in operation. Usually, Peter Unger, one of Anna's brothers who lived nearby, would climb up and replace the ever-failing part in the machinery atop the windmill tower's wooden platform. Dietrich would not climb the tower and declared it off-limits for his children.

Unfortunately, one windmill failure occurred while uncle Peter was away and not expected back for another week. Although Dietrich could see no problem with little Pete pumping water for seven days, the exhausting prospect had little appeal for little Pete himself. To avoid seven straight days of chin-ups, seven-year-old Pete Friesen disregarded his parents' "no tower" command and decided to fix the windmill himself.

Although he had never ventured onto the tower's steel truss-work, Pete was familiar with the replacement part and had often watched his uncle perform the repair. With the part in one hand, Pete began climbing. As he had seen his uncle do, he clambered up the outside of the steel framework, only to experience great difficulty pulling his small body onto the overhanging wooden platform near the top. After finally struggling onto the small ledge, Pete was dismayed to discover he could not reach the windmill mechanism—the repair platform had been constructed with adults in mind. Undaunted, Pete began to shinny up the topmost section of an exposed tower leg. Holding the new part while reaching toward the old one, Pete lost his grip on the steel truss and slipped off. Falling through the center hole of the platform, he managed to grasp its inner edge with his free hand and hold on.

For two years, Pete had been responsible for milking the family's five cows and had already developed the hand strength of a teenager—lucky for him. Later in life, Pete would often credit his survival to the tough teats of one particular Ayrshire cow. For the moment, however, he was grasping the platform with one hand and clutching the spare part with the other while dangling like a rag doll in the prairie wind. He considered his plight. Should he allow himself to drop to the ground through the center of the framework and risk being impaled on the pump stem directly below? Should he try swinging to one side before letting go, in hopes of missing the pump stem, the pump stand, and the well hole? How accurately could he control a thirty-seven-foot free-fall? What if he contacted the inside of the tower framework on the way down? If he shouted for help, Mother would come running, but she would then scream for Father, who would come running only to scream at his son. Pete felt certain of one thing: under no circumstances would his father dare to climb that windmill.

Pete carefully swung the precious part up onto the platform and then edged himself, hand-over-hand, along the inside rim until he reached one of the framing legs. Lo and behold, it had a small ladder attached! Once safely on top, Pete sat down on the platform and hung his head through arms circling his bent knees. "*Dummkopf!*" he shouted at himself just once, as his father would have done. Then, accompanied by his own questions, the child retreated into his first and most illuminating bout of introspection: "Why did I have such a

clumsy hold of that tower and let myself fall? Why didn't I climb the
ladder through the center of the platform in the first place? How many
foolish moves have I made here?"

Pete sat there for a very long time, entertaining thoughts old and
new. Gradually, he came to understand his moment of failure and was
able to put it behind him. With a quieter mind, Pete began to visualize
every move necessary if he was to reach the windmill mechanism,
replace the faulty part, and descend the tower safely. Feeling composed
and resolute, Pete methodically installed the replacement part and was
rewarded by the windmill running smoothly again. A bold young boy
had climbed the windmill tower that day—a much wiser boy came
down. As he would forever profess, this windmill epiphany blessed
little Peter Friesen with a guiding principle he would follow for the
rest of his life: *Derch denche*—think it through, visualize. In fact, Pete's
freshly discovered visualization technique would one day guide him to
the very peak of his chosen profession. Meanwhile, he was on his way
to school for the very first time.

First days at school can be an exciting challenge for anyone; young
Pete's were more challenging than most. As luck would have it, a school
district boundary ran adjacent to the family farm. For little Pete, this
boundary seemed to run along the wrong side of the Friesen home.
Instead of going to a nearby schoolhouse with his Mennonite relatives
and playmates, he would have to trudge four miles to the one-room
Rosenheim School where he was the only German-speaking Protestant
among almost fifty English-speaking Catholic children. When asked
his name, Pete replied with the only English words he knew: "Tommy
Tinker had a dog; it said 'bowwow.'" The fun was on! Needless to say,
little Pete was the odd boy out, a curiosity who bore the brunt of many
practical jokes and much teasing. The preferred goat of the school
bullies, he was also everyone's favorite target during the long snowball
season in cold Provost, Alberta. Although small of stature, Pete was a
tough little nut with a strong body and powerful will. Motivated by
his recent windmill experience, he became keenly interested in school
curriculum while maintaining his new penchant for thinking things
through. Losing several front teeth along the way, he gradually fought
his way through the teasing and bullying stage and, by grade seven, was
acknowledged as the toughest kid in the school. In the process, he also

became the school's best student, excelling at spelling and mathematics. Grade eight was as far as he would get.

In retrospect, the dividing line of the school district boundary was a blessing for Pete. Not only did he learn English and the Catholic catechism as a result, but he also gained understanding of the invisible barrier between ideologies and an appreciation for the similarities of all people. On his favorite horse, Lady, or on foot, the lengthy journeys to and from school offered time for reflection—time to think things through—while providing valuable space between Pete and his father. With wind in his face and snow in his hair, he had deer, hawks, and coyotes to study while his heart rejoiced at many a crimson sunset on a vast and distant horizon.

Back on the farm, things were not going well. Although Dietrich's farm was finally showing some returns, the hard-won gains were poorly invested. Motivated by his aristocratic tendencies, Dietrich had contravened Mennonite doctrine and invested heavily in the stock market, where wheat futures were his preferred option. In 1929, Dietrich's world came crashing down with the stock market. Pete remembered his father coming home about midday with the sad news and both his parents spending the afternoon on their knees in the living room, praying for forgiveness and mercy. Although some of their prayers may have been answered, their situation began to unravel. Confronted by poor weather along with diminished finances, the Friesens were soon at risk of losing their equipment and possibly the entire farm. They held on, through years of poor crops and marginal finances, until 1934.

"[The dust storms] came like a dark cloud as wide as the fields," recalled Pete. "All of a sudden, I couldn't see my hand stretched out in front of me. The air was filled with dirt." Quickly and completely, gale-force winds blew away the Friesen's drought-ridden crops along with any chance these prairie food producers might have had against the Great Depression. Their livelihood had vanished. Once again, Dietrich Friesen was forced to abandon his home and move on. Packing up what they could, the Friesen family followed their blowing soil eastward to Saskatchewan, where they began all over again on a quarter section (160 acres) of land near the community of Glenbush.

As a sturdy twelve-year-old, Pete was now able to participate in adult chores: for hours on end, he wielded a heavy adze while squaring wooden timbers for his family's new house and barn. Although his formal schooling had ground to a halt, Pete's practical education continued; as well as learning to operate and repair most of the farm's equipment, he took responsibility for running the entire farm when Dietrich became disabled by an accident with a heavy sled.

During the next winter, Pete occupied many hours dismantling and repairing his father's cherished but broken grandfather clock. Using only the material at hand, Pete carved out a new gear from a block of hardwood and returned the clock to full operation, albeit briefly. Wooden gears proved to wear out much faster than metal ones. While he may have appreciated Pete's effort with the clock, Dietrich never once let it be known; his anger remained and the beatings continued. The rough treatment no longer bothered Pete. For some time now, he had been thinking things through, and he had come to realize the problem was his father's and not so much his. Persevering through difficult economic times, Dietrich continued to speak wistfully about returning to Russia if he could, seemingly unaware of how much more painful life had become for relatives and friends who had remained behind.

When he found his new house timbers to be infested with beetles and deteriorating rapidly, Dietrich became completely disenchanted with homesteading in the land of beaver and bison. Through friends, he learned of opportunities in a Mennonite community in southwestern British Columbia. Thus in 1936, Dietrich Friesen and his family abandoned yet another farm and moved on. Near the small village of Yarrow in the lower Fraser River valley, the family took up residence in a 320-square-foot grain shed that just happened to be devoid of insulation. This wasn't California, but compared to Glenbush, it was close enough. After renting this farm for some time, Dietrich was able to purchase the nearby Klassen farm in 1938. While drainage of surplus water was a constant concern on this low-lying and extremely fertile soil, it was a problem far more bearable than the relentless wind that had scoured the Provost prairie dry.

While working full-time on the farm, Pete promoted and refined the mechanical aptitude that seemed to come naturally. After watching an electrician work nearby and memorizing information from his invoices and waybills, Pete received permission from Dietrich for a day off, and he headed into the big city by bus. While in Vancouver, Pete found his way to the electrical supply shop and purchased all supplies needed to successfully bring electricity to his family's home, to their barn, to the horse corral, to the chicken coop … and to anything else within the capacity of a surplus Model T ignition coil. As might be expected, Pete's electro-mechanical tendencies did little to alter Dietrich's low opinion of him.

One day shortly thereafter, Dietrich entered the barn and became instantly dissatisfied with what he saw as a lack of progress on farm work. As his temper rose quickly to tantrum level, Dietrich took a familiar swing at sixteen-year-old Pete with a clenched fist. It was the last of those punches he would ever throw. Ducking the intended blow, Pete picked Dietrich up by the lapels of his coat and threw him down across a feed trough. "You will never hit me again!" Pete stated emphatically before walking out of the barn. Although now larger and stronger than his father, Pete refrained from taking physical revenge on his tormentor. Nevertheless, the point had been made, and both men accepted the inevitable end of a long and dysfunctional period.

*The Friesen family in 1938. Seated from left: Anna, John, Jim (son of Katie & Jake),*
*Walter, and Dietrich. Standing: Pete, Frieda, Bill, sister-in-law Katie, and Jake.*

It was now 1939 and another war was on the horizon. Wanting to serve his country while remaining true to his Mennonite beliefs, Pete enlisted as a Conscientious Objector (CO). In this manner, he could participate in his country's war efforts without bearing arms and without inflicting violence on his fellow man. When the time came to leave his family and farm at eighteen years of age, Pete enjoyed a first hug with his father. The times were changing. Once on CO duty, Pete was employed for several years at a variety of tasks on the home front: felling trees, bucking firewood, and cutting railroad ties before becoming a railroad "gandy dancer"—a worker helping pound heavy railway ties into place. Later, while assigned to a cement plant on Vancouver Island, he worked one short, unexpected shift steering a coastal freighter that was short of crewmembers.

In 1942, a change in government policy finally permitted objectors to join the regular Canadian Army. With his heart set on becoming a medic in the paratroop corps, Pete signed up. The army had other plans for Pete. After basic training camp, it assigned Pete to medical corps headquarters at Camp Borden, Ontario, where he served as a typist and bookkeeper. The army was indeed wise. Pete's razor-sharp mind was soon recognized as an invaluable asset: he could memorize mounds of information and easily remembered birth dates, birthplaces, and regimental numbers for many, many soldiers. While so employed, Pete was privy to medical records where he made an astonishing discovery: Conscientious Objectors, a very small percentage of its total complement, collectively raised the total army IQ by a full 5 percent!

Pete's army training then took him to the city of Saint John, New Brunswick, where he became enamored with the possibility of being transferred overseas as a German-language interpreter. While in Saint John, contrary to the dictums of his Mennonite pastors, Pete joined the local Soldiers' and Airmen's Christian Association (SACA) and freely mingled with those of other Christian beliefs. "Any friend of Jesus is a friend of mine," Pete always maintained. Among many new friends at this servicemen's club, Pete was especially attracted to a beautiful young woman with a gorgeous smile: Edith Markham was one of the civilians who volunteered to play piano at the SACA hall. Learning that Edith was in fear of a man who had been following her, Pete and several of his new buddies volunteered to escort her home each night, taking turns on a rotational basis. While it remains unclear where the idea originated or how it evolved, Pete soon became the designated escort of choice. Three months later, on August 12, 1944, Edith Markham and Peter Friesen were married. Needless to say, Pete's desire for an overseas posting had vanished long before. Given Pete's marital status and a war winding down, a gracious commanding officer offered him the option of staying home in Canada. Pete happily accepted.

*Wedding Day—Edith and Pete on the church steps*
*with Edith's parents and brother—August 12, 1944.*

Before being discharged, Pete and his colleagues participated in an army-sponsored course designed to assist their transition back to civilian life. When the curriculum asked each participant to create a personal motto, Pete came up with this one: "If a door of opportunity opens, I will always walk through." While he knew where he wanted to go after leaving the army, Pete Friesen had no idea where this new motto would eventually lead him.

Immediately after his honorable discharge, Pete brought his young bride to British Columbia where, with financial help from the Soldiers'

Settlement Board, he bought the same small dairy farm that his family had worked years before. This low-lying land on Sumas Prairie near Yarrow provided hands-on experience with waterpower and hydraulics. As Pete remembered: "All across the property, from the front to the back, I built trenches and installed culverts so I could retain water and irrigate the farm. Also, I could open the dam and let the water out quickly for harvest purposes. It allowed me to grow early potatoes and gave me good crops."

Edith, excited by the opportunity to learn a new culture, began to learn German to help her fit in with the German-speaking members of their Mennonite Brethren Church. Pete became a leader among the younger church members and was the host of a weekly radio program called *Voice of the Redeemed*. Pete was producing a thirty-minute broadcast with singing groups and guest speakers every Sunday. Unfortunately, many church members were unimpressed. First and foremost was their discomfort at having a non-Mennonite in their midst. Although a devout Christian, Edith was a devout Anglican, and this fact caused her to be isolated within the church and the community. So-called "mixed marriages" were still *verboten,* and church elders schemed to remove Pete and Edith from the congregation. Having borrowed heavily to buy his first herd of dairy cattle, Pete was temporarily unable to contribute the obligatory 10 percent of gross income to the church. While promising to eventually make full reimbursement, Pete refused to sell off his cattle in order to pay the tithe. Pete was immediately excommunicated from the church.

Excommunication hurt deeply, and it was particularly hard on Edith. Sharing her husband's strong Christian beliefs, she had been eager to share his church and excited to experience a different form of worship. For a time, she felt partly responsible for her new husband being kicked out of his own church. Preferring not to linger around a problem, Pete and Edith simply moved on to another place of worship where the teachings of Jesus seemed to be lived as well as preached. They would have far greater challenges to overcome in their lifetimes. Ironically, an epilogue to this unhappy drama occurred about twenty years later when a deacon of the Mennonite church sought forgiveness from Edith and Pete; he had lied about them to their congregation.

Meanwhile, as a recently demobilized serviceman, Pete was

allowed to purchase power equipment that was still too scarce for general distribution. He bought a chainsaw to cut firewood. One of his neighbors, Nick Thiessen, owned a small house-moving business but wanted to go into the logging business. He proposed that Pete buy his house-moving outfit, using the chainsaw as down payment. Thiessen allayed any concerns Pete had about a lack of experience in moving houses by promising to help out with Pete's first project. The deal was made, and they shook hands. Peter D. Friesen became proprietor of Western House Movers. The door of opportunity had opened, and Pete walked through.

# 2

## On the Move

Alongside his small dairy farm, Pete now had a small house-moving business to provide income. At least that was the plan. In January 1948, Pete borrowed $1,882 from the Canadian Bank of Commerce that, together with his surrendered chainsaw, would complete the deal for purchase of Western House Movers (WHM). According to the bill of sale, WHM's assets were as follows: "1930 six-cylinder Kenworth truck with hoist, serial number 177878A, motor number 4723, model BA6; full set of moving trailers; 8 timbers & blocking; 4 pump jacks; 7 screw jacks; 1 hydraulic jack; cable & blocks and 2 logging chains." This rudimentary set of house-moving equipment seemed barely adequate on paper, and it wasn't much to look at either. The truck and hoist were very experienced and tired-looking; the "full set" of moving trailers were more accurately seen as three ancient steel dollies with solid rubber wheels. However, it was enough gear to get started with, and Pete was happy to have it.

While awaiting his first moving job, Pete took on as his business partner another neighbor, Nick Dyck, who was studying to become a preacher and needed extra income. About a month after acquiring WHM, Pete embarked on his first project: a small house in the town of Langley needed to be moved thirty miles east to a site about five miles past the city of Abbotsford. Nick Thiessen had obtained this job and scouted the route before Pete purchased the company. Pete Friesen got his farm chores organized and his house-moving equipment together. Because of prior commitments, Nick Dyck could not be present, but his brother Arthur was available and happy to help. As stipulated by the purchase agreement, Thiessen would meet them next morning at the jobsite and help get them started.

Fuelled by their thermos of coffee, the idle young men of WHM passed most of the morning in casual conversation while waiting for Thiessen. Eventually, their talk turned to the subject at hand. While neither had any previous experience, Arthur and Pete began sharing what they knew about moving buildings. As their discussion gradually drifted toward the particular building they hoped to move, their eyes wandered over the assemblage of trucks and equipment before them. Being intelligent men with considerable mechanical skill, they began examining their tools more closely while speculating on their uses and relationships. Before lunchtime arrived, Arthur and Pete decided to begin the house-moving operation without help from Thiessen. They would simply use their own imaginations, employ the tools available, and think things through. Arthur and Pete put on their caps and went to work.

Although not a large building, this house would contain a lot of lessons for the two would-be house movers, situated as it was in a confined space on challenging terrain. The forty-foot-long structure was oriented north-south on a hillside sloping down eight feet, west to east, across its twenty-eight-foot width. While pondering the challenging exterior scenario, Arthur and Pete began carrying crib blocks into the basement. No matter what happened later, they would first have to work underneath in order to jack the house free of its foundation. While stacking up blocks to form crib piles on which to support their jacks, Arthur and Pete soon became painfully aware that they were short of crib blocks. Their supply, one pickup truck load, would not be sufficient for the amount of cribbing necessary to lift and load this house. The adventurous young men of WHM had much to think about while lugging their supply of heavy blocks into the basement.

They soon had a plan. Using axe and saw, Arthur and Pete cut two large openings in the pony wall at each end of the house between the floor joists and the stepped-down foundation wall. With help from the hoist on their worthy truck "Ken," they inserted their two forty-foot-long wooden beams through these openings and rested them on four stacks of crib blocks erected in the basement. Although these beams were too short to include end walls of the house, their placement immediately beneath existing main floor beams was safe and efficient. Planning to use one under each end of each beam, the avid entrepreneurs selected four of their best-looking jacks. Recognizing the need to disconnect all utility feeds to the building and remembering to remove the hardware holding the structure's baseplate to the foundation, the young men began jacking up their very first house. By quitting time, Arthur and Pete had the company's first project jacked clear of its foundation and up one extra "shot."

As soon as he arrived home that evening, Pete telephoned Thiessen to inquire about his state of health. It seemed to be pretty good. "Did you get started?" asked Thiessen, after making his apology.

"Yes, we did," said Pete.

"Good!" exclaimed Thiessen. "I'll see you there tomorrow."

Although their second day on the job would have its share of challenges, Arthur and Pete were encouraged to see their forty-foot beams still supporting the house along its north-south axis. Without waiting for Thiessen, they began refining their previous day's plan while incorporating renewed emphasis on crib block conservation. Knowing they had insufficient blocks to consider using the down-sloping terrain east of the building, the two movers-in-training soon agreed to sidestep the house directly west and lower it lengthwise onto dollies before towing it straight out the narrow lane. Although the higher ground there would demand fewer crib blocks, an outlying utility shed would severely restrict their maneuvering room. Thiessen was a no-show again, but Arthur and Pete didn't wait around this time. Back inside the basement, Arthur and Pete moved the two southern crib piles slightly north where they would support the south ends of both load beams which were then repositioned to protrude slightly beyond the north wall. By situating their north-end jacks there—outside the north wall, on slightly higher, albeit sloping terrain—Arthur and Pete would require fewer blocks from their meager supply. The westerly, uphill ends of the first course of blocks were allowed to rest on the ground while their downhill ends rested on a north-south block placed across the hill … so far, so good.

To further compensate for the lack of blocks, the ingenious young men decided to insert two forty-foot support/slide beams underneath and horizontally perpendicular to their two main load beams. Calculated to align with eventual placement of their transport dollies, one support/slide beam was positioned about ten feet north of the south cribs and the other was positioned just south of the north wall. The midpoint of both support/slide beams rested on the west foundation wall, allowing their eastern ends to extend slightly beyond the east main load beam. Here, simple blocking would provide almost twenty linear feet of support during jack changes, helping to further conserve their limited supply of blocks. Extending twenty feet beyond the west wall, the two support/slide beams and minimal cribbing would allow the house to slide west where it would then be lowered onto the transport dollies. Having seen no sign of Mr. Thiessen, Arthur and Pete resumed the task of jacking "their" house higher, in accordance with their plan.

At this point in WHM's first house-moving experience, the learning curve of its two workers took a sharp turn upwards as their house took a sudden drop downwards. As they soon understood, the soil under the uphill ends of the north cribs compressed and caused both those outside jacks to lean uphill until they finally kicked out from under the load beams. Fortunately, the house and the load beams were caught by the slide/support beams without damage. The boys were lucky. If the house had kicked in the opposite direction, both it and Pete's house-moving career would likely have come to a sudden and sorry end. Now, it was simply a matter of keeping the structure going in that westerly direction far enough onto the support/slide beams to install the dollies for transport. "This house-moving thing is interesting business," thought Pete, after slowing his heart and catching his breath. "We've already learned about compression and how to 'kick a load' sideways."

As soon as he arrived home that evening, Pete telephoned Thiessen to inquire about his state of health. It seemed to be pretty good. After another apology, Thiessen asked, "Did you get any more done today?"

"Yes, we did," said Pete.

"That's good!" exclaimed Thiessen. "I'll see you there tomorrow."

Partway through the following day, another day of hucking blocks and jacking beams without the tutelage of Thiessen, Arthur remarked dryly, "That Mr. Thiessen, he sure must be a busy fellow."

"Yeah," quipped Pete, "he must be getting good use outta that chainsaw." Anchoring old Ken on the western edge of the work site, Arthur and Pete used its hoist and chain to slowly pull the house structure west along the support/slide beams. By the end of day three, the industrious lads of WHM had winched their house a considerable distance to the west where it was now almost ready for transfer to the dollies.

As soon as he arrived home that evening, Pete telephoned Thiessen to inquire about his state of health. It seemed to be pretty good. "Sorry I couldn't be there," said Thiessen. "Are you ready to roll?"

"Almost," said Pete.

"Very good!" exclaimed Thiessen. "I'll meet you at ten tomorrow morning in the government office and help you with gettin' the highway permit."

At noon the next day, Pete was still cooling his heels—and temper—in the government office. Before closing up for lunch, a considerate clerk asked Pete what he was doing there. Upon hearing his story, the clerk took it upon herself to help him complete the requisite application form. Before closing time that day, Pete headed out the door with the necessary moving permit in his hand.

As soon as he arrived home that evening, Pete telephoned Thiessen to inquire about his state of health. It seemed to be pretty good. "Sorry, I couldn't be there," said Thiessen. "Did you get the permit?"

"Yes, I did," said Pete.

"Good, good!" exclaimed Thiessen. "I'll come by and help when you start actually moving the house."

On the morning of the appointed day, a flurry of activity surrounded WHM's jobsite. Policemen, telephone linemen, electric utility workers, and others were busy preparing for Arthur and Pete's handiwork to be moved under the wires and onto a road leading to the main highway. Having never put a house on dollies before and never having towed anything like this awkward-looking load before, even the imperturbable young men of WHM were a little nervous. If policemen and utility workers had seen the previous day's events, they too would have been nervous.

The day before, Arthur and Pete had had quite an adventure. After the house was slid along the support beams onto dollies, it almost filled the narrow space between its foundation and the outlying shed, such that

Pete could not make the necessary hard right turn to get the truck onto the narrow driveway before heading down to the street. The perceptive young men both noticed how the driveway ran steeply downhill for a spell and how its eastern edge dropped off at alarming angle. Only by repeatedly inching backward and forward with alternating, opposite direction, full steering wheel travel could Pete finally squeeze their load free of its tightly confined space. Only by brushing the house up against its old foundation and hanging the truck's front bumper over the precipice did Pete finally maneuver his long load onto the driveway. Immediately after gaining the driveway, the heavy house on dollies began creeping downhill and soon attempted an illegal right-side pass of its pull-truck. Fortunately, all hitches and welds held firm during the resulting jackknife, but the new formation continued flying downhill like a flock of backward geese. Pete's out-loud prayer was answered when the front dolly tires contacted the rear truck tires to put brakes on the runaways, none too soon. The entire assembly slid to a merciful stop at the bottom of the driveway. There was a lot of sweat on the workmen, but no damage to their load.

"What d'ya think, Art?" asked Pete, after slowing his heart and catching his breath. "Should we think about using some sort of sea anchor on these downhill runs?" This was another important, early learning experience. From then on, whenever the road grade presented any significant downhill threat, Pete would always use a holdback vehicle behind towed buildings.

The next day, with a crowd forming and the authorities in attendance, the apprehensive young men of WHM were hoping for assistance from a neighbor who had house-towing experience. While spending considerable time re-inspecting already well-inspected tie-downs, Arthur and Pete repeatedly glanced over their shoulders. Finally, an exasperated police officer gave Pete some firm encouragement: "Get on the road in five minutes, or I'll shut you down!"

After looking once more for the face of Thiessen in the growing crowd, Arthur turned to Pete and asked, "What are you waiting for, boss?"

Meeting Arthur's eyes and swallowing hard, Pete yelled to no one in particular: "Let's roll!" Cautiously, Arthur and Pete gently edged their awkward-looking ensemble—a big old logging truck sporting an A-frame tail, pulling a forty-foot wood-frame house sitting atop a triangle of ancient rubber-wheeled dollies—out onto the road leading to the main highway. Accompanied by police escort, Arthur and Pete's curious load trundled slowly north toward the Trans-Canada Highway. At a turnout adjacent to the highway access point, the entire entourage came to a halt. On the highway immediately ahead, they saw a bridge with railings higher than the bottom of their extra-wide load. Pushed once again by necessity, the inventive young men of WHM quickly solved the problem by jacking up the house and inserting stacks of crib blocks between the load beams and the dollies. However, soon after starting to move forward, Pete noticed one of the dollies was wandering off from under the house and rolling one of the load beams with it. "Whoa!" shouted Pete. "Stop and try backing up a bit." Fortunately, this timely little maneuver put both dolly and beam back into alignment.

The innovative duo then hustled off to a nearby building supply store and returned with two lengths of 2x12-inch lumber. After being cut to the required twelve feet, these boards were then inserted between the two load beams, one in the front and one behind the rear dollies. By chaining the beams tightly to these spacer planks, Arthur and Pete intended to prevent any more "dolly wandering" under their house. The jury-rig worked. Once across the bridge, they jacked their precious cargo back down onto the dolly bunks and proceeded on their way. Experience being such a great teacher, the conscientious young men had an easier go of things when their newly developed bridge crossing technique was required for a similar situation a few miles down the road. However, time was rolling along faster than their wheels. Five miles short of their destination and only a few minutes ahead of a late-afternoon curfew, they pulled their big rig off the Trans-Canada Highway and into a roadside rest area for the night.

As soon as he arrived home that evening, Pete telephoned Thiessen to inquire about his state of health. It seemed to be pretty good. Pete's words were well chosen and few in number.

"Sorry," said Thiessen, "I'll come and show you how to put the house in place tomorrow."

While not surprised by the absence of Thiessen next morning, the stalwart young men of WHM were certainly surprised by seeing the winding road to their destination. Sumas Mountain Road appeared to be much steeper and narrower than remembered from their scouting mission. This would be challenging, to say the least. Along the road's inside edge, a steeply rising embankment restricted maneuverability; along the outside edge, a steep drop-off threatened them with "unrestricted vertical acceleration of the gravitational kind." Terminal velocity was undesirable at this point, even after their long, slow journey. They knew they needed to think this through, and they did. Once again, necessity blurred the distinction between genius and common sense. With immense risk to themselves and to their precious cargo, Arthur and Pete repositioned the outside dolly in toward the centerline of their load and, by so doing, allowed much of the building's mass to extend out beyond the precipice while keeping all their dolly wheels on the narrow road. Realizing there was now too much weight on the outside dolly, the courageous young men also repositioned the inside dolly in toward centerline to keep their load in balance. However, even with the outside dolly repositioned, the uphill house movers often needed to set blocks into the shoulder of the road to support the outermost dolly wheel.

It took a full day of hucking blocks and swallowing fear, but the relentless young men of WHM slowly and steadily cajoled their precious cargo uphill to its intended place of rest. Once "their" house was finally coaxed onto its new foundation, Pete shook hands with Arthur and declared: "Now we're officially house movers."

Professional structural movers everywhere are entertained by this story about the initial house move by Pete Friesen and Arthur Dyck in 1948. Not only can other movers relate to the trials and tribulations of the process, but they also understand the mental machinations necessary to move past one new obstacle after another. In this particular house move, they can also see how one untrained practitioner taught himself the technical basics before starting on the road to invention and innovation. Following Pete's learning curve up Sumas Mountain, many people recognize the origins of his three-point loading system as well as the seeds of major computer programs he would later design. The courage and imagination demonstrated on this first house move would accompany Pete throughout his long and challenging journey. To help get the proper perspective on this initial project, it is interesting to note that this particularly difficult stretch of Sumas Mountain Road has long been abandoned and closed to motor vehicle traffic of any kind. Although no one knows exactly what Nick Thiessen was up to all those days, he and Pete maintained a lifelong casual friendship.

The second moving project for Western House Movers was also a small job containing big lessons. One day, having gone to obtain permits for the impending move, Pete arrived back at the site just in time to see the wooden granary shed they had raised come thudding down. Similar to their previous such experience, the screw jacks had kicked out from under their main load beams, and the building had "kicked" quickly to ground. This time, however, Arthur was trapped underneath, crammed between floor joists. Using the truck hoist, Pete quickly freed Arthur and was very happy to discover that neither his colleague nor the building was damaged beyond repair. Having no broken bones, Arthur made no bones about continuing the work. The unflappable young men soon completed their second move without further incident.

Obviously, these neophyte house movers had much to learn about height stability, and Pete got to thinking. From this particular "thinking it through" came Pete's 3:1 safety factor ratio, whereby one horizontal unit should not support more than three vertical units. For example, a four-foot square crib pile could be safely built to a height of twelve feet without jeopardizing its stability. This safety factor was designed into the replacement jacks that Pete would soon manufacture, and it remained an underlying principle in all of his subsequent work. Meanwhile, Pete Friesen was a twenty-six-year-old farmer and entrepreneur, taking care of his business on the land while keeping his eyes open for buildings to move. During the preceding two years, Edith had delivered their first two children—sons Peter and Paul. It was now the spring of 1948, and heavy rains were beginning to lash the southwest coast of British Columbia.

It had to happen sooner or later, and it happened soon after WHM had successfully completed its second project. Heavy spring rains washed a deeper-than-usual snowpack down from the interior mountains into the province's largest river system. Rudimentary dikes along the river's lowest reaches were soon breached. Though this was not the highest water level ever recorded in the Fraser River—that was recorded in 1894—the infamous Fraser River Flood of 1948 was a very close second and was far more destructive. The Fraser River floodplain was living up to its name. Beginning in late May, the deluge overcame more than a dozen diking systems and soon put more than fifty thousand acres under water—one-third of the arable land in the floodplain. Along the Fraser's last one hundred miles, from the town of Hope to its mouth near Vancouver, decades of settlement and development were suddenly inundated with water, silt, and debris. Both transcontinental rail lines and many major roads were put out of service. Small cities, towns, villages, and hundreds of farms were completely flooded. In 1948 currency, the damage amounted to CA$20 million. Sixteen thousand residents had to be evacuated.

Suddenly, there were hundreds of houses to be moved, and WHM was flooded with more business than it could handle. Full of confidence from their initial success and inexperienced enough to underbid every potential contract, the enterprising young house movers received the lion's share of flood-related work, moving scores of buildings onto higher ground or back behind hastily repaired dikes and levees. Federal and provincial governments would eventually spend CA$160 million to construct 375 miles of new and improved dikes. As well as keeping his farm going, Pete was busily "on the move" with flood-related projects for more than a year.

In 1950, at the Alliance Church, Pete met a fellow house mover who wanted to retire from the business. At age twenty-eight, Pete Friesen acquired Modern Building Movers (MBM) from a Mr. Entz and began doing business under that name. As well as gaining another complete set of equipment, Pete acquired a larger company with government contracts already in place. Numerous buildings, some as far away as Williams Lake in the British Columbia interior, were in need of timely relocation to make way for upgrading of the main highway running north through the Fraser River's canyon and beyond.

The Fraser Canyon has always been a tough place for humans to travel through. Fur trader and explorer Simon Fraser would have been the first to agree, having remarkably lived to tell the story of his wild canoe and cliff-scaling adventure down it in 1808. The river was bridged for the first time in 1862 as part of a crude wagon road built, with considerable loss of human life, to support increasing traffic between the coast and the goldfields at Barkerville in the interior Cariboo region. With further loss of human life and great hardship, the two transcontinental railways notched their tracks into the canyon walls in 1884 and 1911 respectively. Following portions of the old wagon road, the first terrifying automobile route through the canyon was constructed in the early 1920s, and at the same time, the only bridge across the river was replaced with something more substantial. Fuelled by the irrepressible relationship between humans and automobiles, this new "easy" route to the interior gradually sprouted tourism and a growing population. Following World War II, an unprecedented era of expansion prompted a major upgrade of the Fraser Canyon Road to new "highway" specifications and status.

Enter Pete Friesen and company. The first task for MBM was the relocation of a house and barn in cattle ranch country near the town of Williams Lake, three hundred miles upstream of Abbotsford. It would have been extremely difficult, if not impossible, for Pete and his long, heavy moving equipment—fifty-foot load beams and much more—to negotiate the Fraser Canyon Road at any time. With tunneling and other heavy construction in progress, MBM and its oversized loads were restricted from using this route altogether. Instead, Pete and his crew were compelled to detour two hundred miles east through the Okanagan Valley.

After one hundred miles of tight mountain highway across the Cascade Range, the brakes were beginning to smoke on Pete's big truck and its oversized load. A thirty-minute cooling-off period was deemed necessary before descending the very long and steep grade leading to the city of Penticton, on the valley floor one thousand feet below. Perhaps more than a cooling-off period should have been considered. Soon after starting downhill, the brakes failed completely on Pete's truck. Downshifting like never before, Pete gear-jammed all the way to first gear before reaching the bottom of the big hill. Pete arrived safe and the tractor-trailer remained upright. Inspections there proved his truck's drive shaft and rear axles to be twisted beyond repair and its transmission seriously damaged. The ensuing one-week delay for repairs was a small price to pay for the preservation of a human life.

After they resumed their journey northbound on Highway 97, Pete was in the passenger seat when he became acutely concerned as the same truck gained speed down a steep, seven-mile grade toward the town of Cache Creek. Motivated by recent experience, Pete cautioned his driver to slow down a bit. However, when the clutch was released in an attempt to downshift, the pistons met the valves inside the over-revving old engine and it became instantaneously useless; everything and everyone "rattled" the rest of the way down the hill. It was a two-week delay to locate and install a new engine for this hard-luck truck.

Finally, they were back on the road and traversing the wide-open ranch country on the high, rolling plateau. However, the fun was not quite done. Approaching Williams Lake, Pete was again riding as passenger when, after descending a series of steep switchbacks, the driver lost control of their big rig at a rough railway crossing and they rolled ignominiously into a roadside ditch. Hopping uninjured from the truck cab, Pete and his colleague saw their beams and other equipment scattered far and wide. While his crew shuttled their strewn equipment to the jobsite on other vehicles, Pete phoned home and ordered another vehicle from his recently expanded inventory. Although somewhat behind schedule, the actual move of the house and barn in Williams Lake went off without further problems.

However, back on his farm, things were not going well for Pete. Ever since the big flood of 1948, his farming enterprise had been going downhill, but not for neglect or a lack of effort. Farming was certainly in his blood, and he did not lack for determination or innovation. Admired by many other farmers in the area, Pete's system of dams and irrigation channels allowed him to grow cash crops as well as maintain a dairy herd. He started out with one acre of raspberries and one half-acre of strawberries, producing good financial returns. Later, when a representative from the local food processing company suggested pole beans and corn, Pete obliged and began reducing the size of his dairy herd. Pete soon had fifteen acres of potatoes, fourteen acres of corn, and ten acres of pole beans under cultivation. With experimentation, he proved he could get two crops a year by following his early potatoes with late plantings of turnips and beets that would be overwintered inground and sold for seed in the spring. As it was, his early potatoes were yielding five or six tons per acre and fetching $120 per ton at market. By 1952, Pete's dairy herd was reduced to only a few cows as he committed to growing more fruit and vegetables.

Soon after and without warning, European producers had flooded the berry market and dried up that source of income. Now things really began to go sour on Pete's farm. The very next year, wet spring weather delayed a potato crop, and it came in too late to compete with imports from south of the border. Undeterred, as they were all certified seed stock, Pete stored his potatoes over winter. He had turnips and sugar beets to plant, as well as pole beans to harvest. Although he was able to get his turnips and beets into the ground, he got in just one picking of beans before they were all flattened by a severe windstorm. His first planting of corn did not take because of the wet spring conditions, so he had to replant. This second planting of corn matured late and was destroyed by frost. Then came torrential winter rains and overflowing riverbanks. Pete's dams and the municipal water pumps in Sumas Prairie were all powerless against such a flood; his farm remained under six inches of water for several weeks. Farmer Pete lost all his turnips and all his sugar beets. With all local farmers facing the same problem, there was no market for his certified seed potatoes, and they were dumped back onto the land whence they came. Someone or something was telling Pete Friesen that he was not destined to be a farmer. In one short year, he had lost everything ... well, not quite everything. Pete was still blessed with a healthy family, and he had a source of supplementary income as principal owner of Modern Building Movers.

Immediately after the flood of 1954, Pete sold the farm and moved his young family fifty miles west into the city of New Westminster where he committed to his house-moving business full-time. Edith remained busy with three young sons in their urban home. Born in 1950, Jon was now four years old; Paul was now seven years and Peter eight. As their grandfather had done several times, their thirty-two-year-old father had also left his farm and moved on.

# 3

## The Inventor

Pete's full-time house-moving career began slowly as increased competition accompanied a leveling-off period for provincial infrastructure expansion. Contracts became few and far between for Modern Building Movers. Frustrated by the lack of work for his two crewmen, Vic Janzen and John Loewen, who had relocated to New Westminster with him, Pete occupied himself with maintenance and repair of his equipment. Without an advertising budget, MBM's future did not look promising. During this first year of "full-time" business, Pete developed his trendsetting "Bathtub Marketing Technique." Because the few telephone queries he did receive seemed to always occur during his daily ablutions, Pete began spending more and more time in the bathtub.

Perhaps his growing reputation as a clean operator with well-maintained equipment prompted the big call that finally came in. The call was from Simpson Sears, the large department store chain, needing some houses moved to make way for a new shopping mall in nearby Burnaby. MBM was soon on the job, and Pete was soon taking his turn under one of the houses, slithering around in the mud while attempting to crank the screw jacks a quarter-turn at a time as the crib blocks retreated into the mire beneath. It was dirty and frustrating work done mostly in a prone position, shuttling penguin-like from jack to jack, crib pile to crib pile, with barely enough room to achieve enough leverage. "What are you doing under there? What's taking so long?" queried Vic and John. This particular form of professional cheerleading was, of course, vital to the operation, and it would continue as long as necessary, regardless of which players were on the field.

As Pete's mud-spattered face finally emerged from the darkness, his colleagues were temporarily stunned to hear him say: "Look, guys, next year we'll have a jacking unit that will work automatically. Then, we'll hardly be under here at all."

Seeing nothing but humor in the moment, Vic and John exchanged wide-eyed grins as Pete climbed back into the daylight. "Sure, boss," chided the bemused young men of MBM. "We'll just stand around in our muddy boots and watch the houses levitate."

On his way home to the bathtub, Pete chuckled to himself: "Sure guys, give me a rough time ... but there's got to be a better way to jack up houses." Because of his general curiosity and his interest in most things mechanical, Pete had been keeping up-to-date with developments in the construction industry, especially advances in heavy equipment design. He had become intrigued by industry's transition to hydraulically powered machinery. High-pressure hoses, heavy-duty actuators, and powerful control rods were rapidly replacing the old cable, winch, and pulley systems that had traditionally controlled the business end of bulldozers, excavators, and the like. "Somehow," he figured, "this technology can be applied to the business of pushing up houses. After all, it's just a matter of applying a small amount of high-viscosity, pressurized fluid to a large piston surface that then does the heavy work." Pete was soon able to visualize a simple solution to the house-raising issue: "All we need is a tank of fluid, a pressure pump, some hoses connected to a bunch of those hydraulic jacks, and a way to get all the jacks going up and down at the same time."

Pete's great gift for visualization gave him the ability to see mechanical things in their simplest of forms. Since childhood, he had been taking apart machines, big and small, to see how they worked. Each little success nurtured more confidence to tackle more complex machines. He had a great imagination, and he was always willing to make an attempt. Given his mechanical aptitude and knowledge of house-moving, Pete had little doubt in his mind about the possibility of designing something to do the jacking "automatically." No doubt, he had already started thinking the subject through before making that bold, muddy-faced declaration to his co-workers. The fact that they teased him just made him more determined. *Derch denche!*

Pete had been teased before. The little German-speaking Mennonite kid had been teased mercilessly by the English-speaking bullies at the Rosenheim School. Perhaps Dietrich's early assertions that little Pete would never amount to anything were in the mind of the child who climbed the windmill one day and almost fell to his death with replacement part in hand. In any event, seven-year-old Pete Friesen had the will and presence of mind to carry a three-foot-long part up thirty-five vertical feet to repair a powerful mechanism he had never seen before. The same seven-year-old repaired the farm's grain binder when it proved too much for his father and older brother. Once, out of necessity, he repaired a defect in the grain-delivery component of the threshing machine; another time, he figured out how to fix the knotting mechanism that tied the grain sheaves together in the hay baler.

As a nine-year-old, Pete once "saved his day" by coming up with an original idea while rounding up horses far from home on a very cold winter evening. An uncooperative lead-horse moved away from every fence post Pete tried using to boost his small frame onto the horse's back. With no other boarding options available, Pete became legitimately concerned about his own survival while walking the horses toward home and struggling through shin-deep snow on a desperately cold, moonless night. Fortunately, when the herd stopped to paw and nibble around a remote granary, the young wrangler saw a wind-whipped snowdrift beside a grain shed. Of course, the lead-horse broke through when led into the drift and little Pete did not; he clambered onboard and rode the rest of the way home. While Pete Friesen did not invent the "snowdrift technique" for mounting tall, stubborn steeds on cold, starry nights, the experience certainly helped open his mind to unknown possibilities whenever again faced with trying circumstances.

The family's two-year tenure in Glenbush, Saskatchewan, was also packed with lessons and opportunities for invention. Certainly, during the first month—when the seven-member Friesen family was invited to share a three-bedroom home with a warmhearted family of ten—there were valuable insights into the nature of social order and interpersonal relationships. Tolerance and compassion became deeply imbedded in Pete's soul. During long periods of concentrated physical labor, there was ample opportunity for thinking things through. Also, by being invited into an adult world to help build the family home, Pete began learning what houses were all about.

When Dietrich decided to sell off several horses because of financial necessity and found himself short one complete set of harness, thirteen-year-old Pete decided to become a harness maker. The hide from one of their butchered cows was cut into strips, and Pete built a sewing stand—two short pieces of 2″ by 6″ lumber held vice-like by a nut and bolt on an old sawhorse. This invention held the leather in place while Pete sewed it length by length with heavy tarred string. The new harness was finished in time for spring planting.

Several years later, sixteen-year-old Pete utilized bits and pieces from a child's Mechano set to put an electric fence around the livestock enclosure on his family's farm in British Columbia. While farming in this same area after World War II, Pete designed and manufactured his own cultivator and a six-auger beanpole digger, both inventions being controlled from his tractor's pneumatic system. By then, Pete the designer had taken to drawing his plans out on restaurant paper napkins while drinking mugs of strong coffee. Not long thereafter, motivated by height-stability challenges as a neophyte house mover, Pete was again applying pencil to paper napkins—designing new screw jacks. He wanted something safer and more efficient than the old jacks that were making life so exciting for Arthur and him.

In 1948, twenty-six-year-old Pete Friesen designed and manufactured a new type of screw jack that was noticeably different and far safer than anything he had used before. This new jack's larger, 8″ by 14″ baseplate served as a flange-like collar that rested firmly on top of two crib blocks while allowing the threaded jack ram to protrude downwards between them. These larger baseplate dimensions improved the jack's overall stability and allowed more ram extension while remaining within Pete's self-determined 3:1 height-to-base safety ratio. Designed at home on the farm and manufactured locally, these jacks were almost too simple to be true, but they worked just fine.

With these new jacks, Pete improved operating efficiency and pushed the house-moving envelope for the first time.

Now Pete Friesen was contemplating another, even larger stretch of his imagination. Climbing from the bathtub and donning fresh attire, he stuffed a handful of heavily marked paper napkins into his shirt pocket and headed to downtown New Westminster to see his friendly bank manager. "Sure!" said Frank at the bank, after seeing Pete's ideas. "It looks good to me!"

"But I already have a lot of debt," cautioned Pete.

"Don't worry," countered Frank. "If you can find someone to build these things, I will make sure you get the necessary money."

After filing for patents on his designs for a "Unified Hydraulic Jacking Unit" and for quick-change hydraulic crib jacks, Pete ventured into Peters Brothers, a Vancouver manufacturing firm specializing in hydraulic equipment. Although both items were designed as separate functioning entities, Pete saw the jacking unit and crib jacks being combined into one efficient hydraulic system for raising houses. Predicated on widespread use of their in-stock components, Peters Brothers quoted Pete a cost of $13,000 to manufacture a prototype "Unified Hydraulic Jacking System," combining the proposed new jacks and jacking unit into one dedicated system.

With Pete's simple design and Peters Brothers' comprehensive inventory, it did not take long to assemble the necessary components. Pete had been doing his homework and already knew he was looking for a multi-piston reciprocating pump (as opposed to rotary or diaphragm) to pressurize his positive-displacement hydraulic circuit at 6,000 psi (pounds per square inch). By necessity, Pete's jacking unit had to be compact and portable. Therefore, he designed it with slave cylinders in circular clusters: one slave cylinder encircled by a band of six slave cylinders encircled by another twelve for a total of nineteen. The ends of the nineteen slave piston rods were then welded flush to an end plate on the master cylinder ram that would control them all at once. Fortunately, because of recent advances in heavy equipment technology, most of these components were readily available. Also now available was small-diameter, wire-reinforced, high-pressure rubber hose. To keep his system portable and efficient, Pete decided on a standard hose length of twenty-five feet; to each hose end, he secured one of the quick-change couplings that had recently come on market. Abrasion-resistant and flexible, these hose sections would provide valuable versatility in the supply of high-pressure fluid to his newly designed quick-change hydraulic crib jacks.

A technological generation beyond his screw jacks of 1948, Pete's new hydraulic crib jacks were designed to work with his new unified jacking unit. They were the many *hands* of Pete's unified system that would lift a building by transmitting the hydraulic power generated in the *arms* of the jacking unit. By necessity, these jacks had to be heavy-duty without being too heavy. They had to be strong enough to handle great pressures but light enough to be handled by one man. Pete also wanted to speed up the jack-change procedure between each upward push by the jacking unit. Similar to his screw jack, Pete's new hydraulic jack had a collar-like base that allowed the ram to protrude downward between the supporting crib blocks. However, in this new hydraulic jack, the ram was contained within a hydraulic cylinder that, as a unit, slid through the base. Designed with a ladder-like series of horizontal grooves in its outer wall, the hydraulic cylinder could be locked vertically in a variety of positions by retainer plates, incorporated in the jack base, being slid into the grooves. Repositioning the hydraulic cylinder to a higher position would allow another upward push with the ram without adding blocks to the jack crib. By locking the hydraulic cylinder in place, the jack could provide safety support even when hydraulic pressure was reduced or removed. Allowing for even finer adjustments of up to three inches, Pete designed a threaded screw cap onto the top end of each jack ram. Once all basic design concepts were established, it was time to concentrate on details.

The final specifications of Pete's patented Unified Hydraulic Jacking System would balance the size of off-the-shelf components with measurements attained at the working end. Given the standard crib block measurement of 6″ by 8″ and the desirability of alternating their sides on sequential course placements, Pete wanted ram travel of at least 14″ in his new jack. Allowing for crib compression and working room, he decided that seventeen inches of ram travel would be even better, and he designed his jack as such: a 17.5″ extension of the jack ram, plus a 15.5″ extension of the hydraulic cylinder above the 3″ jack base, plus a maximum 3″ extension of the 1″ head cap gave a total extension of 40″. It seems like a scary amount of altitude. However, Pete had already factored in a large, 11″ by 16″ base for his jacks, remaining happily within his mandatory 3:1 height-to-base safety ratio. Using quality off-the-shelf components, Pete chose jack cylinders with pistons 2.5″ in diameter. With hydraulic pressure of 6,000 psi, the jacks would produce thirty thousand pounds of force. Pete had a fifteen-ton jack in the making.

For the jacking unit at the supply end of his system, Pete found himself with a bit of a problem. Unfortunately, master and slave cylinders with the same 2.5″ piston diameter as the jacks proved unsuitable for the size and strength of the mounting assembly—they overstressed it. Therefore, Pete was forced to choose readily available actuators with 2″-diameter pistons for both master and slave cylinders. To compensate for their smaller circumference, Pete designed a longer, 22″ stroke for his slave cylinders, thus ensuring sufficient fluid for a full 14″ extension of the jack rams within their larger-diameter cylinders. Also part of Pete's design were eight common-pressure hydraulic lines that bypassed the unified pressure provided by the slave units. This supply-side common pressure was not limited by slave cylinder volume and would therefore enable the maximum 17″ extension of the jack rams. As such, main system common pressure could compensate for as much as 3″ of initial crib compression while still allowing a subsequent 14″ shot of unified pressure before having to reset jacks. Adjusting the grooved jack cylinders upward between shots would further postpone the need for additional crib blocks.

One fine day in May 1955, the master cylinder, the nineteen slave cylinders, and a pressure pump were all secured to the deck of a flatbed truck. A gravity-feed hydraulic fluid tank was mounted above the cylinders and a control panel was attached to the front end of the master-slave assembly. Seven months after the project began, Pete Friesen's compact and portable hydraulic jacking unit was ready to roll. With great relief, Pete soon headed back to Peters Brothers with more paper than napkins in his pocket. The money was paid, and the deal was done. The shiny new UHJS belonged to Peter D. Friesen, free and clear. Throwing on a load of his new quick-change hydraulic jacks and numerous twenty-five-foot lengths of high-pressure hose with the fancy new couplings, Pete took his hydraulic jacking unit out for a test drive. He could hardly wait to show his new toy to Vic and John, his skeptical crewmen.

"Congratulations, boss!" they chorused. "You did it, whatever it is." Of course, Pete's colleagues were well aware of what he had been so intently working on for the previous six months, but they were not about to let their boss off the hook so easily.

"Yeah, that's an impressive-looking piece of machinery," continued Vic. "Does it do anything?"

"Yeah, I've always wanted one of those," continued John. "Does it work?"

"Well, we'll soon see," said Pete, leading his colleagues to the control panel and pointing with his hand. "This lever controls fluid to the master cylinder. Selecting it down extends the master piston that mechanically extends the nineteen slave pistons that then supply an equal amount of pressure to all their hydraulic circuits at the same time …" After providing his colleagues with a thorough description of the machine and its capabilities, Pete concluded with, "So, by putting splitters into all the unified and common-pressure circuits, we can have fifty-four jacks under a building—all controlled by one man operating one machine!"

"It sounds good to me, boss," John chuckled, "as long as I don't get laid off."

"Yeah, we'd hate to miss the fireworks when you fire that thing up," laughed Vic.

"Well, you won't have too long to wait," said Pete with a smile. "We'll be using this jacking unit on our next job, and it starts tomorrow morning. And yeah, even though you have lousy senses of humor, you both still have jobs … that is, if you can figure out how to work those quick-change hydraulic jacks over there."

Excitement ran high next day at the jobsite as the two intrigued crewmen of MBM quickly built crib piles, placed the strange new hydraulic jacks into position, and laid out many sections of new rubber hose. Vic and John then exchanged quick smiles and shrugs while watching their mad professor approach the controls of his new machine. After making certain his hydraulic pump was running properly, Pete began his first-of-its-kind hydraulic jacking experiment. By raising the control lever, he directed pressurized hydraulic fluid to the *retract* end of the master cylinder piston. As the slave cylinder pistons retracted with the master piston, a vacuum was created in the slave circuits that quickly became filled, by gravity and suction, with fluid from the tank.

As instructed, Vic and John backed off a small nut valve at the base of each new crib jack, and soon all these jack cylinders also filled with hydraulic fluid by gravity. After all jacks and slave circuits had been preloaded in this manner, Pete closed the slave shut-off valves to prevent fluid from seeping back to the tank. Thus, with each slave circuit isolated while being full of hydraulic fluid, extension of the master and slave cylinder pistons would produce a similar *unified* pressure in all the slave circuits. Pete pushed the control lever downward and directed pressurized hydraulic fluid to the *extend* end of the master cylinder piston. Pushed by the master piston, the slave pistons extended within their cylinders and pressurized the fluid in their unified circuits. Up went the jacks. Up went the house. Up went everyone's arms.

"It's levitating! The house is levitating!" cried the impressed young men in self-mockery. "That's amazing, Pete," they added more seriously, while shaking his hand.

"You have created something totally unique and very, very special," said John.

"Yeah, boss," ventured Vic, "the house-moving business will never be the same again."

"Thanks, guys; it's fun working with you," Pete said with true appreciation. "But there is something we have to look at." Pete closed the master shut-off valve, locking everything in place with blocked pressure. The three of them then crawled underneath the building for a closer look. Although the system had worked according to plan, Pete had been disturbed to see some of the jacks come up more slowly than others. Also, contrary to hydraulic gospel of the day, his hoses had shown signs of expansion. Mildly concerned but undeterred, Pete helped his cohorts install safety blocking and then showed them how to quickly set the quick-change jacks in preparation for another lift. They jacked up that house in record time.

During the next six months, thanks to their new tool, the unified young men of MBM relocated more houses than previously thought possible. Although it was not perfect in Pete's eyes, his unified jacking system operated as intended. When he was not needed at jobsites,

Pete engaged in earnest dialogue with suppliers and manufacturers of hydraulic equipment, and it was soon obvious to all concerned that his trail-breaking innovation was advancing accepted hydraulic practice. Unlike the medium pressures and short hose lengths of heavy construction equipment, Pete's invention was operating at significantly higher pressures and over far greater distances. Yes, as Pete explained to all who would listen, contrary to popular misconception, hydraulic fluid *will* compress and yes, hydraulic hoses *do* expand.

Although his new jacks worked perfectly well, Pete knew it was unacceptable for a building to rise unevenly, if only for reasons of fluid compression and hose expansion. To overcome these inequalities, Pete began pre-loading individual jack circuits with variable amounts of pressure before applying overall unified pressure. Although time-consuming, this additional procedure produced a more uniform lift. Once all the jack circuits had been pre-pressurized in this manner, the hose expansion factor remained constant. The pre-loading procedure went like this: After loading the lines with fluid and after again filling all his slave cylinders by gravity and suction, Pete would very slowly apply pressure from the unified system, carefully noting which jack ram first moved upwards against its load. Once determined, this fast-jack circuit and its slight pre-charge of pressure would be isolated from the unified system by closing its slave shut-off valve. Continuing to slowly apply unified pressure while watching carefully, the crew would similarly isolate the next jack circuit that showed early upward movement. In this manner, each jack circuit in use would receive a specific amount of pre-charge. The last jack to show upward movement represented the heaviest load, the greatest length of expanding hose, or both—and it received the greatest amount of pre-loaded pressure. While leaving all relevant slave shut-off valves closed, the master ram was retracted to fill the master cylinder with fluid. Once main cylinder pressure was re-applied in *extend* mode, all relevant slave shut-off valves would again be opened, allowing unified pressure from the slave cylinders to initiate a more balanced lift. So it would continue, one unified shot at a time.

The big test for Pete's new jacking system came about six months after its maiden liftoff. Two very large and heavy structures associated with a lumber mill needed moving: one building was a one-hundred-foot-long laboratory; the other was a two-story office containing a two-story concrete vault. While already contemplating modifications to his new jacking unit, Pete immediately recognized this job as a true test for his jacking system design as well as for his relocation procedures. As almost every job seemed to, this one would also test his engineering intuition. The lumber company client was very agreeable, cutting and squaring two large trees to serve as the necessary extra-long beams. However, company management was less pleased with Pete's desire to give himself and his crew a day of rest on Sunday. Management made granting of Pete's request conditional upon Pete being the person to inform their employees about losing a full day's pay while their operation was shut down for his move on Monday.

Pete relented. The little Mennonite kid from the prairies was in the big leagues now, and at times, he had to rethink more than one aspect of his life—*derch denche*. As it turned out, this would be his first Sunday on the job, but not his last. As he began moving larger and larger buildings in bigger and busier cities, Pete often accepted Sundays as the best available moving day in terms of traffic and street closures. Although pushed to their limits on this job, Pete and his machine passed the test, successfully moving both difficult buildings in the allotted time frame. As a bonus, MBM now had sufficient funds to fully repay the manufacturing loan. It had been a busy and profitable six months. Pete's invention had proven itself and more than paid for itself. The world's first unified hydraulic jacking system was alive and well and working in British Columbia, Canada.

However, in Pete's mind, the UHJS was already an old tool ready to be re-invented. When the return of winter rains signaled the approaching slow season, Pete pulled his jacking machine off the road and began a comprehensive overhaul, actually a re-build, of the entire system. His quick-change hydraulic crib jacks were tested and true, but they required immediate attention. Signs of rust, inside and out, prompted Pete to clean and chrome-plate every operating surface of every jack cylinder and piston. He also insisted on uniform operating surfaces by imposing a maximum tolerance limit of three-one-thousandths of an inch on every one of them. On the jacking unit itself, the gravity-feed hydraulic tank was replaced with a much larger reservoir that, for space considerations, completely encased the master cylinder. To simplify the jacking circuit pre-loading procedure, additional hydraulic lines were installed from the pressurized main system through additional shut-off valves directly to each of the nineteen slave circuits. Thus, the time-consuming procedure to sequentially pre-pressurize each jack circuit was significantly quickened. By referring back to recorded initial pre-load pressures, the operator could now quickly pre-pressurize each jack circuit without having to employ gradual amounts of master ram pressure each time and without having to carefully monitor each jack for initial movement on every lift.

For its time, this Mk II UHJS was high technology. While hardly a sports car, the 1956 model UHJS was now self-contained in the box of a dedicated pick-up truck, and it definitely had a somewhat racier look. Pete and his well-convinced colleagues at MBM were back on the road, better than before. They also had a new motto: "Big or small, we move them all!"

In 1956, Pete Friesen created Modern Hydraulics Limited (MHL) to manufacture and distribute the new UHJS from a facility in New Westminster, British Columbia. Although Pete had built the UHJS for his own use, it was obviously a tool of interest for other building movers, and he was encouraged to make more units available. Pete was not then, and never would be, a person to withhold his knowledge and experience from others, especially from fellow house movers. The unified jacking system was a giant leap of technology, an innovation of revolutionary proportion that would forever benefit structural movers everywhere. It had to be shared.

Robin Renshaw, a young mechanical engineer, was hired on and given a 10-percent share in the company. He would facilitate production and help refine MHL's product. However, his first task was the transcription of those paper napkin files into acceptable engineering formats. Later, Robin would improve design of the jacking unit by organizing the snakes' nest of hydraulic hose behind the control panel into more manageable blocks. In 1958, the chassis beams of the jacking unit truck would be replaced with deeper beams allowing for installation of components beneath the deck surface. To improve accessibility, jacking unit controls were mounted on a side panel of the truck.

Bill Friesen, one of Pete's younger brothers, volunteered to spearhead the marketing department and began traveling throughout North America with their product. His reception was lukewarm in most places. Notwithstanding their unfamiliarity with hydraulics, many old-timers were also disturbed by the potential fourteen to seventeen inches of jack extension in the newfangled UHJS. Many of them were reluctant, if not unwilling, to accept more than six or eight inches of jack height as prescribed by their mentors. Although comprehensive safety testing would eventually dispel these fears, acceptance of Pete's invention was slow in coming. It took a number of years before his jacking machine and jack heights were finally accepted industry-wide. Continually updated and modernized, Pete's UHJS is used by almost every structural mover today.

The fact that such revolutionary technology originated in a small city in western Canada created inherent problems. The few Canadian firms that could afford the new equipment were often reluctant to buy anything unless it came from the epitome of progress, south of the border. Ironically, people south of the forty-ninth parallel were then balking at the exchange rate of 13 percent on the higher-valued Canadian dollar. Then as now, many American citizens simply mistrusted any so-called progress that came from north of the border. Those who gave Pete's invention a chance recognized a good thing when they saw it, and they wanted it—especially if they could capitalize on it. That's exactly what happened. Almas International, a structural moving company in California, purchased one of Pete's original jacking units and along with it, received joint-distribution rights with MHL for sales in the western United States.

Another American company, Belding Engineering of West Chicago, Illinois, having been around since 1878 and obviously not averse to new technology, recognized that good thing when it came by; company directors immediately ordered one of Pete's 1956-style unified hydraulic jacking units. They also immediately obtained Pete's partnership in future manufacture of such units in the United States.

In 1958, after building six of his unified jacking systems, Pete Friesen turned his attention from MHL of New Westminster to his stake in Modern Hydraulics Incorporated (MHI) of West Chicago. Chip Belding, Hartley Belding, and Herb Bromstad collectively owned 50 percent of MHI; Pete Friesen owned the other 50 percent and served as the company's first president. Honoring his original commitment, Pete gave 10 percent of his half-share to Robin Renshaw, who also joined the staff of this new company. However, Pete's involvement with Modern Hydraulics

Incorporated of West Chicago was short-lived. In 1960, believing his partners wanted to build a degree of obsolescence into the jacking-system design, Pete sold back his share of the company along with all of his patents. Pete Friesen had much on his plate, and he moved on.

On the subject of obsolescence: Frank Leonard, a house mover from Florida, met Pete at the 1996 International Association of Structural Movers convention and reported that, after thirty-eight years of reliable service, his original MHL-model jacking system from New Westminster was finally being overhauled for the very first time. General Motors of Detroit, having purchased several of these original units for separating molds and making patterns, tested Pete's jacks and found them exceptional: between the heaviest and lightest loads, variation of the fourteen-inch stroke amounted to only three-one-thousandths of an inch—the breadth of a human hair. As of this writing, the first unified hydraulic jacking unit built in 1955 remains in active service with Nickel Brothers House Movers in southwestern British Columbia.

*Fifty years after its manufacture, Pete's original unified hydraulic jacking unit is still on the job with Nickel Brothers House Moving in British Columbia—Peter Rowlands.*

After his newly modified jacking system had taken to the road in 1956, Pete turned his attention to another facet of his house-moving operation that could use improvement: the dollies.

The heavy, steel, single-axle, solid-rubber-wheeled dollies of the early days had already evolved, thanks to new metal alloys and reliable, air-filled tires. Lighter and stronger dolly units were on the road, each riding on dual axles and eight wheels. With the advent of hydraulic power, some of the newer dollies had articulating rear axles to improve maneuvering capabilities. They were better, but they could be better yet. Pete, with his inventive colleague and best friend, Karsten Vegsund, designed and built fully steerable dollies in which both axles could pivot beneath the load bed. Hydraulically controlled from the pull-truck cab, these innovative units gave Pete and MBM a vastly improved range of maneuverability that would prove extremely important on many of their subsequent projects. Once again, a Pete Friesen invention had pushed his company to the forefront of the best-equipped outfits in the structural-moving industry. Unfortunately, this particular new dolly design never did make it into mass production; the manufacturer dropped the ball, and both Karsten and Pete were too busy elsewhere to go looking for it.

By the early 1960s, Pete and his company had already moved several buildings by barge in the Queen Charlotte Islands and were contracted to move another fifty prefabricated houses up the coast from Vancouver for a mining company. Given the narrow operating window allowed by the tidal extremes in the area, Pete began looking for a more efficient way of transferring buildings between ship and shore. Yet again, Pete responded to necessity's push by inventing and building something. In this case, it was a totally new truck-trailer design that would do the ship-to-shore transfer and do it remarkably well.

The rear axles of a standard flatbed trailer were replaced by two of Pete's dual-axle, eight-wheeled, fully steerable dollies; they were attached, side-by-side, with one dolly under each girder of the trailer mainframe. On each side of the trailer frame, three hydraulically powered steel outrigger arms were installed where they could extend and retract horizontally; one arm was located behind and two were located ahead of the newly integrated dollies on both sides. Topping the whole thing off were six small hydraulic jacks, one being inserted into a pocket at the end of each outrigger arm. By these modifications, Pete had created a highly maneuverable, compact, and flexible 40' by 14' house-moving platform.

When backed underneath the broad side of a house sitting on cribbing, the trailer with extended outriggers and jacks would lift the house and transport it crossways. Backing onto the barge, the trailer would then lower the house crossways onto another set of cribbing. One barge could accommodate five regular-sized prefabricated homes in this orientation. Under normal sea conditions, one tugboat could comfortably tow two loaded barges. After all houses and cribbing were firmly secured, tractor and trailer were loaded onboard one of the barges for the long sea journey north. Several days later, Pete and three MBM crewmen flew north by chartered aircraft into the town of Stewart, British Columbia, to meet the tug and barges coming up Portland Canal, the ninety-mile fjord bordering southeastern Alaska.

As high tide approached its peak (twenty-five-foot maximum), Pete and his crew would go to work backing the tractor-trailer under each individual house, lifting it crossways off the barge and onto more cribbing at a staging area onshore. By quickly off-loading each house in this manner, all ten could be unloaded from two barges in one two-hour interval. During the low-tide cycle, all ten houses were then transported lengthways and lowered onto their foundations at the mining company's residential site. At the next high tide, twelve hours after unloading, tractor and trailer were secured back onboard the returning barge before Pete and crew reboarded the airplane to fly south to Vancouver. Repeated five times, this cycle would move all fifty homes. Designed and assembled by Pete Friesen, this structural-moving truck-trailer invention was immediately seen as another winner on the west coast. Wherever he went in life, Pete was destined to take along his good friend "inventiveness."

Pete's father, Dietrich, died of intestinal cancer in 1955 without once setting eyes on his son's engineering invention, the unified hydraulic jacking system, that was about to revolutionize an entire industry. Ironically, in designing this machine to "do it automatically," Pete was adhering to his aristocratically minded father's long-stated advice: "Organize the work for others so everything gets done and you have your *self* left over."

# 4

## The Builder

In 1954, when Pete and his family moved from their Yarrow farm and left the Alliance Church, he had become accustomed to donating generously, within the confines of his income, to church-sponsored missionary work. Joining the Evangelical Free Church after the move to New Westminster, he continued to donate generously from a gradually expanding income. It was discovered the Friesen family had donated more to that church's missionary convention funds than all other parishioners in the district combined. Pete was asked to serve on national, district, and university boards as well as on his own church board, while continuing to volunteer as Sunday-school superintendent and teacher.

In 1958, the same year MHI was formed in Chicago, baby daughter Joy joined one-year-old Eric, eight-year-old Jon, eleven-year-old Paul, and twelve-year-old Peter in the busy New Westminster household. It is easy to understand what Edith was doing; Pete, on the other hand, was all over the place. When he was not inventing something, moving something, or attending to business in New Westminster and Chicago, he was out doing church work. While modern hindsight might fault him for not making enough family time, one could never fault Friesen's commitment to his community. By the late 1950s, business was brisk, rising with the tide of Pacific Rim economic development and an ever-increasing population. Pete's Modern Building Movers had several jacking units and crews on the go, almost every day of the year.

The jobsite crews of Modern Building Movers were heterogeneous collections of workingmen. They spanned a broad range of ages and came from very disparate social, ethnic, and economic backgrounds—from hardened European immigrants to Bible-school students on summer employment. While his crews were busy on the road, Pete was busy running the company: scouting for new business and submitting the critical bids for prospective jobs. Although he had full-time office help and two estimators, he was occupied "in office" much of the time. Nevertheless, he also showed up on the job, especially difficult ones, and particularly for the move itself. Whatever else he might take on, Pete was always there to steer the dollies while keeping his experienced eye on the various obstacles to be found along the route. One of those Bible-school students who found summer employment with MBM between 1958 and 1962, Rod Wilson remembers it well: "Although Pete was a church-going man, there was nothing very churchy about the job or the outfit. However, I do recall a noticeable lack of profanity on the jobsite—unusual, given that house movers are stereotypically such a rough and ready, rowdy bunch."

As a relative youngster, Rod Wilson was impressed by the quality of men Pete hired, especially the "old sweats" like John Loewen and Vic Janzen who "like Pete, were very bright and could figure out almost anything." Elaborating on this point, Wilson provides insights about his foreman, Vic Janzen, who was older than anyone else on the crew. Having grown up in a Mennonite agricultural community in Ukraine, Janzen got drafted into the Russian army as a truck driver during WWII. After being captured, he was forced to serve in the German army. After the war, he made his way to Canada and started out as a sharecropping farmer in the lower Fraser Valley. Although he never had a course in engineering or anything like it, Janzen was known for his analytic turn of mind and prowess on the jobsite. "Although farm boys are well known to be broadly capable, Vic was a special case," continues Wilson. "He was bright and keenly observant. He was also tenacious, never giving up on a problem until it was solved."

Although highly occupied with administrative details, Pete knew his people and knew his jobsites were in good hands. According to Wilson, "Pete was very clearly an exceptional inventor and entrepreneur; he was also very much a man's man, a working stiff, a man who literally exuded strength. He may not have been doing much bull work anymore, but we all knew that he had, and there was no doubt in any of our minds that he still could." Rod Wilson knows whereof he speaks. He and his forty-year-old boss got into a "friendly" five-minute wrestling match in the office one day. Rod says he was glad to come away with a draw, but Pete claimed he went easy on the 6'5", 240-pound, twenty-year-old kid.

Now retired from the Department of Anthropology at the University of Alberta, Wilson still reflects warmly on moving experiences of the distant past. His most memorable story is about Pete and his crew moving a two-story, wooden hotel down a steep mountain road in the Coast Range, about one hundred miles north of Vancouver. A mining company wanted it moved onto their site near the village of Gold Bridge, probably as accommodation for their employees. As pointed out by Wilson, Pete's jacking system greatly increased the odds of successfully lifting the heavy, well-aged, complex structure, and his steerable dollies made negotiating the tight switchbacks on the mountain road seem an almost reasonable thing to attempt. "Although the structure itself was very challenging, the week-long job was straightforward from a worker's perspective," says Wilson, sharing his personal experience. "As always, the hardest part was getting started, digging out enough room to get the timbers in and the jacks started. We spent a lot of time on our stomachs in the dirt, and sometimes the days were measured in inches gained. But the main thing about it was being part of something that we were quite sure no other house-moving company would even attempt. Even though the trip down the mountainside was on the edge of madness, Pete and his crew got it done."

Apparently, more than one road leads to the edge of madness. Pete was always willing to share an experience from the late 1950s that he called "My Hard-Luck Story". The tale begins with a house on the west side of Vancouver, near the University of British Columbia, being moved to a location farther east and south, down near the Fraser River. The building was an ordinary story-and-a-half, wood-frame house about twenty-eight feet wide and forty-four feet long. The outside walls extended about two feet above the ceiling of the first floor where they met a steep roof. The relocation route was about six-miles long, and almost the entire distance was under an electric-bus trolley line. About three miles of this route went south down Granville Street, one of Vancouver's main thoroughfares, which presented a fairly steep downhill grade for the last mile to its destination.

In order to get under the trolley lines with the building on beams and dollies, Pete's crew had to make adjustments to its roofline. First, they separated the two sides of the roof at its ridgeline. Then, after removing the gable ends from the house, they lowered one roof section on top of the other by "hinging" their rafters at the eaves. With both roof sections lying flat, the "uncrowned" house met the exact height limitation specified by the electric company who owned the trolley lines.

Because bus service would be suspended while they were on the street, the MBM crew began moving the house at four o'clock in the morning. Traveling down the hill on Granville Street before five o'clock, they were surprised to see a trolley bus coming uphill towards them. The house movers immediately pulled their entourage over as far as possible and stopped. If the bus driver was surprised to see them and their house on the street, he gave no indication—the bus kept coming. When it pulled even with the middle of the house, the bus stopped suddenly, as if its driver had suddenly become aware of a drastic reduction in available road space. "That's when it flipped its trolley-boom off the overhead wires, and that's when the overhead wires started bouncing up and down," Pete exclaims, picking up his storyline. "The bouncing wires contacted a piece of metal flashing; it was from around the removed chimney, and it was sticking up a bit from the house roof. Pfft! With a bright flash, the electrified supply-wire burned in two. One end fell on the house roof and started a fire next to the flashing at the chimney opening. As it fell forward off the roof, this end of the "hot" wire started another fire at the front of the house. When it hit the ground, the line jumped and crackled. Then it turned red, right back up to the anchor on the overhead support cable that was strung across the road between two posts. Then the overhead wire started turning red up to the next anchor in line, and the wire started stretching. It soon broke and fell to the ground. Pfft! This continued on down the street, as far as the eye could see. Pfft! Pfft! Pfft!"

Pete and his crew could only gape in awe as one overhead wire segment after another burned bright red and dropped to the ground, all in sequence, all the way down Granville Street. Uphill, behind their house on dollies, MBM's newest truck—a late-model International five-ton—maintained holdback tension on the load while its driver leaned out his window and peered skyward. "The other end of the power line that severed on the rooftop metal fell on the rear of the house and started the shingles burning there," Pete continues. "When this end of the hot wire fell on the ground, it bounced back up under the holdback vehicle. Pfft! Somehow, that wire burned a hole into the bottom of the truck's gas tank. Whoosh! Suddenly, there were flames shooting thirty feet into the air around the cab. The hole in the tank turned out to be about the size of my little finger, and the gas tank happened to be full. Whoosh! The driver pulled on the hand brake and jumped to safety."

Fed by a steady stream of gas, the flames continued shooting thirty feet in the air. It took only a short time for the friction band on the mechanical hand brake to heat and expand. Like an apparition in a bad dream, the fire-breathing truck began creeping very slowly downhill toward the house and dollies. The driver, a newly arrived Dutch immigrant, was having none of that. Without hesitation, and probably not thinking much about his safety, he released the holdback cable, jumped back into the cab of the burning monster, and turned the steering wheel away from the house. After grazing the side of the house, the burning truck rolled downhill toward a gas station where it knocked down a corner canopy post and one gas pump before finally coming to rest against the other gas pump. "I stood back, and I looked around," recalled Pete. "Above me, burned and blackened wires were hanging down. In front of me, the house was still burning in three places. Just down the street, the gas station canopy was sitting on top of my new truck that was on fire beside a flattened gas pump. How much worse could it get?"

Fortunately, the gas station did not explode, and Pete was relieved to see his heroic truck driver escape with only minor burns. Accepting responsibility for the rogue trolley bus that was not supposed to be there, the city and the electric company assumed the cost for almost all repairs, while Pete accepted responsibility for repairing his "new" truck. The house-in-transition arrived at its new site several days later than planned. More than fifty years after the fact, Pete's anecdote still seems like the storyline for a soon-to-be-released animated film.

In between church board meetings and early-morning entertainments, Pete made time to help found a university. It began as an idea in the minds of Pete's fellow parishioners for a post-secondary educational institution where their children could continue faith-based learning in

keeping with the beliefs of their church. When the time came, Pete pro-
cured several buildings, including surplus construction trailers, from
his long-time client BC Hydro and moved them onto several acres of
acquired farmland near the town of Langley. He then brought in electricity and installed plumbing and sewer systems—just in time for the
first sixteen students. This was 1962, and the new school was known as
Trinity Junior College. Not surprisingly, Pete was on another board of
directors, serving as chairman of the building committee. Forty years
later, on a substantially expanded campus, Trinity Western University
is a fully accredited degree-granting institution with more than three
thousand students in a variety of disciplines.

By the mid-1960s, Modern Building Movers was a going concern.
With three full-time people in the office and as many as seven crews
in the field, MBM was relocating as many as four hundred buildings
per year. Perhaps Pete became bored with the routine, or perhaps he
had temporarily run out of inventions for the house-moving industry.
In 1965, having recognized the burgeoning demand for prefabricated
housing in remote areas of British Columbia, Pete Friesen decided to
go into the business of building and transporting those prefabricated
dwellings. Keeping his recently designed "barge trailer" and other
relevant equipment, Pete sold MBM and its remaining assets to one of
his competitors, Gordon Litz of Litz Brothers.

Renting a former sawmill site near New Westminster, Pete began
doing business as the sole proprietor of Coast Homes and set about
designing an assembly-line factory beneath almost two acres of roof.
As with his jacking system and other inventions, Pete's house-building
assembly line was a model of efficient simplicity. The first of seven
assembly areas, all connected by a track of rollers, produced a rigid shell
able to be hand-pushed to subsequent stations. The floor-frame of each
house was designed to include laminated beams that rolled well on the
assembly-line track before serving as main load beams during transport
and continuing as integral parts of the structure once located on site.
All electrical wiring as well as all plumbing and heating conduits were
installed at down-line stations in the factory; furnaces or fireplaces, or
both, were also included in each unit. The free-floating nature of Pete's
assembly line permitted construction of one-story and two-story units
ranging from one thousand to three thousand square feet in size. Soon,
one ready-made house was rolling off the assembly line every day.

Every ten working days, two barges were loaded with ten homes for a journey by sea. Pete's super barge-loading truck and steerable trailer with extendable outrigger arms and jacks made many trips up and down the coast of British Columbia. Of course, Pete and his high-flying colleagues at Coast Homes enjoyed many an exciting airplane ride through the Coast Mountains of western British Columbia. In tried and true fashion, ten houses would be rapidly unloaded in the two-hour high-tide window at their destination. The ready-to-inhabit homes were then placed on their foundations during the low-tide cycle before crew and equipment returned south. The coastal communities of Prince Rupert, Powell River, and Gold River each received fifty houses in this manner. Another fifty units were delivered to various small settlements and logging camps dotting the coast. All told, two hundred complete living units, including twenty-four larger bunkhouses, were constructed and moved hundreds of miles by barge in one short year. A conservative estimate puts the total barge travel at fifteen thousand miles.

Then came a call from Montreal. The rush was on to complete construction in preparation for the World's Fair—Expo 67—opening there in 1967. Organizers were seeking help to provide sufficient accommodations for the many visitors anticipated at this world-class exposition. Pete did not hesitate; he contracted with a Montreal-based company to supply four thousand motel-style living units within three months. For Pete's newly established house-building business, this contract was almost too good to be true. The assembly line was immediately reorganized, and more workers were hired on. Pete created one of the most efficient industrial operations ever. Coast Homes was soon producing forty-eight living units *per day* with only fifty-seven employees. A manufacturing plant in Seattle was supplying plumbing fixtures; some wood products were imported from Asia. Every available flat car on one of Canada's transcontinental railroads was being directed toward New Westminster in order to carry completed housing units east to Montreal in the province of Quebec. The ninety-day time frame was more than a bit tight, but Pete was on schedule to deliver all four thousand units on time.

Inspired by the magnitude and efficiency of Pete's undertaking, the Canadian Broadcasting Corporation aired a televised report praising his operation and celebrating the interprovincial cooperation in helping to build a national dream. Pete soon received a telephone call from a government official in Quebec City, the eastern province's capital. Fueled by protests from their electorate, provincial legislators were unhappy: a small company in western Canada was making a profit and getting nationwide attention by supplying "their" World's Fair. It did not look good: "La Belle Province" seemed dependent on a little guy from "out west." At the same time, many members of the province's workforce and business community began complaining loudly about losing revenue because of Pete's successful and distant enterprise.

Regional prejudice notwithstanding, the provincial legislators did what provincially minded legislators have usually done: they took care of themselves with little respect for broader issues concerning the nation or its citizens. Pete Friesen became collateral damage in a struggle he didn't know existed and would never fully understand. Without delay, a Quebec provincial representative gave Pete an ultimatum: he could sign over 51 percent of his house-building company to that provincial government, or the province would cause default on his contract to supply the living units. Having contracted with a company in the private sector, Pete protested. It was no use. He tried to reason, but the government would not listen. It was soon apparent that people within the provincial government somehow influenced the Montreal-based company Pete had contracted with. If Pete refused to cede control of Coast Homes, financing could be withheld from the Montreal-based company and Pete would not get paid in turn. Forty-eight living units were already heading east by train.

Pete did not back down, and neither did his opponents. Unfortunately, there is rarely a tie when wrestling with the government. The door of opportunity slammed shut in Pete's face. Highly respected legal advisers from both ends of the country convinced Pete that any pursuit of "justice" would be futile. The Montreal-based company had suddenly gone out of existence, and there was no person or corporate entity available to honor Pete's contract. Any attempt to connect his now-defunct contracting company with the provincial government in power would require many years of legal effort and many, many dollars. It was an impossible situation: even if such legal process eventually proved successful, any and all blame would probably be assigned to one individual who, by then, would be financially unable to reimburse

Pete's legal fees, let alone his business losses. Although he didn't have the time or money to prove it, Pete strongly suspected the Montreal-based contractor to have been a shell company, siphoning funds from provincial coffers. "One thing is for sure," Pete remarked dryly. "Just because there are a lot of laws in the country doesn't necessarily mean there is a lot of justice in the system."

With millions of dollars in outstanding orders, Pete was cornered by insurmountable personal debt. He was forced into bankruptcy with Coast Homes, having to sell off all the company's equipment and put all his employees out of work. In the process, Pete was also forced to forfeit a recently signed $8 million contract to provide prefabricated buildings for a large resource company on the west coast. As Pete soon discovered, bankruptcy courts proceed much faster than parliamentary legislatures or court actions in his favor. With a minimum of delay, Pete was pushed outside his country's economy. For Pete, it was not as harrowing as being excommunicated from his church, but it was close. In a token gesture of mercy, the court allowed Edith to keep the family's furniture, because she had bought it. Pete was permitted to keep his watch, his golf clubs, his hunting rifles, his briefcase, and his camera. All else was lost. Married with five children, forty-five-year-old Pete Friesen was bankrupt.

*The Friesens at Christmas 1963.*
*Seated from left: Eric, Pete, Edith, and Joy.*
*Standing from left: Peter, Paul, and Jon.*

Being bankrupt weighed heavily on Pete, and it came with an added insult. In 1967, on the eve of his country's biggest celebration ever, he suddenly found himself persona non grata among many former friends and colleagues. Aghast at Pete's bankruptcy, the fellow directors of Trinity Junior College demanded that he resign from the board of the school he had helped create five years prior. Suddenly, his groundbreaking initiatives and his years of dedication appeared worthless in the eyes of those who now controlled this rapidly growing institution. They would not even entertain his fervent request to complete his current term of office, due to expire in only two months. Instead Pete was unceremoniously fired from the board and, figuratively speaking, kicked out the door. Although far less painful, this act was almost as drastic as excommunication from the church or exile from the economy. According to Pete: "It was bad enough being out of money, but what really hurt was finding out that some people who I thought were my friends were not my friends at all."

Before long, Pete decided to go "up north" and get out of everyone's hair while thinking things through. Up north he certainly went— Pete went about as far north as possible while remaining in the same province. He went almost one thousand miles away from his former New Westminster house-building factory, to the town of Fort Nelson in the far northeastern corner of British Columbia.

Founded in 1805 by the North West Company that later merged with the Hudson's Bay Company, this old fur-trade post was named in honor of Admiral Horatio Nelson, who was mortally wounded at the battle of Trafalgar that same year. Despite such auspicious labeling, business at Fort Nelson got off to an inglorious start. In 1813, a tribe of disenchanted indigenous people massacred the eight company inhabitants and burned the place to the ground. Eventually re-established as a fur-trade post, "The Fort" slowly developed as a northern supply center for wilderness travelers and resource explorers. With the outbreak of WWII, it became a major supply hub for construction of the Alaska Highway, also known as the ALCAN. Situated at mile 300 of that 1,500-mile marvel of engineering tenacity, the hardy little community enjoyed a short burst of hyperactivity before settling back into its role of regional distribution center. With a road and an airport, this town of several thousand residents at fifty-nine degrees north latitude continues to host explorers from oil and gas industries as well as summertime motorists. Surrounded by dense forests of very small trees hiding endless acres of "bottomless" muskeg, Fort Nelson is the kind of place where a person can get some serious thinking done.

Just before freeze-up in the autumn of 1967, Pete Friesen came to town with his wife, Edith, and their three youngest children—Jon, Eric, and Joy. Fortunately, Pete was also able to bring a grubstake. Learning of Pete's financial plight, a sympathetic Vancouver businessman had loaned Pete $25,000 to help get re-established. Finding rental accommodations on the old army base, Pete applied the loaned monies toward purchase of a gravel pit and equipment to start up a small batch-plant for the production of ready-mixed concrete. With a newly purchased (if well-used) front-end loader, Pete built a high drive-up gravel berm from which to pour gravel, sand, and cement into his newly manufactured mixing unit. Ready-mixed concrete would pour out into his delivery truck parked below. For long-distance transport of sand and gravel, he bought back one of his old house-moving trucks and welded a steel box onto its deck. With acquisition of another used flatbed truck for general haulage, Pete's fleet was soon complete.

Joined by his son Jon and one occasional employee, Pete was soon supplying ready-mix concrete to the local construction industry, as minor competition to a larger, long-established company doing the same. Pete's batch-plant was nevertheless busy, operating every day of the week except Sunday and bringing in a modest profit. His vehicles were being paid for, and he was providing for his family. Things were not going as smoothly on the home front, however. The old army base had been designated for development, forcing Pete and Edith to find alternative accommodations. This is not an easy task in the north, where options are very limited and prices are extremely high. It was decided Edith and the children would return to the Vancouver area, and Pete would commute for reasonable intervals every month or so. It was not to be. After finding a place for his family to live in Vancouver, Pete returned to Fort Nelson only to witness the beginning of the end for his batch-plant business.

Pete remembered it well: "It was September 12, 1968. I returned from Vancouver and soon learned what rolling stock was. The ready-mix truck had slid off a rain-soaked dike and rolled into the ditch with a full load of concrete in the mixer—rolling stock. Of course, the concrete set long before anything could be done about the truck, and it was all pretty much a write-off. About five days later, the driver of my flatbed truck used too much brake on an unexpectedly icy curve, and the whole rig sailed off the highway and into the bush—rolling stock. Soon after that, I was pulling out of the pit with a load of gravel in my old haul-truck when all hell broke loose. Suddenly, I was going full speed down a hill and my brakes didn't work! I had to force the truck into an embankment, and it flipped over—rolling stock. As I soon discovered, somebody had loosened all the bolts on the drive shaft flange. They snapped off under stress, and the drive shaft kicked around and tore off the brake line. I felt uneasy about this suspected sabotage, but I soon felt a whole lot worse.

"Now that we were pretty much out of the concrete business, I found a job for my front-ender loader in one of the nearby mines and hired another driver to share the twenty-four-hour shifts with me. This new driver became distracted when he was driving down a hill one day. He was not too experienced with rear-wheel steering and probably over-reacted when he got too close to the bank. Over went the loader. Sadly, the driver was caught underneath the loader and was killed. I can't tell you how bad I felt. In all these years around heavy equipment and such, none of my people had ever been seriously injured before. I felt really sad for this man's family. Not only did I feel really bad, I was ruined. I had nothing left—no money, no trucks, no business. My family was a thousand miles away, and I was in a sleeping bag on the floor of a friend's garage. That's about as down as you can get."

Then came a call from Watson Lake in Yukon. A company there had heard about Pete's rolling-stock situation and offered him work, hauling logs for their sawmill. Pete traded the remnants of his damaged fleet for one truck and headed west through the northern fringe of the Rocky Mountains to this small town situated "north of sixty" at mile 635 of the Alaska Highway. While shuttling back and forth between the bush and the sawmill that winter, Pete got wind of an upcoming large contract for manufacturing railway ties. When logging finished in the spring of 1969, Pete drove back east and then south past Fort Nelson while collecting bits and pieces of used sawmill equipment along the way. His destination was mile 50 of the Alaska Highway.

Here, on the outskirts of Fort St. John, the primary administrative center and bustling distribution hub for northeastern British Columbia, Pete and his new partner from Vancouver quickly assembled their railway-tie manufacturing plant. Pushing out hundreds of new railway ties per day, their high-efficiency sawmill was soon part of the local buzz, employing about a dozen workers and turning a reasonable profit. However, by autumn of 1969, a disagreement about operating principles was creating friction between Pete and his partner.

Then came a call from Chicago. Pete's erstwhile associates at Belding Engineering desired his services and made an offer he could not refuse. Being faced with the need to quickly move fifty houses and a number of fragile heritage buildings, the boys at Belding could find no one better qualified than the man who had invented the unified hydraulic jacking system and whose company was known to have once moved fourteen houses in a single day. With special dispensation from the U.S. Department of Immigration as a person necessary to the industry, Pete Friesen would be the new manager of Belding Engineering's structural moving division, for which he would receive a portion of operating profits along with a comfortable salary. Pete's days in the bush were done. Mercifully, his difficult period of self-banishment was now over. Reflecting back on this trying chapter in his life, Pete calmly stated: "God brought me down, and he allowed me to come back up so I would know I could do it."

# 5

# Highland Park

Chicago's suburbs have been around as long as the city itself. The 1833 treaty between the Potawatomi people and the U.S. government allowed pioneer settlers to move into a large piece of territory immediately north of the newly incorporated town of Chicago. Beginning this same year, a narrow trail was surveyed and blazed north to Milwaukee and on to Green Bay. With years of gradual improvement, this rough track eventually replaced the Lake Michigan beachfront as the preferred north-south route for horse-mounted mail carriers and arriving settlers. It became known as the Green Bay Road. At frequent intervals along this new road, the government constructed log houses to serve as resting places for wayfarers. About twenty-five miles north of Chicago, one such roadside stop became an inn and tavern known as Green Bay House. A church, schoolhouse, and post office were soon built nearby. In 1850, the first township meeting and election of officials took place in Green Bay House, now only a half-day's carriage ride from Chicago on a much improved road. Two years later, more refined accommodations became available with construction of the Highland Park Hotel.

Powered by wood-burning locomotives, the Milwaukee & Chicago Railway Company (later, Chicago Northwestern) arrived in 1854 and named the new stop Highland Park. Suddenly, this budding new community was but an hour's train-ride away from Chicago. By then, the community already contained a sawmill, furniture factory, steel foundry, and machine shop as well as two brickyards. Two large piers on the nearby lakeshore had already linked this community with many others around Lake Michigan. Available land was soon enthusiastically acquired and developed. In no time at all, many of Chicago's well-to-do citizens had erected very permanent and often auspicious summer homes on the lakefront. In 1869, the Illinois state legislature granted a charter to the City of Highland Park.

While this new and rapidly expanding city escaped the fiery wrath that rampaged to the north and south in 1871, some of its citizens took notice of the threat that fire posed. Community protection began with a public subscription and the grand sum of twenty dollars that placed two water tanks at strategic sites in the downtown core. Budget constraints prevented the young city from undertaking further fire-protection measures for almost twenty years. However, when fire almost destroyed the entire business district in 1888, the city fathers became convinced of the need for some level of organized protection.

The following year saw formation of the Highland Park Volunteer Fire Department, equipped with two hand-drawn hose carts and a bunch of buckets. Under direction of its new chief fire marshal, two volunteer units were created: "Irish Company" manned one hose cart based in a shed affixed to the city building, while "Dutch Company" operated the other hose cart from a nearby livery stable. Apparently, there was a great rivalry between the two companies. Whenever the alarm sounded, volunteers ran to their respective bases and dragged their respective hose carts to the fire scene as quickly as possible. History suggests the fire was often less important than the five dollar reward given by city council to the first company arriving at the scene. More often than not, the reward winner was determined only after prolonged argument and sometimes by open fisticuffs—on occasions, rival company members were seen to fight each other before fighting the fire. However, as soon as the fire was extinguished and tempers had cooled, the losing company would always buy a round of beer that was shared by all.

After another series of fires almost destroyed the business district early in the twentieth century, Highland Park became even more serious about fire protection. The city's first sole-purpose, stand-alone fire station was constructed at Central Avenue and Green Bay Road in 1904. Funded mostly by private subscription, the city later purchased a brand new, four-cylinder, forty-horsepower 1912 LaFrance fire engine for $5,500. By 1924, a dozen full-time firemen were serving a fire department that continued to grow with its community.

By 1974, the Highland Park Fire Department employed three dozen firemen and operated a vast array of specialized equipment from four fire stations. However, with construction of new and improved facilities, one of these stations was no longer needed. Constructed in 1940 as a replacement for the 1904 fire station, the recently vacated second edition of Station #1 (Central Station) was now standing in the way of plans for urban redevelopment. Having purchased the property from the city in 1975 to expand their grocery store on the corner of Green Bay Road and Central Avenue, the Cortesi family offered to donate the fire station back to the community, on the condition that it was moved off their property. The Highland Park Youth Committee had already expressed interest in using the vacant fire station to provide a much-needed activity space for teenagers and pre-teens. After a year of meetings and paper pushing, a permit was finally acquired to move the old fire station two hundred yards west, to the edge of Sunset Park, where it would gain new life as a community youth center. Everyone was onboard, and fund-raising began. All they had to do now was move the building.

In November 1967, when recently bankrupted Pete Friesen and his family were settling in for a long, cold winter at Fort Nelson, U.S. President Lyndon B. Johnson signed a federal bill authorizing construction of a national accelerator laboratory in the westernmost suburbs of Chicago. Dedicated to research at the frontier of high-energy physics, this particle-testing facility would soon be on the leading edge of nuclear research, hosting the world's highest-energy particle accelerator. Meantime, an entire village and 6,800 acres of farmland would be assimilated to make room for the necessary facilities which would eventually include the Tevatron—an accelerator four miles in circumference. Although a number of barns and other farm structures would remain on site for recreation and storage purposes, many others would be relocated from a large area near the city of Batavia. Belding

Engineering of nearby West Chicago was the main contractor for these moves. Accepting the invitation and arriving from the backwoods of northern Canada in 1971, the new manager of Belding's Structural Moving Division, Pete Friesen, was soon on the job. Back doing one of the things he did best, Pete supervised the delicate relocation of approximately fifty farm buildings, some of which were large, multi-story, wood-frame structures dating from the nineteenth century.

Dedicated as Fermi National Accelerator Laboratory (Fermilab) in May 1974, the laboratory honors Italian-born Enrico Fermi (1901-1954), preeminent physicist of the atomic age. Defecting to the United States in 1938, the Nobel Prize winner Fermi subsequently joined the faculty at the University of Chicago. On December 2, 1942, Fermi and scientists from his laboratory had achieved the first controlled release of nuclear energy—on the squash court beneath the stands of Stagg Field at the University of Chicago.

Following the busy and profitable year of relocating buildings for the Fermilab project, Belding's structural-moving division became very active in and around Chicago. As well as organizing men and equipment on numerous, often simultaneous projects, division manager Pete Friesen was also dedicated and energetic in the pursuit of new business. Pete's agreement with Belding Engineering for a share of moving-division profits soon paid off handsomely. After less than two years as manager, Pete could afford to buy the structural-moving division free and clear. Together with operating partner Marvin Wasmund, Pete Friesen began doing business as Advance Moving Contractors (AMC) of West Chicago. Although AMC was a recent entry in the area business directory, its owners were already known for bringing a wealth of experience to the business of moving buildings.

When contacted, AMC co-owners Marvin Wasmund and Pete Friesen went to check out the fire station in Highland Park. While Marv sensibly cautioned against trying to move the heavy and fragile two-story brick structure, his more experienced and somewhat adventurous partner had other ideas. Although the old building would require considerable care and attention, Pete was confident it could be moved successfully using his three-point loading system in conjunction with hydraulic-powered lift. While the method of three-point loading is fairly intuitive and widely employed, Pete had recently refined the principle into a workable system with mathematical calculations. However, as far as anyone knew, the three-point principle had never been used in conjunction with hydraulic jacks to move a building.

Though not particularly well-defined or identified, three-point loading has been in use for millennia. An early example is the *travois*—a triangle of three sticks—for pulling a load behind a dog or larger animal. A more modern example is the tricycle—a triangle of wheels. Being the strongest of geometric forms, the triangle provides rigidity in its plane. Having only three sides, the triangle also allows for displacement of one corner into another plane without disrupting the entire form. For example, if one of four wheels on a moving wagon falls into a hole, one of the other three wheels usually pops free of the ground because of the two rigid axles; however, a travois or tricycle leans toward the errant corner without forcing the other two out of plane. Three points are more dynamically stable than four.

In 1948, after mechanically jacking up that first house with arm-powered screw jacks, Pete instinctively loaded it on three points for transport: his old logging truck carried one end of the house and two ancient dollies carried the others. Near the end of a thirty-mile journey with that house, the Sumas Mountain Road filled Pete with thoughts about loading methods, building weights, and centers of gravity. He became intrigued and would forever enjoy exploration of these critical issues; aided by his wealth of hands-on research, he gradually developed a system of calculations to help understand them better. By 1975, Pete was seriously chewing on the idea of implementing *hydraulic* three-point loading for his next relocation project: instead of a truck and two dollies, he wanted to use three distinct points, or zones, of hydraulically pressurized jacks under the moving load. Pete knew the fire station in Highland Park was heavier than any other building he had attempted to move. It would also be the first major project for Advance Moving Contractors. Regardless of any remuneration offered, Pete Friesen probably took this fire station job because of the challenges it presented.

Having calculated the 38' by 56' fire hall and all the necessary supporting steel to weigh about 570 tons, Pete refined a plan to employ heavy-duty dollies with removable fifty-ton jacks to transport and maneuver the two-story brick building into place. However, Pete was soon thinking about Plan B. The large transport dollies and jacks he intended to rent were already committed elsewhere. Never one to shy away from innovation, Pete Friesen once again decided to try something different: instead of hauling the fire station on rubber-tired dollies, he would glide it to its destination with heavy-duty rollers riding on steel tracks. During transit, the building and its support beams would be "floating" on Pete's hydraulic three-point loading system. Of course, Pete and Marvin still had other issues to consider: without use of the intended fifty-ton jacks, they had to determine how many smaller capacity jacks would be required and where they would be placed. Then there was the matter of finding roll beams strong enough to support a load of 570 tons. Also of concern was a fifteen-foot drop in elevation across the six hundred feet to the new location. Then there was the question of how to rotate the building into its proper alignment at the new site. While Pete pondered Plan B, a subcontractor was hired to cut the fire station free of its foundation.

On March 18, 1976, the Concrete Drilling and Sawing Company began drilling and sawing through fifteen-inch concrete foundation walls. By positioning the cut line two and a half feet below level of the main floor, a substantial concrete flange remained attached to the base of all four exterior walls. This solid perimeter frame would help keep the building aligned as well as all the bricks in place during subsequent lifting, moving, and lowering procedures. Below the separation line, notches were cut into the foundation sidewalls to allow insertion of fifteen cross-steel beams, one every four feet across the building's long axis. Immediately beneath and horizontally perpendicular to this cross-steel, four longer beams were similarly inserted through openings in the foundation end walls. Because of issues related to weight distribution and jack placement, Pete had these four beams arranged as two pairs with a six-inch space between paired beams. Each stitch-welded, two-beam pairing was regarded as one main load beam and was positioned directly above the planned roll-beam track. While Pete continued thinking things through, the well-organized workers of AMC began hucking four-foot crib blocks into the fire station basement.

The best jacks Pete could find for this job were his own. Although less than ideal in terms of capacity, these fifteen-ton jacks originally manufactured by Modern Hydraulics in the mid-1950s from Pete's design were the only available hydraulic-powered crib jacks with a fourteen-inch stroke under unified pressure and a baseplate wide enough to satisfy his 3:1 safety ratio. Also, the fourteen-inch stroke would simplify jack-resetting procedures by the alternate stacking of crib blocks on their six-inch and eight-inch sides. Using forty-eight of these fifteen-ton jacks, Pete would have a potential lifting capacity of 720 tons to raise 570 tons of building and support steel. As such, each of his jacks would be working at about three-quarters of its maximum rating, and there would be less risk of jack failure. The extra 150 tons of lifting capacity provided a 26 percent safety margin in the event of unforeseen failures.

After estimating total weight as well as the weight differentials between various sections of the building, Pete identified three distinct areas, or zones, for jack placement in accordance with his three-point system. The lightest section of the building, the front end with wooden garage doors and vehicle bays, was designated Zone One and would contain twelve jacks. The heavier left rear section was designated Zone Two and would contain sixteen jacks. The heaviest section, under the brick bell tower extension in rear right, became Zone Three and would contain twenty jacks. Although arranged in balance around the building's center of gravity like wheels on a tricycle, Pete's three centers of lift were not simply three points of support. More accurately, the jacks represented forty-eight points of support arranged into three distinct zones that were responsible for carrying the load in a balanced manner. As such, Pete Friesen's three-point loading method can also be correctly regarded as a *three-zone* loading system. Regardless of what the system is called anywhere else, all forty-eight jacks in these three zones under the fire station had to go up the same amount at the same time.

Having recently purchased the structural moving division of Belding Engineering, Pete had re-acquired one of his original jacking units; in fact, it was the one he had manufactured in New Westminster and sold to Belding in 1958. By segregating and combining adjacent outlets within this unit, Pete and his plumbers realigned many of its nineteen slave circuits into three consolidated and zone-related sections. Through a splitter connection, each of these three new sections supplied two manifolds distributing pressurized hydraulic fluid to every jack in its particular zone. Thus, by the pre-loading and isolation of each jack circuit with its particular amount of hydraulic pressure according to its carried weight and ram speed, all forty-eight jacks would operate in unison with application of unified pressure through the slave circuits of this one jacking unit. With appropriate hose and valve adjustments, the three zones could also be isolated from each other; as such, each zone would contain its particular amount of locked-in pressure serving as a common pressure to all jacks within that zone. Once the jacks were arranged in established zones, the building could be raised with three zones of *unified* pressure and, after appropriate hydraulic adjustments, it could then be moved horizontally while riding on three distinct zones of independent *common* pressure. In other words, during the transport phase, all jacks in any one zone share the same pressure, but the amount of this zonal "common" pressure might be different in each of the three zones.

For Pete, there was another question to answer. How do you simultaneously move forty-eight hydraulic jacks holding up a 570-ton load—horizontally? Never one to shy away from innovation, Pete Friesen decided to try something new: he turned his jacks upside down. Instead of resting on crib blocks, the bottom of all jack bases would be pressed against the bottom of a main load beam while their ram ends extended downwards onto supplemental support beams mounted on top of heavy-duty rollers, also known as creeper-dollies, riding on the roll beams. Located according to zones, the jacks would be arranged in three straight-line groupings under each main beam and held in place from beneath by three short, supplemental support beams. Laid end-to-end and parallel to the main beam, these supplemental "shoe" beams would each support one group of jacks. Each horizontal shoe beam came with a six-inch-wide vertical beam welded to each end. These vertical "guide" beams would be inserted into the six-inch space between main load beam pairs and thereby keep the shoe beam and its jacks properly aligned. By design, this space between each main-beam pair would also accommodate the higher "bottom" ends of the adjustable jack cylinders extending upwards through their bases while downward-projecting jack rams would be held in place by the shoe beams. With assistance from vertical guide beams, the shoe beams would keep everything properly aligned on the creeper-dollies riding along the straight and narrow roll beam below. *Visualize.*

*The fire station sitting on cross-steel beams above a main load beam and eight inverted 15-ton jacks supported by one shoe beam carried by two creeper-dollies riding on a roll-beam track.*

Resting on independent crib piles, three shoe beams were installed beneath and parallel to each main load beam. The shoe beams came in lengths of ten or sixteen feet, depending on the number of jacks they needed to support. The twelve inverted jacks of Zone One would be equally divided between two shoe beams, with one shoe beam beneath the front section of each main beam. The sixteen inverted jacks of Zone Two would be shared between two shoe beams beneath the rear section of the left main beam. Similarly, the twenty inverted jacks of Zone Three would be shared between two shoe beams beneath the rear section of the right main beam. To facilitate jack resetting, four "reset" beams were installed across the building's width, immediately beneath and horizontally perpendicular to the main beams. Resting on independent cribs, these reset beams would support the load while adjustments were being made to jacks and shoe beams. When necessary during these transitions, any non-pressurized jacks would be held in place against the main load beams by mechanical hand jacks working against the bottom surface of the shoe beams. *Think it through.*

There was another problem. Where do you find rails or roll beams sturdy enough to support such a heavy building and all the weighty steel beneath it? Never one to shy away from innovation, Pete simply built his own. By welding steel plates to the flange-ends on both sides of a fourteen-inch-deep, wide-flange steel beam already weighing one hundred pounds per foot, he created a very rigid, heavy-duty "boxed-beam" roll-track. Welded flush to the top flange of the boxed beam, a ten-inch-wide strip of hardened "T-1" steel plate created a track surface capable of withstanding the pressure of hardened rollers on the creeper-dollies. Fabricated in forty-foot lengths, six of these identical boxed-beam sections would provide two 120-foot roll-tracks. The forty-foot sections would be bolted together through drilled steel plates welded to each section end. As the load progressed onto the second pair of sections, the used first pair would be removed and leapfrogged forward. Coincident with repositioning roll-track sections, every so often, the load would be jacked down several feet to roll-tracks installed at a lower elevation. In this manner, the old fire station would step down the necessary fifteen feet during its six hundred feet of horizontal journey. *Derch denche.*

On Pete's command, the control lever was selected downward and unified pressure pushed through the jacking unit's modernized plumbing. At the ends of forty-eight black hoses snaking into the fire station basement, forty-eight hydraulic jack rams extended downward against six shoe beams resting on crib piles. Up went the two pairs of main load beams. Up went the fifteen cross-steel beams. Up went the old brick fire station, slick as a whistle. Once the forty-eight jacks were fully extended, a six-inch-high course and an eight-inch-high course of blocks were hastily added to eighteen independent crib piles beneath the four reset beams, which were soon shimmed tight and level beneath the main load beams. With a subsequent slight reduction of hydraulic pressure, the main beams and load settled firmly onto the reset beams. Further release of hydraulic pressure allowed the shoe beams to be raised and blocked higher against jack rams retreating upwards into their cylinders. When all crib blocks were in place and all jack cylinders had been reset, the jacking machine was reloaded for another upward shot.

So it went. In small increments, the old fire station was jacked higher and higher atop crib piles growing taller and taller. As soon as sufficient space was created above the severed foundation, preparations were made for transition to horizontal movement mode. With reset beams supporting the load and lengths of chain around the main load beams holding shoe beams and jacks in place, the former main-beam crib piles were transformed into roll-track crib piles ready to accept the first pair of boxed roll-track sections installed parallel to and directly beneath the two main load beams. Once these forty-foot sections of roll-track were in place, their forward end plates were bolted to the second and third sections that were laid out directly behind the fire station, defining the first eighty feet of intended travel. Resting on several independent cribs, each section of roll-track was shimmed level and shimmied into line while, beneath the building, two creeper-dollies were installed under each shoe beam as it was lowered onto its respective roll-track. Also known as a skate, crawler-dolly, or roller, each creeper-dolly is a series of heavy-duty steel rollers in a connected chain circulating around a heavy plate set into a squat, but strong, steel framework. Measuring 21″ by 7″ and weighing 235 pounds, one late-model creeper-dolly is capable of carrying seventy-five tons while occupying only six inches of vertical space.

Under this fire station, there were two creeper-dollies positioned under each shoe beam for a total of four creeper-dollies in each zone, with six on each roll-track. These twelve "mighty midgets" would easily carry the fire station home. A front-end loader with a cable hooked to a bridle assembly would serve as tow vehicle. Attached by a chain to the load's other end, a semi with loaded trailer would be the holdback vehicle. Before the load was moved, however, adjustments at the jacking machine and to the hydraulic circuitry established three independent zones of common pressures for jacks already properly positioned around the load's center of gravity. The amount of pressure in each zone depended on the weight being carried by that particular zone. By instinctively extending or retracting to maintain the common pressure of their zone, the jacks would automatically adjust for any disturbance of the load from its level plane. For example, if one corner of the fire station began dropping out of horizontal plane, unweighted jacks in the opposite corner would begin retracting to maintain their zone's common pressure and, thereby, they would help level the load. At least, that's how Pete Friesen envisioned his hydraulic three-zone loading system would function. It had never been tried before.

After the fire station had been gently towed onto the second and third sections of roll-track, it was time to deal with the issue of rotation. While reset beams supported the load and chains around the main load beams held shoe beams and jacks out of the way, Pete and his crew built additional crib piles either side of both roll-tracks. On top of these crib piles, they laid 4' by 8' sections of one-inch steel plate level with the upper surface of the roll-tracks. After each creeper-dolly had been re-aligned at a predetermined angle to the roll-track, the shoe beams were lowered into place on top, and their jacks were re-pressurized to take the load.  By using the tow vehicle and the holdback vehicle pulling at opposite ends, the building was gently rotated about its vertical axis. During this very small but necessary rotation, the angled creeper-dollies rolled onto the steel plates atop their independent crib piles that now supported the load. After being tweaked around the necessary few degrees, the load was then returned to the reset beams while the steel plates and temporary cribbing were removed. With the fire station now rotated to the proper angle for its new site, the four sections of roll-track beneath it were then re-aligned to take it directly there. After the roll-track was repositioned directly below and parallel to the load beams and shoe beams, the creeper-dollies were returned to the direction of travel along the roll-track. Once again, pressurized hydraulic fluid from the jacking machine extended the jack rams downwards and transferred the load back onto the shoe beams riding on the creeper-dollies. With reset beams soon retracted out of the way, Pete and his crew were again ready to roll.

Because the terrain sloped down fifteen feet across only six hundred feet of intended travel, the fire station would be moved in four level stages and jacked down at several transitions with support from the four reset beams on their independent cribs. Although each roll-track section and each segment of travel were perfectly level according to their instruments, the crew experienced difficulty keeping the load totally on the level. There is no such thing as a compression-proof crib block, and each block in the cribs beneath the boxed roll-track would compress one-quarter of an inch, plus or minus an eighth, under the heavy load. Of course, the downhill cribs containing greater numbers of blocks would experience more total compression—as much as two and a half inches in some cases. Furthermore, the soft spring-season soil around the original site caused the first sets of cribs to settle a half-inch below grade. Although the soft soil was not a factor along the mostly paved route, it was nevertheless tricky to predetermine the possible compression over any particular stage. No one wanted to tow more than a million pounds uphill.

When the load was towed forward onto one particular section of track, its weight compressed all supporting crib piles underneath, especially the taller ones farther ahead of the load. Having thereby created a slight downgrade, the fire station began creeping forward almost of its own accord while being held in check by the holdback vehicle. Without warning and for reasons never known, the driver of the holdback vehicle temporarily released his brakes, and that holdback vehicle rolled forward toward the load while the cable turned to slack. Inspired by encouraging words from Pete, the driver quickly stomped on his brakes, and the holdback cable began regaining tension behind the load that was still creeping forward. When it suddenly snapped tight, the steel holdback cable stripped all the bolts and ripped the heavy-duty bumper assembly free and clear of the now-stationary holdback vehicle. Loud exclamations and silent prayers pursued the 570 tons of two-story brick building trundling solemnly toward its own demise over an abrupt four-foot drop to receding terrain. "Golly, gee whiz!" (or some such thing) exclaimed Pete's crewmembers, almost in unison.

Recognizing a crisis in progress, an alert young foreman on watch beneath the suddenly accelerating load removed a large crescent wrench from his coverall pocket and slapped it purposefully atop one of the roll-tracks between the roller guide tubes of an advancing creeper-dolly. Cla-runch! At first, nothing changed except the crescent wrench. Finally the forces of friction, fusion, and good luck prevailed. The fire station "scree-runched" to a halt before going off the end of the tracks. For a moment, there was only silence. "I don't know how the good Lord works," sighed Pete, after slowing his heart and catching his breath, "but God is certainly looking out for us."

The rest of the move went off without a hitch. Within two months of the first cut into the old foundation wall, the two-story fire station and its precarious bell tower arrived at their new home with nary a brick out of place. Pete Friesen's hydraulic three-zone loading system had worked like a charm. Any tendency for one part of the building to drop from level plane during transit had been instantaneously countered by increased pressure in the affected jacks on the downside while the upside sank onto jacks of relatively lower pressure. Although many weeks of hucking blocks, hoisting beams, and moving tracks proved the process more difficult than it sounded, the fragile old building had indeed been "floated" home on fluid.

With great faith in his own abilities and believing anything built by man could be moved by man, Pete Friesen had accepted a challenge few would have dared to undertake. Driven by necessity and employing tools he had invented twenty years prior, Pete accomplished something many of his peers considered impossible. Given then-current technology and accepted methods, the fire station move could have been considered impossible. However, Pete had moved "outside the box" many years before, and he had been thinking laterally ever since. Following his instincts and believing in himself, Pete discovered the best possible way, if not the only way, of moving the fragile fire station. Although subsequent research would discover that similar methods had been used earlier in Europe, this was the first known use of hydraulic three-zone loading on "rails and rollers" in North America. Once again, through courage and conviction, Pete Friesen had blazed a trail into unexplored territory. A 1976 entry in the *Guinness Book of World Records* listed Central Avenue Fire Station as the heaviest building ever moved on rails and rollers.

While he did appreciate the recognition afforded his efforts, Pete remembered the fire station project mostly because of the innovation it inspired. First were adaptations of the interpersonal kind, as he and his new partner learned to accept different points of view about their first major project together. After agreeing to accept the job, they were faced with challenges known and unknown, expected and unexpected.

Neither Pete nor his partner had used shoe beams or made boxed roll-beams before. Finding themselves unexpectedly without maneuverable transport dollies, they implemented a near-static rotation of their load around its vertical axis. This was one of several small inventions on this large and complex project. While adept at deflecting skepticism, Pete well understood that this first use of the hydraulic three-zone loading principle with roll-tracks and creeper-dollies was unknown territory or at least unproven ground. If his new idea didn't work, Pete knew he would be picking up bricks for a long, long time.

A daring realignment of hydraulic plumbing behind the operating panel of Pete's beloved old jacking unit opened up a new frontier. Subsequent models of his unified jacking machine would manifest ever more complex zoning within the machine itself, allowing for completion of ever more complex tasks. Similarly, his use of splitters and manifolds would shine light on a whole new world of possibilities in the future. Pete's innovation of a boxed roll-beam track with a hardened steel running surface paved the way for many successful moves of far greater magnitude, some of which he would go on to direct. It is easy to overlook the contribution made by the UHJS designed and manufactured by Pete twenty years earlier; without it, this job may not have been worth attempting. What more could be said about Pete's idea for inverting his jacks? Pete Friesen turned conventional thinking upside down and got the job done.

In his later years, Pete took great comfort in remembering his contribution to the young people of Highland Park. After being moved to its new location on the edge of Sunset Park, the fire station underwent eighteen months of intensive redesign and refurbishment while the Highland Park Youth Committee campaigned to stimulate interest and raise funds within the community. The city and its citizens can be proud. Approximately $200,000 and many hours of volunteer labor were ultimately donated to the youth center project. A new basement returned the old building to its original three-floor plan and provided a large area with a performance stage suitable for dances. Upper floors provided activity and meeting rooms as well as a games room and reception area. On September 21, 1978, the old redbrick fire station re-opened its doors as the new Firehouse Activity Center.

*At the edge of Sunset Park, the Firehouse Youth Activity Center
serves the young people of Highland Park—Peter Rowlands.*

The Firehouse Activity Center is a tribute to the people of Highland Park who recognized a good idea when they saw it, rallied behind their youth committee, and stayed the course for three years to get the job done. They are all to be congratulated: the youth committee that conceived and promoted the project; the family that graciously donated the building; the city council that stretched the rules and its own pocketbook; the local business people who donated material and professional services; the family of volunteers who hammered and painted the place into shape; and, most of all, the parents who cared.

Surrounded by trees at the edge of Sunset Park, the old fire station is now serving its second generation of Highland Park youth. "Please tell Mr. Friesen," says Charlotte Landsman, Manager of Youth Services for Highland Park, "hundreds and hundreds of young people have benefited greatly from the work he did here in the 1970s."

# 6

## Joliet

On the return leg of an epic 1673 canoe journey mapping much of the Mississippi River, a Jesuit priest and a fur-trader from New France—Father Jacques Marquette and Louis Jolliet—followed their Potawatomi guide northeasterly up a river known as *Illinois* and into one of its tributaries flowing from the north. Climbing a prominent hillock beside this small river, the explorers surveyed the surrounding plains as well as much of their intended route north. Naming the knob of higher ground *Mound Jolliet*, the adventurers continued up the small river they now called *La Riviere des Plaines*. Forty miles farther upstream, after carrying their gear and two canoes easterly across one and a half miles of swampy ground, they put into the short river *Checagou* and were soon discharged into the great lake *Michigami*. While Father Marquette remained in the region to tend his new flock, Jolliet hurried back to Quebec with a report of their discoveries.

The governors of New France emphatically denied Jolliet's request to establish a fur-trading post at the strategic *Portage Checagou*, but the leaders of the new United States would not make the same mistake. One hundred and fifty years later, settlement and commercial enterprise would be enthusiastically promoted at that very place. In 1822, within four years of becoming the twenty-first state in the Union, Illinois received a grant from Congress toward construction of a shipping canal across Chicago Portage to connect Lake Michigan with the Mississippi. In 1834, three years before Chicago was incorporated as a city, canal commissioners had already surveyed a new town site on the banks of the Des Plaines River adjacent to that prominent mound of higher ground. In and around the new town site, bedrock had proven to be an extensive layer of Silurian-age limestone that could easily be quarried for construction of bridges, locks, and retaining walls. From Mount Joliet and a multitude of nearby quarries, "Stone City" was soon supplying building materials for the ninety-six-mile shipping channel being dredged out beside and within the shallow Des Plaines River. Completed in 1848, the Illinois and Michigan Canal connected the Chicago River and the Illinois River with fifteen lift locks and five aqueducts along with miles and miles of roadbed and retaining wall.

In 1852, the hustling young community beside the diminishing mound of high ground was incorporated as the City of Joliet (one "l" was lost in the transition to English) and became the seat of Will County, Illinois. To clear up any confusion regarding their city's name, the city fathers passed a bylaw recognizing "joe-lee-**ette**" be the official pronunciation— as opposed to "**jolly**-ette" or, heaven forbid, "zho-lee-**eh**."

Long after completion of the canal, Joliet limestone was a preferred building material for many civic buildings and commercial establishments, as well as for many a grand residence in the city and surrounding district. After the great fire of 1871, much of the rebuilding in downtown Chicago came about with the help of this bluish-white limestone from only forty miles away. By that time, Joliet had a steel mill and an active railroad industry. Local quarries began shipping more than three thousand stone-laden railway cars each month to Chicago and elsewhere. On recently leveled terrain south of Joliet's downtown core, a suburb called Rockdale would soon emerge—Mound Jolliet was no more. Along with factories and a large labor force came service industries and merchants. Among the latter was a jeweler named Feagen who advertised far and wide for help in his growing enterprise. Answering the call was a young engraver and diamond-setter from Detroit, Louis August Liebermann.

After working five years with Mr. Feagen, Louis Liebermann started up his own business, and by the turn of century, he was well established in downtown Joliet, which had become an influential manufacturing city with a population of thirty thousand. Born in 1903, his son Louis Arthur began working at the family store very early in life. Born in 1923, Louis Arthur's own son, Louis Arthur Jr., also followed in father's footsteps; working part-time after school, this youngster known as "Art" became the third generation to work at the family store. After serving in Europe with the U.S. Army's Thirteenth Division during WWII, Art returned home to work full-time at the jewelry store. With his father's passing in 1966, Art became the proprietor of Liebermann's Jewelers, a business that was still growing with its community. By then the population of Joliet was approaching seventy thousand.

In 1970, motivated by necessity, Art made plans to modernize the family business. With help from his friendly banker, he purchased a three-level store on South Ottawa Street in the downtown business core. After gutting the interior, he had it remodeled to suit the needs of his business: the basement was re-organized for improved storage of inventory; the main floor featured custom-made cherry-wood display cases as well as office and work space; the top floor was leased out to provide supplementary income. Business continued to grow. Life was good. In 1977, things turned sour. Motivated by necessity, the City of Joliet made plans to modernize its downtown core by demolishing a city block of storefronts to make way for a new parking garage. Liebermann's Jewelry was one of the stores slated for removal. Being somewhat attached to his cherry-wood display cases and his relatively modern retail space, Art was not happy with the city's offer of $150,000 as compensation to relocate. "It was fine for the other merchants who were all renting," declared Art. "But the amount of compensation was far too little for a store owner, such as myself, with hundreds of thousands of dollars invested in the business. I wouldn't be able to pay off the bank, let alone secure another space anywhere near comparable."

For the structural moving division of Belding Engineering, several issues were raised by the Fermilab experience of moving a relatively large number of buildings in a relatively short time interval during the early 1970s. Division manager Pete Friesen, accustomed to working with a small nucleus of personally trained house-moving colleagues in British Columbia, now had to manage a large work force of relative inexperience and unproven ability. These employees were mostly experienced *equipment* movers unfamiliar with the leading edge of house-moving technology. Furthermore, very few, if any, of them had ever worked for such a bold and intuitive risk-taker. None of them were present on that Sumas Mountain Road back in 1948, where Pete was learning his art the hard way and being pushed by dire necessity toward new inventions. They did not see the grain shed come down on Arthur Dyck, and they did not see development of Pete Friesen's revolutionary crib jacks. Prior to learning Pete's background, many of these employees thought the UHJS was an American invention, manufactured only in Chicago.

In 1973, Pete organized a series of experiments to get everyone in his operation on the same page. In order to maximize productivity while maintaining a safe working environment, Pete needed to have confidence in his workforce; his employees had to be familiar with every theory and technique being employed as well as with all the equipment being used. Given the controversy generated by the height of his jack cribs and by the length of his jacks' ram extension, Pete's 3:1 height-to-base safety ratio seemed like a good place to start. Although the following description is somewhat tangential to our story, it is included for several reasons. By proving the validity of Pete's major safety guideline, this experiment instilled confidence in his co-workers and helped get everyone on solid footing for the many challenges ahead. This experiment and Pete's related equipment demonstrations were essential on-the-job training. This is also one of Pete's favorite technical stories.

Using standard 6″ by 8″ crib blocks four feet long, Pete and his crew built two crib piles, each four feet square at the base and twelve feet in height. Placed on top of each crib pile was one of Pete's personally designed hydraulic crib jacks, having a baseplate measuring 11″ by 16″ and a full ram extension height of forty inches. Placed atop the two jacks and bridging the distance between the crib piles came an 8″ by 8″ steel beam, sixteen feet in length. Slung over this arch beam, four and a half feet either side of its midpoint, two steel cables hung to the ground where their ends were connected to corresponding ends of two steel lift beams, both nine feet long, lying parallel to the overhead beam. A 26,000-pound, single-axle crane truck was then parked across the nine-foot lift beams between the jack cribs. When hydraulic pressure was supplied, extension of the crib-top jack rams raised the sixteen-foot beam that raised the cables, which in turn raised the nine-foot beams that then raised the 26,000-pound crane truck off the ground. Heavy ballast attached to the truck's telescoping boom provided an adjustable counterweight to keep the airborne truck in perfect balance. Hooked to the front of the suspended truck, a cable ran to the large winch on the back deck of a 17,000-pound, double-axle winch truck that would pull the suspended crane truck far enough forward to upset the jacks and/or destabilize the cribbing.

After instructing his crew to carefully watch for the first point of disturbance, Pete ordered the winch operator to start winching. The suspended truck did swing forward some, but the winch truck moved farther—sliding backward toward the center of the experiment. After chocks had been placed at each wheel of the winch truck, Pete again ordered the winch operator to start winching. Although the suspended truck did swing forward a bit more, the winch truck just pushed its chocks out of the way and kept sliding backward toward the crane truck calmly suspended between two crib piles. After the crew inserted the chocks into short trenches dug before each wheel of the winch truck, Pete again ordered the winch operator to begin winching. He did. He winched, and he winched, and the winch truck held firm until something finally happened. THUNK! THUD! The sixteen-foot steel lift beam slid off the jack rams, and the crane truck and the support beams returned unceremoniously to earth. However, the jacks and the jack cribs stayed perfectly upright and perfectly stable. The test was not repeated. Pete's 3:1 height-to-base safety ratio remained intact and unquestioned.

*Pete Friesen, an innovative structural mover, at work.*

With a well-trained and motivated workforce, Pete Friesen and Marvin Wasmund were soon doing business as Advance Moving Contractors of West Chicago. Six months after successfully relocating a two-story brick fire station in Highland Park, they received a telephone call from Art Liebermann who was hoping to move his jewelry store in Joliet. When Art had refused the compensation offer and refused to relocate, the City of Joliet had condemned that entire block of buildings and begun tearing down the stores, one by one. Before they got to Liebermann's, they had a deal. In exchange for their current property, the city gave Liebermann's another one nearby—across the street and south a bit—on the southwest corner of Van Buren and South Ottawa, where an old hotel had been leveled into a parking lot. Having agreed to the city's offer, all Art had to do was move Liebermann's Jewelers to the new site. When research suggested this would not be a simple matter, he was advised to contact AMC in West Chicago. Marv Wasmund and Pete Friesen were soon in Joliet checking out the jewelry store. Art Liebermann and Pete Friesen were soon on the golf course checking out each other. "All you have to do is lift it up, turn it around, and plunk it down beside that other building across the street," suggested Art.

"Yup," countered Pete. "All you have to do is excavate a new foundation beside that other building across the street."

"Okay," continued Art. "Will you be responsible for all the men and equipment necessary for the move?"

"Sure," countered Pete. "Will you be responsible for all the necessary permits and paperwork?"

"No sweat," responded Art. "I know lots of people at city hall." Each recognizing an accomplished sandbagger when they saw one, Art and Pete became good friends during their first round of golf and would enjoy many more rounds together. Meanwhile, the deal was done. Art had already realized that Pete was probably the only person who could wedge the store into exactly the right place. Pete Friesen probably took this jewelry store job because of the challenges it presented.

For one thing, estimated to weigh about seven hundred tons, Liebermann's Jewelers and its supporting steel would be about one hundred and thirty tons heavier than the fire station load in Highland Park, the heaviest Pete had yet tried to move. Fortunately, the steerable dollies and removable fifty-ton jacks he had wanted for the fire station job were now available. After quick mental arithmetic, Pete immediately reserved twenty-four of these Regent dollies from Almas International, a California-based company that had been using them on pipeline related projects in Alaska. Having already purchased one of Pete's original unified jacking units from Modern Hydraulics of New Westminster in the late fifties, one of the company's owners, Everett Almas, was now interested in seeing how Pete's newfangled three-zone loading system might work with these rubber-tired dollies. He was not the only curious party. Having learned of Pete's innovative success in Highland Park, engineers and structural movers from all corners of North America came to see what Pete Friesen was doing in Joliet, Illinois.

The first thing Pete was doing, after pouring himself a cup of strong coffee, was drawing lines on a paper napkin. He began the jewelry store move by designing a new model of unified hydraulic jacking machine capable of lifting the heavy building with its triple-layered brick walls; he needed a jacking unit with greater capacity in order to adequately pressurize three zones containing the larger fifty-ton jacks. Also, as his fire station experience had shown, it would be highly advantageous for the hydraulic fluid to be segregated into three distinct zones at the source—within the jacking unit itself.

Unlike previous jacking units, powered from the engine of the truck carrying them, a more powerful version would be driven by its own internal combustion engine. Instead of one hydraulic pump pressurizing a master-slave system, this unit would have three identical hydraulic pumps, each directly supplying its own distinct hydraulic circuit or zone. Mounted to framework around the engine, the three hydraulic pumps would be driven by a large gear affixed to the engine output shaft. As such, all three pumps would produce approximately the same amount of hydraulic pressure, each drawing fluid from the same large-volume reservoir. A common control lever would activate three control valves, directing pressurized fluid from each pump to its zone or back to the common reservoir. When the control lever was left in the neutral position, pressurized fluid would be locked in the downstream circuits to block the fluid and any load in place. Pressurized fluid from one pump would be routed through manifolds to all the jacks in one particular zone. While differentials in load weight might dictate slightly different pressures in each of the three zones, all jacks in any one zone would operate with the same amount of common pressure. Although not designed to supply unified pressure to all the jacks for lifting a building, this new jacking machine could very capably provide three zones of common pressure for supporting and moving heavy loads. *Visualize.*

Known by the color of its power plant, Pete's "Blue Brute" would be manufactured by Modern Hydraulics Incorporated. While awaiting assembly of his new jacking machine, Pete joined Art Liebermann for another round of golf on a nearby course. "Tough putt, Art," remarked Pete, watching Art's ball curve past the hole. "What are you going to do with all the stuff in your store during the move?"

"'Dunno, Pete," said Art, after finally getting his ball down. "There's a lot of fragile inventory in there that'll need a temporary home ... and a lot of lugging to and fro."

"Well," said Pete, lining up a short, tricky putt of his own, "you could always leave it in the store. It won't get damaged."

"Really?" asked Art, also sizing up Pete's current putting challenge.

"No, it'll be fine. I guarantee it," responded Pete.

"Sounds good to me!" declared Art, putting the pin back in its hole. "You can pick up your ball, Pete. That's a gimme." Back at the store, Art and his sons began hucking boxes of inventory out of the basement and up to temporary storage on the main floor. The decision had been made: their entire inventory, including the stemware on the shelves, would be left in the store during its move.

Meanwhile, Pete began planning for placement of his beams and jacks. Applying the jewelry store's dimensions to mathematical equations he had developed through years of experience, Pete was able to estimate the weight of each building section according to its size and its construction material. By knowing the relative weight of various materials, Pete could easily approximate weights of buildings and sections of buildings. After estimating the weight of each section, Pete then searched for the building's center of gravity by comparing section weights and the distance between them. Visualizing disparate building sections to be children of different weights on a seesaw, Pete would determine the exact point of balance between each pair of sections. By applying his teeter-totter principle across all opposing sections and plotting each point of balance, Pete was able to find the common point of balance for the building as a whole—its center of gravity. Once this point was known, Pete could organize his three loading zones around it for best balance, like three wheels around the seat of a child's tricycle.

Unlike the Highland Park fire station with its corner bell tower, Liebermann's 44' by 96' jewelry store was of fairly uniform construction, three bricks deep. Similar to the fire station, however, the store's front wall was relatively light because of a doorway and a large display window. Zone One would therefore encompass the entire width of the store's front section while Zone Two and Zone Three would equally share the weight of the back section. Years of experience and an acquired distrust of unfamiliar hydraulic jacks encouraged Pete to plan for almost twice the necessary jack-power to raise this load. Given the building's fragile contents, he considered a generous safety factor to be necessary, especially given the guarantee he had made to Art on the golf course.

Twenty-four fifty-ton jacks would provide 1,200 tons of lifting power under a load of seven hundred tons. With jacks operating at only 60 percent of their rated capacity, ample reserve pressure would be available should problems develop during this first attempt at using Pete's hydraulic three-zone loading system with rubber-tired dollies. Because the hydraulic pumps on Pete's Blue Brute would each supply approximately the same amount of hydraulic fluid at approximately the same common pressure to each of the three zones, Pete would need to use the same number of jacks in each zone. Therefore, Zone One would contain eight jacks, four under the forward part of each main load beam; Zone Two and Zone Three would each contain eight jacks under the aft part of their respective main load beams. *Derch denche.*

Although Art had soon cleaned out his old basement, his new basement was an untidy affair. Unbeknownst to Art and everyone else, a solid block of Joliet limestone lay beneath the asphalt surface of the parking lot that would soon be the new home of Liebermann's Jewelry. There were no options available other than dynamite and expensive labor. For this new basement alone, Art was now into the bank for almost as much money as he had refused in compensation. So far, all he had to show for his efforts was a big hole in the ground at the corner of West Van Buren and South Ottawa Streets. Meanwhile, once the city works department had removed all the buildings from both sides of Liebermann's store across the street, Pete brought in his crew and equipment. The hard-working men of AMC were already busy inserting cross-steel beams through notches in the old foundation walls when Pete received some bad news: workers had gone on strike at the steel mill manufacturing his heavy-duty main load beams. There was nothing to do but wait. One week stretched into two. "Nice drive, Pete," declared Art from beside the tee.

"Thanks, Art," responded Pete. "That one got the sweet spot."

"Yeah, great when it happens," commented Art, as they set off down the fairway. "Pete," continued Art, "I'm not in a very sweet spot right now. We're way past the deadline for moving the store, and the city is charging me $900 a day for being on what is now their property. What with cost of the new basement and all, I'm in a real financial bind. My lawyer is recommending that I sue you for the city's nine hundred a day."

After a moment to think it through, Pete turned to Art. "Okay, Art, I understand," he began. "If you sue me, I will sue the steel mill. They will probably lobby the government for more money, and the feds will probably lean on the state ... they'll get the money out of the city somehow. Strike or no strike, we'll have your store in place before anyone has to pay anyone anything," Pete concluded. "Your shot, Art."

The next day, Pete departed for California to complete the rental arrangement with Almas International and make certain the two dozen Regent dollies made it to Joliet without delay. While not quite in panic mode, Art was certainly somewhat stressed. He immediately took out a $1 million life insurance policy on Pete. "I had no choice," declared Art. "The city is charging me nine hundred bucks a day for my own store that's punched full of holes and sitting in a pile of rubble while the only guy with any chance in hell of moving it is away tending to some dollies in California. If anything happens to Pete Friesen, I'm a long way up the proverbial creek ... and it will take more than a paddle to get me out of this mess!"

Pete arrived back unscathed with the dollies loaded on the deck of a flatbed semi-trailer. The Regent dolly was a magnificent-looking item: a strong steel housing supporting two axles in tandem, each carrying two pairs of 8.25″ by 15″ rubber tires pumped up to 85 psi. Steerable front axles offered maneuverability; a fifty-ton hydraulic jack mounted on the center bunk promised strength. With each rubber-tired wheel weighing about seventy-five pounds, these dollies weighed in at almost three thousand pounds each.

The strike at the steel mill finally ended and eight fifty-foot sections of twenty-one-inch-deep, wide-flange steel beams eventually found their way to Joliet. Welded end-to-end, two of these sections made a girder one hundred feet long; two of these girders welded side by side created a one-hundred-foot boxed beam. Two of these one-hundred-foot boxed beams were the necessary main load beams. Soon installed beneath and horizontally perpendicular to a layer of cross-steel, these two long main beams were parallel to the store's long axis and ideally spaced to balance all three zones while accommodating the dollies that would eventually be rolling underneath. Meantime, Pete's crewmen were building crib piles to support twenty-four fifty-ton jacks, in three zones, beneath the two main load beams.

The Blue Brute worked well. Down went the control lever and up went the jacks, the main load beams, the cross-steel, and the stemware on the shelves, all as smooth as silk. Three working days later, after the old basement had been filled with crib blocks, all twenty-four Regent dollies and their twenty-four fifty-ton hydraulics jacks were in position, twelve beneath each main load beam. Pete and his crew soon had everything in order, and they were ready to roll. Because of limited maneuvering room enroute, they would begin an immediate ninety-degree turn as soon as they started forward from the old site. "You should have seen it!" exclaimed Art. "As soon as the front dolly reached the sidewalk, the concrete caved in and the front wheels dropped through, down to their hubs. Ee-yow!"

Unbeknownst to Art or to anyone else, there was a large security vault beneath the Ottawa Street sidewalk, probably installed by the original owner and accessed by a long-abandoned passageway through the front basement wall of the store. While Pete's crew worked to remove the forward outside dolly from under his building, Art remained frozen in time, visualizing hundreds of thousands of dollars in inventory, especially the crystal stemware last seen standing on his shelves.

After slowing his heart and catching his breath, Pete smiled briefly with the thirty-year-old memory of another errant dolly trying to slide a main load beam out from under his first house move. Here in Joliet, Pete knew he could not have designed a better test for his hydraulic three-zone loading system if he had tried. As the forward outside dolly began descending from under the load, its jack ram began extending to maintain Zone One's common pressure while the unweighted jack ram under the rising front corner began retracting to maintain that zone's common pressure. Similarly, any jacks back in Zone Two or Three that became unweighted would retract in order to maintain their zone's common pressure and thereby help keep the load level. This sudden vertical deviation at the extreme end of a turning moment had not upset hydraulic equilibrium one little bit. Whether on rails and rollers or on rubber-tired dollies, Pete Friesen's hydraulic three-zone loading method was here to stay.

After checking in vain for financial treasure that might help Arthur back from the brink of despair, Pete and his crew began hucking crib blocks into the hole. As soon as the vault had been stacked to the top, Pete's crew realigned the front outside dolly and prepared to roll onto a street made level with heavy wood planking. Pulling their load gently, they executed two tight turns to face the storefront in the desired opposite direction and then slowly nudged it into position above the new basement foundation. Using an old trick he had discovered by accident in 1948 and used many times since, Pete angled his jacks and gently kicked the load sideways, tight against the north wall of the adjacent structure. While everyone else was admiring the resultant "seamless" transition, Art was squirming in his lawn chair, thinking about crystal stemware that was last seen standing on the shelves of his repositioned store.

After the Blue Brute had softly lowered the building into place, the AMC crew collected their beams, blocks, and jacks, while the Regent dollies were loaded back onto their flatbed semi trailer for the return journey to California. Once again, Pete had pushed the envelope and completed a task few would have attempted and many thought was impossible. The Blue Brute jacking machine was one innovation. The application of hydraulic three-zone loading for seven hundred tons on rubber-tired dollies was significant. While something similar may have been done elsewhere or beforehand, written descriptions are hard to come by. Although Pete may have employed the hydraulic three-zone system on a smaller load before this one, it doesn't stand out in his mind or on paper anywhere. As evidenced by the number of house movers from across the country that came to watch, Liebermann's Jewelry seems to have blazed a short, new trail in structural-moving territory. Meantime, Pete temporarily excused himself and followed Louis Jolliet's route north along the Des Plaines. He and Marv had another job to look at—an old wooden mansion in downtown Chicago.

Looking at the exterior, it is almost impossible to see any sign of Liebermann's "new" store being moved up against the existing structure alongside it. When Art finally got inside, he found everything exactly as he had last seen it. Nothing had moved. The crystal stemware was still standing upright on the shelves where he had left it. Had the goblets been filled, nary a drop would have spilled. When asked if the exhausting and expensive relocation exercise had been worthwhile, Art responded without hesitation. "We're still here, and we're still in business!"

The Liebermanns are, indeed, still here and still in business. When he had returned to Joliet after serving with the U.S. Army, Louis Arthur "Art" Liebermann Jr. had married his sweetheart, Jean Slack. In 1950, the first of their four sons, Louis Blair, was born. Once of age and sufficiently educated, Louis Blair found employment at his family's jewelry store. In 1977, the year of the big move, Louis Blair's first-born son, Louis Eric, arrived on the scene. By the time young Louis Eric joined his father, two uncles, and a grandfather in the family store, it was time for another move.

The modernization of downtown Joliet had proved a spur to the city's economic resurgence, but not without some adverse effect. The new parking facilities proved to serve far more midnight gamblers than daytime shoppers. Large urban casinos and their support facilities had gradually squeezed many small retail operations out to shopping malls on the edge of town. An era had come to an end. "I remember farmers congregating in my grandfather's store like old friends," Art recalled. "It was a bit of a meeting place for people who came to town for supplies every week or so. Even in my dad's time, people were always dropping in to say hello. Downtown Joliet used to be full of people … now, there is hardly anyone around during daylight hours. There is no retail business to be had."

Philosophical about the new business reality, Art calmly abandoned the downtown store he had fought so hard to keep thirty years before. By this time, Art Liebermann was known as "Art Senior"—a man who would go quietly, taking his beautiful cherry-wood display cases with him. By 2000, Art and his sons had completed relocation of their family business to a small plaza in the northwestern part of town. "It took a while for business to find us," says Art, "but some days, you can hardly find a spot in the parking lot. It's a busy little mall."

Life is good at Liebermann's, where one can usually find three generations of active Liebermanns at work. Having failed at retirement, Art comes to "the office" four or five afternoons a week, usually after a round of golf. The family business is now managed by three of his sons, who are introducing several of his ten grandchildren to the business. A fifth generation of Liebermanns is already at work in the family store. Although Louis Jolliet never returned to Illinois, and Mound Jolliet has long since disappeared, there has always been a Louis at Liebermann's jewelry store.

# 7

# Chicago

The Potawatomi people who first guided French-Canadian explorers to the area in 1673 knew it as *Checagou*—a small river that flowed into the southwest corner of a very great lake. The low-lying land at the river's outlet subsequently gave rise to a series of forts and missions. In 1779, Jean Baptiste Pointe du Sable, an African-American from Sainte-Domingue (Haiti) became the first pioneer settler in the area. By 1833, the settlement had become a town of three hundred and fifty hardy souls who understood Checagou to mean something "strong or great." In 1837, with slightly more than four thousand inhabitants, the bustling community became incorporated as the City of Chicago. During the previous year, hardware merchant Henry Clarke and his wife, Caroline, having recently relocated from New York State, built their new home on twenty acres of prairie land they had acquired on the municipality's southern outskirts.

For this new residence at Sixteenth Street and Michigan Avenue, Henry and Caroline opted for traditional timber-frame structure—large squared timbers with mortise and tenon joints secured by wooden pegs. However, in keeping with contemporary fashion, the Clarkes chose Greek Revival-style architecture—tall Doric columns supporting a large portico and well-proportioned pediment, large shuttered windows, and an imposing entrance. Inside, a wide central hall opened to ornately decorated main-floor rooms while six bedrooms occupied the second story. When Henry died bankrupt in 1849, Caroline sold part of the property to help support her children and finance completion of the family home. During the next decade, a complementary second portico was constructed on the west side of the house, and a parapet with Italianate finials was added to the roofline. To increase light and ventilation, a moderate-sized cupola was incorporated into the rooftop.

Chicago was booming. By 1860, with a twenty-five-fold increase in twenty-three years since incorporation, the city population had surpassed one hundred thousand. A well-established police force and a free public school system were key components of the city's burgeoning social fabric. Canals had already connected Lake Michigan with the Mississippi River system, and boat traffic was brisk. Chicago was well on its way to becoming the world's largest railroad center. The city's first opportunity for hosting a national political convention saw Abraham Lincoln of Illinois nominated as the Republican candidate for President.

When the American Civil War ended in 1865, the city re-energized its commitment to infrastructure improvements while experiencing another large surge in population. By 1870, a three-fold increase in ten years saw almost three hundred thousand people living in a dynamic community continuing to build at a near-frantic pace. Under Lake Michigan, a brick-lined tunnel five feet in diameter was constructed to channel clean drinking water from two miles offshore. A central facility with a landmark 150-foot limestone tower was built to distribute water citywide. Vehicle-traffic tunnels were built beneath the Chicago River to service the busy central core, now blossoming with a multitude of new brick and masonry structures. Streets and avenues pushed the city energetically in every possible direction. On the periphery came communities of new homes being rapidly constructed by the city's first suburbanites.

The Midwest was booming. European immigration and westward migration were pushing roads and railways through the forest and across the prairie. At railheads and river junctions, old forts and trading posts were all but disappearing beneath the construction projects of the vibrant young cities growing around them. With the harvest of the forest and turning of prairie sod came the need for sub-distribution centers and the rise of new, remote communities. Myriad towns, villages, and hamlets were sprouting everywhere across a seemingly limitless land where almost everything constructed by man was dependent on wood from the northern forest.

Following a summer of drought, the autumn of 1871 continued hot and dusty. On Sunday, October 8, graying skies over the southwestern horizon suggested the possibility of rain and relief for the hundreds of thousands now living along Lake Michigan's western shore. Instead, disaster struck. Strong surface winds, associated with a low-pressure weather system sweeping northeasterly across the Great Plains, suddenly whipped new life into hundreds of intentional farm and forestry slash burns smoldering along the frontier. In a region of intense commercial forestry around Green Bay in northern Wisconsin, the situation was soon out of control. Many small brush fires erupted into one gigantic forest fire that consumed entire logging communities and 1.5 million acres of vegetation before burning itself out at the edge of the big lake. Within a 2,400-square-mile area of devastation, approximately two thousand people burned to death, including half the 1,600 village residents of Peshtigo, Wisconsin.

Meanwhile, down in the big city, the 334,000 residents of Chicago also experienced a night never to be forgotten. Soon after darkness fell on that warm Sunday evening, a suddenly strong wind began whirling through the streets and back alleys of the mostly wooden metropolis. While a thief, a gambler, and even a meteor shower remain suspects, most histories have taken Catherine and Patrick O'Leary's cow off the hook as the "goat" for initiating a blaze that ravaged downtown Chicago on that October night. Wherever the spark came from, it ignited a tinderbox—a conglomeration of closely spaced, multi-level, wooden buildings surrounding the business district. Although many were of newer brick and masonry exteriors, most downtown buildings were wood framed and were connected by wide and solid boardwalks. Everything was very dry and well seasoned, like the cords of firewood stacked beside wooden homes and barns in preparation for winter's inevitable return.

Miraculously, because of the wind's direction, the O'Leary home survived the small fire that began in or near their barn before raging northeasterly across the city's core. A few masonry buildings survived, but almost everything else in the fire's path was leveled. An antiquated fire-alarm system and a glitch in administrative communication were contributing factors to an emergency that quickly became a disaster. Like falling dominoes, wooden structure after wooden structure exploded in spontaneous combustion from the radiant heat. Superheated winds launched cluster bombs of burning embers and timber far ahead of the flame front, often onto fleeing citizens who crammed the remaining river bridges while attempting to outrun the advancing horror. When the fire jumped across the river and destroyed the waterworks, the city's water supply was cut off. Overwrought firefighters finally laid down their hoses and sought safety. The rain finally arrived late on Monday. On Tuesday, the wind dropped and the flames finally ran out of fuel. At the edge of the great lake where the small river comes in, heavy smoke lingered above two thousand acres of newly blackened landscape.

Best estimates suggest property valued at $200 million in 1871 currency went up in smoke during this disastrous forty-eight-hour period that claimed approximately two hundred and fifty human lives and left almost one hundred thousand people homeless. Although the city would later witness other tragedies with far greater loss of human life, the Great Chicago Fire of 1871 remains a touchstone in its history and a turning point in its development as a progressive and energetic community. The enduring notoriety and mystique attached to this event attests to Chicago's civic pride. The speed and direction of the city's reconstruction can be seen as testament to the will and bravado of its citizenry.

Caroline Clarke had passed away eleven years prior to the fire of 1871. Although her spacious wooden home was spared, the inferno devastated much of the city that had grown out to surround the Clarke house. One year later, her children sold the family home to Mr. John Chrimes, who had it moved, by a team of horses and good-sized log rollers, four miles south to East Forty-Fifth Street at Wabash Avenue. The city continued growing outwards. By 1890, more than one million people called Chicago home; by 1910, there were more than two million inhabitants; by 1930, there were more than three million. In 1941, Mr. Chrimes's grandchildren sold the old Clarke house to Bishop Louis Henry Ford and the St. Paul Church of God in Christ. After being used as a parish hall, parsonage, and community center, it was purchased by the City of Chicago in 1977. By then, the Widow Clarke's house had been identified as the oldest family home in the city. Wanting to preserve this 141-year-old Greek Revival survivor, city officials decided to return it to its original neighborhood, at Sixteenth and South Michigan, where it would be refurbished as part of the Prairie Avenue Historic District then under development.

Having moved numerous buildings in and around Chicago, and after being recognized industry-wide for recent relocations of a fire station and a jewelry store, Advance Moving Contractors was invited to submit a proposal for moving the Clarke House back north. While considering the project and scouting possible routes, Pete discovered two major problems that he needed to literally "go over" with his colleagues. One problem was Interstate 55, the Stevenson Expressway: this very wide and very urban highway would have to be crossed on a long overpass bridge of limited weight-bearing capacity. Chicago's renowned elevated rail system, locally known as the "El," presented the other major difficulty; its original north-south segment, the Green Line, was fully elevated along its entire length and operating twenty-four hours a day. Obviously impossible to get around, the Green Line was also too low to get under. They would have to go over it. Regardless of any remuneration offered, Pete probably took the Clarke job primarily because of the challenges it presented.

In late 1977, Pete and his AMC crew went to work at 4520 South Wabash Avenue, having contracted to move Chicago's oldest house almost four miles along big-city streets in a very urban environment. While his men began removing the cupola from the rooftop and severing the porches from east and west walls, Pete continued to examine all possible routes and to study every available option for dealing with his two major hurdles. Needless to say, Pete had many a powwow with city officials and jumped through more than one hoop to get this job done. The city insisted on employment of unionized equipment operators and a $500,000 damage deposit for any attempted crossing of its elevated rail system. Fortunately, Pete's former parent company was able to help out on both counts. As well as supplying some of the necessary equipment and unionized operators, Belding agreed to post the required bond, insuring the city against damage to its treasured historic building or its beloved transit system.

One thing was certain, regardless of the route taken: this relocation would demand major diversions of vehicle traffic and at least one disruption of train service on the elevated Green Line. One of the wider thoroughfares nearby, Martin Luther King Jr. Drive was recognized as the most desirable north-south artery for transport of the oversize load. However, between the house on Wabash Avenue and the chosen route, there was an El of a problem. Everyone was soon in agreement: the best place to cross the elevated railway was the Green Line bridge over Forty-Fourth Street, a bit more than a block north and just around the corner from where Pete's crew was already hard at work. "Better sooner than later," Pete mused, while visualizing his fragile cargo "flying" over this steel-and-concrete obstacle. "One thing's for sure," he muttered to himself, "we're gonna need a pile of crib blocks." After yet another meeting with city officials, it was time for Pete to check back in with his crew.

With porches and cupola removed, the Widow Clarke House was just another rectangular wood-frame structure to be lifted and moved by methods long tried and well proven. Measuring 28' by 46' and estimated to weigh slightly more than one hundred tons, the main house shell was not problematic, even with its four fireplaces. After chimneys and other protuberances were removed and after all doors and windows had been battened down, the heavier work began. Jack-hammered holes notched into the top of foundation walls allowed insertion of the cross-steel: ten pieces of wide-flange steel beam, thirty feet in length, were spaced every six to eight feet across the building's width and immediately beneath its ground floor timbers. Two main load beams, sixteen inches deep and fifty feet long, were then inserted on the building's long axis, immediately beneath and horizontally perpendicular to the cross-steel. Equidistant from centerline and fourteen feet apart, these main beams would receive upward pressure from the hydraulic jacks and carry weight of the building. Pete and everyone else present watched carefully as the UHJS control lever was selected downwards, pushing twelve circuits of unified pressure out to twelve carefully placed quick-change crib jacks. The delicate house rose smoothly from its foundation and, after subsequent jacking cycles, was soon sitting on the rear bunk of a large pull-truck and six rubber-tired dollies. The next day, the entire ensemble began creeping slowly northward along Wabash Avenue.

Around the corner on Forty-Fourth Street, quite a scene was

unfolding at the Green Line rail crossing, where a small army of personnel was shuffling equipment and erecting lights inside temporary fences and barricades. Over on the east side of the elevated track, four horizontally cross-shaped wooden crib piles were growing out of the asphalt where hundreds of eight-foot-long wooden blocks were being layered ever upward. In cross-section, these expanded crib piles resembled an inflated plus sign (+), or Greek cross, measuring 8' by 8'. To conserve crib blocks while maintaining his mandatory 3:1 safety ratio, Pete had devised a more open crib pattern whereby eight-foot blocks were laid, two or three at a time, across the center four feet of the preceding course while four-foot blocks were laid across their ends. When completed, the structure was a tall, stable, and well-ventilated crib pile.

Back on the west side of the tracks, the Widow Clarke was donning her skates, also known as creeper-dollies or rollers. Eight of these amazingly strong, low-profile units would easily carry the Widow Clarke house along the two roll beams, from one side of the Green Line tracks to the other. Meantime, in ground-level preparation, two sections of roll beam with skates already in place were being strap-welded to the bottom of the two main load beams under the house. The skates and roll beam sections would be jacked upwards with everything else. Someone had been *thinking it through.*

Once the skates and roll beams were fastened into place, workers began importing eight-foot blocks to build four horizontally cross-shaped crib piles, two beneath each main load beam. Twelve of Pete's fifteen-ton hydraulic crib jacks were then installed, three on each crib pile, and connected to AMC's unified jacking unit, representing 180 tons of lifting potential. As such, Pete was well satisfied with a 50 percent safety margin for lifting the house and steel beams, a load weighing 120 tons. All twelve hydraulic circuits were soon pre-loaded with pressure according to their positions and weight-bearing responsibilities. As soon as everyone and everything was ready, the jacking unit control lever was selected downwards, directing high-pressure hydraulic fluid to the *extend* side of the master cylinder piston. Pushed by the master piston, the slave pistons extended within their cylinders and pressurized the fluid in their unified circuits. Up went the jacks. Up went the oldest house in Chicago. Up and up it went.

Although refinements to the jacking unit and Pete's quick-change crib jacks made the task much easier than it otherwise might have been, it was still a tedious process for the crewmen to repeatedly jack and block their way skyward, one layer at a time. It took six men manning the machinery, hucking blocks, and resetting jacks to make it all happen. It was difficult and dangerous work. Course after course, they layered the house upwards. The higher they got, the shakier-looking the crib piles got. Several dozen hours and 650 crib blocks after they began jacking, Pete and his crew had their house exactly where they wanted it. The shell of Chicago's oldest home was perched on ten cross-steel beams resting on two main load beams supported by eight creeper-dollies riding on two roll beams sitting on four twenty-four-foot-high crib piles. West of the Green Line rail bridge, the Widow Clarke house was hovering twenty-seven feet above Forty-Fourth Street. On the east side of the bridge, two roll beam extensions were waiting to receive the house load onto the top of four additional twenty-four-foot-high crib piles. From a bridle assembly attached to the back end of the load, a strong cable extended to a loaded tractor-trailer serving as holdback vehicle. From a similar bridle assembly at the forward end of the load, another strong cable stretched over the tracks to the rear-mounted winch on a heavy front-end loader. This tow vehicle would slowly winch the load across.

Pete was concerned because the limited amount of cable available on its winch drum would require the front-end loader to reposition forward several times while towing the load across. When Pete approached the loader's operator to emphasize the importance of maintaining tension on the tow cable, he was brushed off. "Get outta here!" commanded the operator. "I'm a union man, and I know how to operate my equipment."

At midnight on Saturday, December 4, 1977, trains stopped running and electricity was cut off from the center power-rails along the section of the Green Line between the Forty-Third Street and Forty-Seventh Street stations. For the first time ever, Chicago's historic elevated railway was shut down. While night-owl train riders shuttled between these two stations by bus, Pete's crew quickly installed the two roll-beam center sections across the two sets of track, where they would be bolted to their crib-top extensions. Atop the four west-side pillars of wood, other workers severed the bar straps holding creeper-dolly skates and roll beam stubs under the main beams. By 2:40 AM Sunday, the center beam sections were in place across the tracks and the crew was ready to roll. Pete had visualized this part of the move many times. He had checked and rechecked many things many times. He had thought it all through, and there was nothing else to do but get on with it. Suppressing a chuckle in remembrance of the crib test episode from a few years back, Pete ordered the loader operator to start winching.

*The 120-ton Widow Clarke heritage building appears to float across Chicago's elevated railway on a bright beam of floodlights—Chicago Sun-Times.*

Slowly but surely, in the glare of floodlights and with the rapt attention of all present, the old building and two layers of steel beams riding on squat creeper-dollies inched across the El. Soon, it became time to move the tow vehicle farther forward, and when the loader operator released the lock on his rear-mounted winch mechanism, the situation quickly became unraveled. Suddenly released of tension, the winch drum rotated in reverse and started spewing slack cable. On top of the roll beams on top of the railway tracks, one hundred and twenty tons of wood and steel sitting on the El began to roll solemnly backward—in the direction it came from. During the elevation process, the west-side crib piles had compressed together and into the road; the railway bridge had not. The resulting slight difference in elevation was drawing the house toward an ugly ending just beyond its starting point. "Golly, gee whiz!" (or some such thing) exclaimed Pete's crewmembers, almost in unison.

Encouraged by an additional series of loud words emanating from Pete's mouth, the unionized loader operator quickly regained control of his wayward winch and, like a frenzied fisherman, began reeling in slack cable. He made it—his line regained tension and his trophy catch remained hooked. However, in giving up its western escape, the old house gave the line a good yank and jerked the rear end of the front-ender loader high into the air—an added punctuation to the proceedings. With thanks to the energy absorbed by elevating the loader, the cable did not snap. There were no deaths or decapitations; there were no severed limbs or injuries of any kind. Very fortunately, there was also not a catastrophic end to the 141-year-old house. "I don't know how the good Lord works," sighed Pete, after slowing his heart and catching his breath, "but God is certainly looking out for us."

Slightly before four o'clock that Sunday morning, one hour and ten minutes after the El crossing had commenced, the Widow Clarke House was "safely" perched atop the four east-side crib piles, twenty-seven feet above the ground. As soon as the two middle roll beam sections were unbolted and removed, electrical power was restored to the conducting center rails, and trains resumed operation along the Green Line as if nothing had happened. While Pete gave his crew the remainder of the day off, the large weather-beaten structure sitting at eye-level must have caused a stir among early-morning train riders. In fact, thanks to Mother Nature, Green Line commuters had ample opportunity for glimpses of the weekend's handiwork. When Pete and his rested crew returned to begin jacking down the house, they were dismayed to find their jacking system unusable. Cold temperatures had found water in the circuits and turned it into ice. Minute quantities of moisture, often from condensed water vapor, are common in fluid-based operating systems subjected to repeated changes of temperature and pressure. Like a chain's weakest link, one frozen or faulty hydraulic circuit could destroy the reliability of any complex hydraulic-based system. Pete extended the rest period for his men and their machinery.

A few days later, the weather warmed. Somewhere in the hydraulic circuitry, ice melted to water, and the jacking system returned to normal operation. So too did Pete and his well-rested crew. Jacking the old house down from its lofty perch was equally as tedious and possibly more dangerous than the jacking-up process. Once again, six men were actively employed atop the four crib piles under the load or operating the machinery below. Hydraulic hose and electric cable hung down from the wooden towers and covered the ground below. One at a time, course after course, hefty eight-foot-long blocks were extricated from beneath jack-supported load beams and lowered to ground. While safety blocking was in place on all crib piles under the load, the twelve crib jacks were once again removed and reset to a lower course of blocks. Then, on command from the unified jacking unit, the jacks would again raise the house slightly, relieving weight from the topmost layers of blocks that could then be removed. After two days of demanding toil, the old house—minus creeper-dolly skates and roll beams—was back aboard the six dollies and the original tow vehicle. Along with an entourage of police and other escorts, Caroline and Henry Clarke's house was soon trundling east toward Martin Luther King Jr. Drive. After the removal of fences, barricades, and lights, vehicle traffic was flowing under the elevated rail bridge on Forty-Fourth Street for the first time in several weeks. As it had been doing for all but four hours since 1893, the Green Line kept rolling along.

Three miles to the north, Pete Friesen was studying another bridge. During the previous few weeks, he had spent considerable time here, where Michigan Avenue crosses the multi-lane Stevenson Expressway on two long spans of concrete. Although this was considered the best available route across the wide expressway, legitimate concerns were raised about the bridge's ability to hold up under the narrow footprint of Pete's load, now trundling west along Thirty-First Street from Martin Luther King Jr. Drive. With all the beams, jacks, dollies, and a truck underneath the house, the total load now weighed about 250 tons. Having thought the problem through and visualized a solution, the former Alberta cowboy rounded up an additional herd of rubber-tired dollies. Before his heavy load ventured onto the Michigan Avenue bridge, Pete had an additional six dollies installed under the steel main beams supporting the old house. Now relieved of all weight-bearing responsibility, the pull-truck was removed from underneath and repositioned as far as possible ahead of the dollies, from where it would winch the load across. In so doing, Pete doubled the number of rubber tires under his load and virtually doubled the size of its footprint, spreading the weight more evenly over a broader area. Riding on ninety-six rubber tires, the Widow Clarke house reportedly depressed the Michigan Avenue bridge a mere one-hundredth of an inch while it crossed over the Stevenson Expressway. Once across, Pete cut the extra dollies out from the herd and sent them on their way.

After negotiating one tight turn to the east and another to the north, Pete's crew towed their fragile load to its new home on the east side of Indiana Avenue, just south of Eighteenth Street. Here, the house was carefully raised from the dollies and slid onto its new concrete foundation. The cupola, porches, and other accessories arrived by flatbed truck. On December 18, 1977, the entire Greek Revival structure was back "home" in time for the Christmas holiday, two city blocks away from where it had been built 141 years before. Now located at 1827 South Indiana Avenue, the Widow Clarke house became an integral part of the Prairie Avenue Historic District. During the latter half of the nineteenth century, this part of town had been the place to be for many affluent Chicago families. The grand old neighborhood had gradually lost its appeal during intensive industrialization over the next one hundred years. A few of the grand old homes and a surprising amount of original architecture remained. Encouraged by the city, the area is regaining residential appeal. While the Clarke family's prairie vista has long been replaced by a mélange of masonry, steel, and glass, there are now trendy shops sprouting beneath warehouses full of loft apartments, and stylish new homes are growing beside the old mansions, some of which have evolved into living museums.

Today, the Clarke house is one such museum. Completely refurbished and refurnished, it presents the residential ambiance of a middle-class home in the era prior to the American Civil War. The oldest house in Chicago offers warm welcome to visitors from all parts of the globe. As well as commemorating its builders, this superbly renovated structure celebrates the foresight and commitment of the city. The Clarke house lives on, sharing stories of the past with all who enter. It also stands in silent testimony to the people who moved it there. Twentieth-century technology aside, the Clarke House Museum exists because of a very dedicated structural-moving crew led by Pete Friesen.

*Chicago's oldest wooden home undergoes restoration while open to the public as Clarke House Museum in the Prairie Avenue Historic District—Peter Rowlands.*

# 8

# Minneapolis

Late in the year 1679, six years after Father Marquette and Louis Jolliet had paddled up from the Mississippi, another party of French-Canadian explorers and missionaries made its way down the Illinois River. After hastily constructing winter shelter, expedition leader René-Robert de La Salle dispatched three inexperienced men to explore the Mississippi River as far as possible upstream. One of the three "volunteers" was a Belgian-born Recollect Franciscan priest, Father Louis Hennepin. In April 1680, after following the Illinois River downstream and turning up the mighty Mississippi, the three neophyte explorers were taken captive by a tribe of Sioux Indians who then took them farther upriver into *Minnesota*—Land of Milky Waters. Dragged around the countryside by this band of nomadic hunters, Hennepin was the first European to see and describe what eventually proved to be the only major waterfall on the Mississippi River main stem. Known to the locals as *Owamniyomni*— The Whirlpool—this cataract was promptly, if not politely, named Saint Anthony Falls by Hennepin in honor of his patron saint.

That September, the three captives were finally rescued by Daniel Greysolon du Lhut, more simply known as Duluth, who was on an unofficial peace-making mission among his colony's aboriginal fur-trading partners south and west of Lake Superior. While successfully arranging peaceful relations between the Ojibwe and Sioux nations, Duluth negotiated release of three grateful explorers and escorted them back to "civilization" in New France, after claiming the upper Mississippi watershed for Louis XIV, King of France. Meanwhile, after a brief return to Quebec, La Salle resumed his official journey of discovery down the Illinois and Mississippi Rivers. After reaching the Gulf of Mexico in 1682 and naming the new territory *Louisiana* in honor of his king, La Salle returned to France.

At its peak in the early eighteenth century, New France encompassed almost all of explored North America beyond the thirteen British colonies, extending from Hudson's Bay to the Gulf of Mexico and from the Atlantic Ocean to the Rocky Mountains. However, by end of the French and Indian War (also known as the Seven Years' War), the political landscape of the New World had been irrevocably altered. Under the terms of the 1763 Treaty of Paris, France ceded all mainland North American territories east of the Mississippi to Britain. After the American War of Independence, the 1783 Treaty of Paris recognized these territories east of the Mississippi River and south of Canada to be part of the newly formed United States of America.

After the 1803 Louisiana Purchase gave the United States control of all former French territories west of the Mississippi River, the government in Washington initiated an aggressive campaign of westward expansion, spearheaded by a series of military forts along and beyond the Mississippi River. One such outpost was constructed in 1820 at the confluence of the Minnesota and Mississippi Rivers, just below Saint Anthony Falls. Bringing law and order to the wild Minnesota territory, the soldiers of this Fort Snelling also introduced agriculture and industry to the area. Hundreds of acres of wheat and vegetables were soon cultivated; a gristmill and a sawmill began operating by waterpower from the fifty-foot drop of the falls.

Wave after wave of settlers followed close behind. Farmers and ranchers, loggers and miners, lawyers and doctors, merchants and millers all found their way up the Mississippi or followed the trail west from Chicago. By 1858, when Minnesota became the thirty-second state in the Union, town sites had been established on both sides of the big river where Saint Anthony Falls already powered numerous sawmills. In the early 1860s, a short vicious war saw the dispossessed Sioux and Ojibwe dispersed to reservations far removed from Owamniyomni. Then came the railroad. The lure of abundant waterpower soon saw twenty-three flourmills, seventeen sawmills, and numerous woolen mills, cotton mills, and iron works operating near the falls. In 1867, the industrious community on the Mississippi's west bank was incorporated as the city of Minneapolis—Water City. With subsequent absorption of the village of Saint Anthony on the river's east bank, the new city contained almost fifteen thousand residents. By 1880, the population had tripled; by 1890, it had tripled again. By the early twentieth century, more than three hundred thousand people were living in this city, the largest saw-milling center in the nation and the largest flour-milling center in the world.

Growing in harmony with twentieth-century industrialization, the population peaked at more than five hundred thousand. By then the sawmills were all long gone, and the flourmills had all shuffled off to Buffalo. By the mid-twentieth century, the birthplace of the city had become its blighted backyard. The once-industrious riverbanks above and below Saint Anthony Falls were now host to idle factories, abandoned rail depots, and scores of vacant buildings. Large areas of underutilized land had become isolated from the city by a network of barely used railway lines that also separated citizens from their river. With urban renewal in mind, the city began dispensing with the old, obsolete, and vacant structures; within a decade, it had razed approximately two hundred buildings across twenty-five city blocks— about 40 percent of downtown. Eventually realizing the newly created spaces were coming at the expense of historic architecture and buildings of heritage significance, city fathers began rethinking their options. Having identified the central riverfront as an area in need of redevelopment, the city undertook an ambitious revitalization of the former industrial core. Spurred by the Clean Water Act and other environmental legislation of the early 1970s, redevelopers based their vision of urban renewal around the river. Reducing levels of pollution and rehabilitating riparian zones were fundamental steps on the way to a cleaner and healthier riverscape. A system of public riverside parks and trails would provide citizens with renewed access to their river.

In 1972, a committee of concerned municipal and state agencies laid the cornerstone of a long-evolving process to complete the conversion of the river from "a practical utility to a public amenity that is once again a vital part of the city." While miles of railway track and many derelict structures were removed to create space for the envisioned redevelopment, some historic buildings were restored and integrated into the plan. One such building was an old livery stable destined for new life in the revitalized Saint Anthony Village part of town. Built in 1880, the Brown-Ryan Livery Stable was now standing in the way of a major renewal project on East Hennepin Avenue. The developer of the new megaproject offered to restore the livery stable if the city could move it to another location. City planners soon came up with an ideal site, just a few hundred yards downriver. Although there was justifiable concern about the century-old structure's vulnerability to the stress of relocation, almost everyone involved was excited by the idea of moving it.

A local structural engineering company with experience in the restoration of historic buildings, Bakke Kopp Ballou & McFarlin (BKBM), was hired by the city to evaluate the livery stable and oversee its relocation. It would not be a cakewalk. While developing ideas of how to keep the building in one piece, BKBM were soon looking for a qualified structural moving company—preferably one with experience on older masonry-style buildings. They were soon on the phone to AMC of West Chicago, the relatively new outfit that had recently moved the old Widow Clarke house over the elevated railway in Chicago. Apparently, this company had also relocated a 700-ton brick jewelry store in Joliet the previous year and a two-story brick fire station in Highland Park the year before that. "Okay, we'll come and take a look," said the voice on the phone.

Pete Friesen was soon standing on a Minneapolis sidewalk looking at the Brown-Ryan stable. It was not a pretty sight. Abandoned for decades, the one-hundred-year-old livery stable looked to be on the verge of collapse, as it may have been. Standing aloof in a field of new buildings and newer excavations, it looked out of place, a relic from a different time. However, having determined there was still sufficient life in the old building, the Minneapolis Housing and Redevelopment Authority (MHRA) was determined to move it about two hundred yards south, across Hennepin Avenue where it would be rehabilitated as part of a rejuvenated riverfront complex. The development firm of Kajima and Boisclair, whose large project on Hennepin Avenue included both the current and the intended site, had agreed to fully refurbish the old livery stable, if the city could get it from A to B in one piece.

"Not a pretty sight," Pete muttered to himself, already beginning to think it through. "Surely, though," he continued, "if it was built by man then man should be able to move it. Anyway, let's go see what the consultants have to say."

The gentlemen of BKBM outlined their plans to stabilize the structure inside and out with wooden timbers and steel rod. The city's assigned project manager, Dick Victor of MHRA, was on hand to navigate through myriad administrative channels while coordinating the entire project on behalf of the community. Once reassured about the smooth ride offered by Pete's three-zone loading system, all concerned became united in their determination—they would do their level best to move the old stable in one piece. To augment his company's inventory of jacks, beams, and crib blocks, Pete presented a must-have list: bulldozers, backhoe, front-end loader, yards and yards of steel chain, yards and yards of steel cable, equipment operators, experienced welders, and willing workers. Within a few weeks, everyone and everything was organized. Although they had recently left AMC to start their own company, former partner Marvin Wasmund and foreman Corbin Klug agreed to help Pete with this very delicate job. Also on the crew was Pete's twenty-two-year-old son, Eric. They were soon all on the jobsite, and the physical work began in late summer 1980.

The Brown-Ryan Livery Stable was a challenge for all concerned. Having been criticized for demolishing too many old downtown buildings, the city of Minneapolis was under pressure to save this one. To earn their keep and to maintain their reputation, BKBM had to keep this collection of old limestone blocks together long enough and well enough to qualify it for refurbishment. Confronted by restricted operating space at both the origin and destination sites and by a significant downslope along the route, AMC had another challenging move. The old building presented a challenge in size as well as its shaky condition. Although similar in footprint to Liebermann's, this 46' by 94' relic was three hundred tons heavier than the jewelry store. With the addition of supporting steel beneath, the stable would weigh about one thousand tons: it would be the heaviest and most fragile load Pete had ever attempted to move. As with the recent jewelry store project, he would use Regent dollies and their fifty-ton removable jacks in his now-proven three-zone loading configuration.

First things first: following through on BKBM's plan, the building would be "packaged" for shipment. Long wooden beams were bolted vertically on twenty-foot centers to the exterior of all four walls, followed by three horizontal bands of timbers bolted to all exterior walls and secured to the vertical beams. With any luck, this exterior cage-like arrangement would prevent the wobbly old walls from falling outward. To protect against inward collapse, all interior walls were angle-braced by wooden timbers from the floor to the height of the mid-wall outside horizontal band. For good measure, steel rods were inserted across the interior space and attached to the interior bolt ends that secured the external strapping. Even though the precious cargo had been properly crated for transport, more than one person held their breath when the first saw cuts screamed through its ancient foundation.

Through notches cut into the top of the foundation walls, Pete and his crew inserted sixteen pieces of cross-steel, each forty-six feet in length, across the stable's long axis and tight beneath its squared-timber floor joists. Known in the business as dual 16WF60s, each piece of cross-steel was actually two sixteen-inch-deep, wide-flange steel beams welded together, weighing 120 pounds per linear foot. Below the cross-steel, Pete's plan called for two main load beams parallel to the stable's long axis, followed by nine horizontally perpendicular "rocker" beams riding on nine rows of three-abreast dollies. The rocker beams would unify and align each row while accommodating a greater number of dollies under the load.

Fortunately, good basement height and reasonable grade access allowed most of the required dollies to be positioned underneath without having to raise the building. By opening part of the southwesterly facing end-wall of the foundation, Pete's crew could roll dollies directly into the basement and arrange them into three equally spaced columns along the building's long axis. Across each row of three dolly-borne jack rams came one of the nine rocker beams, which were actually two 14WF145 steel beams welded into one beam. The two main load beams were then inserted on the structure's long axis, above and horizontally perpendicular to the rocker beams. The two one-hundred-foot main beams required for this job were each comprised of two fifty-foot sections of thirty-six-inch-deep wide-flange steel beams welded end to end. Weighing 280 pounds per linear foot, these 36WF280s were the second-heaviest steel beams available at the time.

In an ideal situation, twenty-seven dolly-mounted jacks could raise the building with all layers of steel already in place. However, very close to the northeastern front end of the stable, an embankment and associated road easement had been declared off-limits for excavation and encroachment. Therefore, at this end of the load, Pete could not position his last row of dollies as far outside the building's perimeter as he would have liked. Instead, he would use crib piles under that end of the main load beams while jacking and then put the last row of dollies into position prior to transport. Even so, the rearmost four rows of dollies would be positioned closer together than normal.

Having calculated the weight of each building section and located the center of gravity, Pete arranged his jacks according to his three-zone principle. The number of jacks in each zone was determined by the total weight being carried by that zone; in this case, the stable's fairly uniform construction suggested nine fifty-ton jacks in each zone. Zone One, at front of the load, would contain the nine jacks in the first three rows of dollies. Zones Two and Three would share the larger rear section by each having six jacks in its outer column and alternate jacks in the center column. Widely distributed in order to minimize stress on the fragile building, the twenty-seven jacks were capable of lifting 1,350 tons at their normal operating capacity of fifty tons each. With their maximum rating at sixty tons each, these jacks more than satisfied Pete's desire for a healthy margin of safety. *Derch denche.*

At locations convenient for each zone, three portable hydraulic jacking units were affixed to the cross-steel and main load beams. Independently supplying one of the three zones, these jacking machines would supply pressure for raising the building and would travel with the load before jacking the building down at destination. It was almost time to jack up the old building and move it clear of its moorings. Beforehand, Pete and his crew shimmed the support steel tight beneath the building by their now-common procedure of wedging fifteen-ton jacks on the bottom flange on each side of the main load beams and working upward against two adjacent pieces of cross-steel before inserting shims between the two layers of beams. In this manner, the main beams were shimmed tight and level against the cross beams that were now also preloaded as necessary to counter increased flex at their ends, directly beneath the heaviest load—the walls.

On Pete's signal, three control levers simultaneously moved downwards like bows in an orchestra's string section. In harmony,

twenty-seven jack rams eased upward in unison against the bottom
face of nine rocker beams that pushed two huge main load beams and
sixteen pieces of dual cross-steel up tight against a floor of aged wooden
timbers. The symphony had begun. Fortunately, no limestone blocks
fell out of tune. After re-establishing the baseline with another layer of
crib blocks on the safety cribbing, the conductor signaled for another
uplifting chorus. The old arrangement of limestone blocks was taken
to yet another level: the one-hundred-year-old livery stable was soon as
high as it would ever be. With their overture complete, the musicians
immediately began rearranging themselves and their instruments.

Where terrain had been a limiting factor at the rear of the load, the
jacking cribs were dismantled and replaced by dollies three abreast. As
dictated by restricted space at that end, the rearmost four rows of dollies
were positioned unusually close together, almost all within the building
footprint. At the front end of the load, dolly spacing was normal with
the very front row ideally positioned slightly outside the building's end
wall. Once again, everything was shimmed tight and level. A front-end
loader and two tractors were then attached to the front of the load as tow
vehicles. Laced through pulleys on the load and the tow vehicles, one
continuous length of steel cable provided a flexible network to evenly
distribute the pulling power of these three different towing machines.

The first movement was about to begin. Taking their positions
around the stable, the players exuded an aura of calm before a gathering
audience that fussed and murmured in anticipation. Closest to the
stage, at a safe and respectable distance, was the large supporting cast of
structural engineers, project managers, and city officials with clipboards
and cameras. Mingling slightly behind was a group comprised of the
players' families, friends, and supporters. Somewhat removed from
either group, members of the informed public exchanged pleasantries
and excited theories about the proceedings, while hoping to catch a
whisper from the authorities closer in. Surprised by the sight of the
crowd, curious passers-by joined the assemblage. Also present were
history buffs and the technically minded. To be sure, the gathering
throng also included those seeking only entertainment; for some, a
resounding crescendo would have been fantastic fare. A local radio
station, WCCO, was on hand doing play-by-play. Drifting through the
crowd, several structural movers from near and far were sneaking a peak
at Pete Friesen and what he was trying to accomplish in Minneapolis.

The conductor raised his arms, and there was movement. Introduced by chugs of diesel exhaust and chunking of gears, three pull vehicles inched forward, straining taut their steel cable … and eventually, 216 well-compressed rubber tires reluctantly overcame inertia and rolled slowly forward. After one hundred years in the same place, the Brown-Ryan Livery Stable was moving on. "Whoa! Whoa!" yelled Pete. Calling his colleagues into an immediate huddle, he then explained: "She's starting to crack, high up in the center near the chimney. Let's think about this for a minute."

It did not take long for Pete to understand and explain the problem. In fact, he had been anticipating something like this for some time. The necessity of bunching the rear rows of dollies closer together and positioning the last row barely outside the building footprint had messed up his loading profile. Although his three-zone principle remained intact, the center of pressure, or lift, in the two rear zones had been moved forward by the unusual dolly placement. As a result, too much force was being exerted under the center of the load relative to that under the rear of the load at the stable's front wall; because of the differential in support pressures, the thinly mortared old blocks high up near the building's midpoint were beginning to separate. To correct the problem, Pete immediately removed the center row of dollies while maintaining the status quo elsewhere. The loss of these three dolly jacks made hardly a dent in Pete's safety margin. Although Zone Two was a jack short and Zone Three was two jacks shy of a full load, more than sufficient lifting power remained under the load. More importantly, the loading was now in better balance. Although slightly reduced, the total lifting force was now more evenly distributed.

Once again, the conductor raised his arms, and once again there was movement. During the first several feet of resumed forward travel, the old stable walls relaxed back together and the crack disappeared. It was never seen again. "Lo and behold," said Pete, "it worked."

Coincident with all this activity on the north side of Hennepin Avenue, another hard-working crew was completing preparations at the building's new site, two hundred yards south and adjacent to Main Street. Having excavated and poured a new foundation, the crew there was putting finishing touches to some serious landscaping in accordance with Pete's request. Because the stable was to be positioned with its rear end wall tight against another structure, the Saint Anthony Warehouse, Pete had a slight problem: it was impossible to tow his load onto the new site, and the idea of pushing or kicking this fragile structure lengthwise into place seemed to invite disaster. Instead, Pete decided to let gravity do the work. The landscaping project now in progress created a gentle, well, fairly gentle downslope of about seven degrees off Hennepin Avenue. This shallow downramp would be paved with crib blocks to support the rubber-wheeled dollies that would roll down of their own accord, while being held in check by repositioned pull tractors serving as holdback vehicles behind the load. In this freewheeling mode, Pete would be responsible for steering the dollies by use of sixteen small, hand-operated winches, known as "come-alongs," attached to ends of the cross-steel, eight per side. Controlling a bridle assembly chaining together the steering tongues of all three dollies in each row, Pete would take care of the stable's direction, link-by-link. *Visualize.*

*The 1,000-ton Brown-Ryan Livery Stable on Hennepin Avenue in Minneapolis while preparations are underway for the down-sloping route to its new location.*

On a Sunday morning, with vehicle traffic detoured away from the scene, structural movers and civic shakers were busily engaged around the old limestone building they had come to love. In all its glory, the Brown-Ryan Livery Stable was now perched lengthwise across Hennepin Avenue, sitting on three layers of steel beams resting on twenty-four tandem axle dollies. The associated 192 rubber tires were riding on hundreds of wooden crib blocks that leveled the route and protected the street's surface. Remnants of an early snowfall melted from the curbs where supporters and spectators began to assemble. Having positioned their load just over the crown of Hennepin Avenue, Pete and his crew began "paving" the down-ramp to destination with hundreds of used crib blocks brought forward from the route already traveled. While the high-riding livery stable was being held in place by chocks and dolly brakes, the loader and the two yellow "pull-dozers" were repositioned to the rear of the load. A long steel cable secured these holdback vehicles to the support beams in a series of ten short spans. Operation of the pneumatic dolly brakes was rechecked and the air supply topped up. It was now or never.

On Pete's signal, the wheel chocks were removed, and the assigned operator, Marv Wasmund, released the dolly brakes. The Brown-Ryan Livery Stable began rolling forward of its own accord while drivers of the holdbacks applied very light braking. A minute later, the carefully monitored load reached the seven-degree downslope leading to its final destination. Seconds after that, there was panic. As the self-motivated livery stable began to accelerate downhill, a chorus of human voices erupted in loud surprise. "Golly, gee whiz!" (or some such thing) exclaimed the crew, almost in unison. Riding a multi-layered skateboard sporting a multitude of wheels, the thousand-ton heritage building was schussing straight for the north wall of the Saint Anthony Warehouse building. Dragged along with it were a front-end loader and two yellow bulldozers. In no time at all, the collective imagination of those present visualized the impact the fragile livery stable was about to have on the historic building below.

"Put on the brakes, Marv, put on the brakes!" hollered Pete to the assigned dolly brake operator. Encouraged by a long string of encouraging words, Marv Wasmund leapt and ducked through multiple strands of fast-moving steel cable. Though not internationally recognized for his athletic ability, Marv's effort on this day was something Olympian, if not Herculean. Slightly injured in the process and hanging over the last span of cable, he could barely reach the dolly brake control lever. But he did it! With a slight jolt, the old Brown-Ryan Livery Stable snapped to a halt. So too the front-end loader and the two bulldozers slid to a halt, and all the screaming stopped. "I don't know how the good Lord works," sighed Pete, after slowing his heart and catching his breath, "but God is certainly looking out for us."

Perhaps because of recent precipitation, the coefficient of friction on the asphalt surface of Hennepin Avenue was less than ideal. Having been laid down to protect the road surface, wooden planks had become slippery slats that skied the tractors across. After a few minutes for the musicians to debrief and retune, the load was incrementally eased forward again by judicious use of dolly brakes, now controlled by a very attentive operator. Once the holdbacks had cleared the street, it became a walk in the park. It was more like a run in the mud for Pete, who scrambled to and fro among his come-along winches, steering the freewheeling load into place. Once it was there, men and machines began jacking their precious cargo down. Days later, as the old livery stable settled gently onto its new foundation, the conductor crossed his arms above his head—the finale.

*Pete "Toggle-meister" Friesen steers the livery stable load by adjusting come-along winches attached to dolly steering tongues linked by chain.*

Immediately after this successful relocation, the city re-mortared all the limestone blocks of the old livery stable and installed vital municipal services. As agreed, the development company completely remodeled its interior into a comfortable venue for light retail and office space. The Brown-Ryan Livery Stable became part of Riverplace, a commercial, entertainment, and residential complex fronting the Mississippi River on historic Main Street in the revitalized core of old Saint Anthony. Occupants and patrons of Riverplace are only a few steps from the magnificent system of parks and trails now gracing both banks of the city's revered waterway.

As summarized by project manager Dick Victor: "The building's condition and the associated elevation change made this a near-impossible move; the risks of failure were extremely high. However, with knowledgeable consultants, expert movers, and backing of the city's redevelopment agency with support staff and almost $1 million in funding, the building was saved. As I recall, our efforts were recognized with awards from the Minnesota Historical Society, from the Preservation Alliance of Minnesota, and from the Consulting Engineers Council."

Minneapolis has been subsequently recognized as a model for urban rejuvenation. A parkway for cars, a bikeway for riders, and a walkway for pedestrians run parallel courses along the fifty-two-mile route of its Grand Rounds National Scenic Byway. Numerous side trails connect with other natural attractions including a botanical garden, a bird sanctuary, and the renowned Minnehaha Falls. Blessed with twenty lakes and wetlands within its jurisdiction, the city has made most of them accessible for year-round recreation, many connected via walking and cycling trails. Not surprisingly, the company that popularized the sport of inline skating, Rollerblade, took its first strides here. The "Water City" park system has become the envy of many other large communities. Graced by a generous canopy of trees, the city has brought a playground within reach of most children and a park within six blocks of every home. Today, 15 percent of the city area is dedicated to parks, providing 770 square feet of green space for each resident. Surely Father Hennepin would be pleasantly surprised to see his name attached to a major thoroughfare running through such a fine example of civilization. Certainly, Thomas Jefferson and his colleagues would be satisfied with the results of their Louisiana Purchase. Mind you, Baldwin Brown and John Ryan would probably shake their heads to see the roller-blading cappuccino drinkers who now hang out in their old stable.

"The Brown-Ryan Livery Stable move was a rallying point," concludes Dick Victor. "Having successfully moved this one, the city realized that almost any public building could be relocated and saved. Thereafter, relocation of historic architecture became a viable option in urban redevelopment plans that were really taking off."

Years later, having become even more enamored by the possibility of preserving historic architecture, Pete Friesen returned to Minneapolis and helped relocate another of the city's treasured buildings. By then, he had become even more impressed by the durability of the old livery stable building and even more thankful for the good fortune of being able to move it without breaking it. Forevermore, Pete remained deeply inspired by a photograph of this historic limestone building nestled comfortably into place against the north wall of the warehouse. "Whenever I think about that incident … when the stable almost got away on us," Pete shared, with a semblance of a sigh, "it makes me shudder and makes my hair stand on end … and I have to say, 'How great is God.'"

*Thanks to good steering and brakes, the old livery stable is*
*part of Riverplace complex in the Saint Anthony district.*

# 9

## The Unlucky Fifties

Back in 1970, when he first took charge of Belding's structural-moving division, Pete immediately found himself in need of additional equipment. Beginning with the Fermilab project near Batavia, Illinois, scores of buildings would soon require relocation within a restrictive time frame. Anticipating the need to equip several crews working at different sites simultaneously, Pete knew he would need a large working inventory: several jacking units, scores of jacks, hundreds of crib blocks, and a few extra sets of load beams. After rounding up all the necessary vehicles, chains, cables, and manpower, Pete Friesen went shopping for new beams. "They smiled at me as soon as I walked in, and I bought them," Pete recalled, referring to the spanking-new beams that caught his eye in a yard full of steel. There were four of them, each fifty feet long and sixteen inches tall, measuring eight and one-half inches across the flange and weighing sixty-four pounds per linear foot (known as 16WF64s). "These sixteen-inch, sixty-four pounders looked real good, and they were pretty much what I was looking for," remembered Pete. "By welding them side-to-side in pairs, I knew I would soon have two very strong fifty-foot main load beams. I was proud of them."

Although these pretty new beams were not used on any of the major projects already described in this story, they would certainly claim a notoriety of their own during some of Pete's more "routine" moves in the Chicago area during the same time period. "Looking back at my feelings of pride," Pete wistfully declared, "I should have known there would be trouble." Trouble was just around the corner. Soon after completing the Fermilab project, Pete found himself at odds with the owner of a home he had contracted to move in a Chicago suburb. Contrary to Pete's normal operating policy, the homeowner had already determined the route to be followed during transit, and Pete was not happy with it. "We would have to go down a steep hill and cut up too many trees on that route," Pete declared to the homeowner. "Let's go downtown and check with the building department."

"I am the building department!" declared the homeowner bluntly. "And, as building inspector, I have already decided the best route for this move."

"Okay, okay!" responded Pete. "You seem to be the boss around here ... we'll do it your way." On the assigned moving day, they did not get very far. Halfway down the undesirably steep hill, the police arrived on the scene and ordered the operation halted. Apparently, a number of citizens had become alarmed about the many trees being mutilated and managed to get the move stopped. With some difficulty and barely a hint of annoyance, Pete's crew maneuvered their awkward load back uphill a short distance into a vacant lot. There, the house and Pete's cherished new fifty-foot load beams sat on dollies for more than a week, while the municipal administrators decided upon a better route for the move. Pete was never consulted on the subject.

"The new route they came up with was down an even steeper hill and on a gravel road," remarked Pete. "But there was nothing I could do about it, so we just hooked back up and got moving again." Anticipating the need for some serious braking on this section of the "better" route, Pete attached two fully loaded semi trailers as holdback vehicles for his vulnerable cargo. In customary fashion, the front end of the load was secured to the aft deck of the pull-truck while the bulk of the load was carried on dollies. These dollies did not have brakes, and the brakes on the pull-truck were off-limits, for fear of jack-knifing the load. Successful descent on this gravel surface would be entirely dependent on efficient braking by the holdback trucks. Sure enough, as momentum increased on the downward slope, brakes on the holdbacks were soon locked full on, and two fully loaded semis began sliding on the loose surface, dragged by an old house sitting on the new fifty-foot beams atop numerous rubber-tired dollies, pushing an old pull-truck.

Encouraged by loud exclamations from Pete, the driver of the pull-truck ignored all previous advice and began tapping lightly on his foot brake. The ensuing action was not pretty to behold. Flying out of the dust from churning tires came small stones and large shrieks. It was over in a matter of seconds. Judicious use of the front vehicle brakes and some fancy wrangling by the outriders had skidded the whole assembly to a halt on more level ground below. "I don't know how the good Lord works," sighed Pete, after slowing his heart and catching his breath, "but God is certainly looking out for us."

After wiping his brow on his shirtsleeve and replacing his cap, Pete smiled in remembrance of the lesson learned on another gravel-surfaced hill during his very first house move, twenty-five years before. "Okay boys, that's enough excitement for today," he called. "Let's organize our gear and get this show back on the road to where it's going." Without further ado, Pete's crew soon had the house properly situated on its new lot. However, the very next day, Pete received a telephone call from the homeowner and building inspector who had changed his mind: he now wanted to dig the basement two feet deeper. "Okay by me," Pete responded; "I've got lots to keep me busy elsewhere. Call us when you're ready, and we'll come and jack her down." They never got to jack this house down. It fell down. The excavator coming on site to dig out the basement brushed up against a corner crib pile, and the house came tumbling down, disintegrating into many smaller sections, some smaller than others. "There was nothing more we could do there," recalled Pete. "We just collected our blocks and jacks and moved them and my new fifty-foot beams to another job."

More trouble was just around the corner. Pete's favorite new fifty-foot beams were soon under a house being moved in a northern suburb of Chicago. The building was lifted and moved without problem. However, having situated the house over its new foundation, the crew was experiencing difficulty in removing the pull-truck from underneath the load. Recent heavy rains had soaked the surrounding soil, and the pull-truck's tires were spinning in the mud. A winch truck had been attached to the pull-truck in the hope that the additional tension would extricate the mired vehicle. Pete and his estimator arrived on the scene after checking out another job, just in time to see the winch operator start winching. Everyone winced as the house collapsed into a pile of rubble.

Apparently the wallowing pull-truck had become hooked to something on or under the building. The newly moved house had become a write-off in no time flat. Although they were certainly present at the scene, Pete's favorite fifty-foot beams could hardly be accused of this calamity. Nevertheless, two of Pete's men exchanged furtive glances over a comment that included the word "jinxed." "C'mon boys, there's nothing more we can do here," called Pete. "Let's collect our gear and get outta here. We've got another job waiting for us down south."

More trouble, as you might surmise, was lurking in the suburbs south of Chicago, where Pete's favorite new fifty-foot beams were soon under another home to be relocated. This house also lifted easily and traveled well to its new location on the bank of a small urban stream. Here, the house remained for more than a month, resting on Pete's favorite fifty-foot beams and the requisite number of crib piles. A coalition of citizens lobbying for this section of urban stream to be included in a proposed recreation area had succeeded with an eleventh-hour injunction. The entire move was put on hold while the homeowner and the city negotiated a resolution. This delay was not a huge concern for Pete because business was not particularly brisk at the time and he had more than enough equipment to go around. Besides, his company was collecting $37.00 per day for the rental of equipment under the stationary house.

It is unclear what arrangement was finally reached between the homeowner and the city. However, Pete's crew was finally instructed to move the house to an alternate site—on the edge of a suburban swamp. The house remained at rest near the swamp for approximately six months, being supported by Pete's favorite fifty-foot beams and the requisite number of crib piles while Pete's company collected thousands of dollars in equipment rental. When business started picking up again, Pete removed his beloved fifty-foot beams and used them for another job. The new job was also a house that lifted easily and traveled well atop Pete's fifty-footers, up to a point. Several blocks down the street from where they had started, the client suddenly showed up to explain how a problem with his permit had forced temporary cancellation of the move. "We were told to park it," remembered Pete. "We found a suitable field close by and left it there. That is where this house burned down several days later."

A week or so after rescuing his fifty-foot barbequed beams from the ashes, Pete received a phone call from an administrator of the previously mentioned community with that new recreation area along an urban stream. "Come and salvage what equipment you might have left. Your house by the swamp has burned to the ground."

✳  ✳  ✳  ✳

The degree of scrutiny applied by insurance investigators to these two house-in-transit fires remains unknown. What is known is that these fiery mishaps were regarded with no small amount of suspicion by several of Pete's crewmembers. So too were Pete's charred fifty-foot beams. Although still looking straight enough, these welded pairs of steel appeared to have been twisted ever so slightly by the heat of their recent experience. "I know what you guys are thinking," said Pete, before cutting the paired beams apart. After reversing their edges of contact to diminish their twist, he welded the pairs back together. "There!" he declared to his men. "I've cut the bad vibrations out and welded some good vibrations in."

"Say what you like, boss," countered one of the men, "but as far as some of us are concerned, these fifties are an unlucky pair of beams, and we're afraid they could be jinxing us."

"Nonsense, guys!" said Pete. "That's just superstition." Undaunted, Pete hustled his reconfigured fifty-foot beams and his growing crew of skeptics off to their next assignment, a house move west of Chicago. As you may guess, trouble was also lurking in the western suburbs of Chicago. This next move went smoothly and according to plan until the very last day. While backing the house down a slight grade into position over its new basement foundation, the brakes on the control truck failed. The building rolled off the basement crib piles and came to rest slightly beyond its intended point of landing. Although damage was minimal, the level of concern was not. Why would dependable truck brakes fail for no apparent reason? Although Pete's suspect fifty-foot beams could hardly be blamed, they were there.

The fifties were also present at the next job. The community leaders of another northern suburb wanted to preserve an old commercial bank building from their main street, but they didn't quite know where they wanted to put it. Pete and his crew obligingly took the lead. Taking great care with the old masonry structure, they lifted it with kid gloves and slid it softly to a temporary storage site, where it was last seen resting serenely atop those fifty-foot beams. Well over a year later, the call finally came. "Come and get your beams," voiced the city administrator. "We've torn down the old bank building."

So it went. By this time, almost all the men on Pete's crew were suspicious of those fifty-foot beams and were now referring to them as the "Unlucky Fifties." "See, boss, those beams *are* jinxed!" became their refrain. "Something bad happens to every building they come in contact with. We should bury them while we still can."

"No way, guys! That doesn't make any sense," came Pete's standard response. "You're talking about superstition, and I don't believe in any of that stuff."

After doing such a fine job of holding up the bank, Pete's favorite fifty-foot beams were soon under a house being relocated in the same northern suburb. The house had lifted easily and had traveled well. However, the design of the destination basement required the structure to be jacked higher than anticipated. "We were within a quarter-inch … the men had just measured it," Pete remembered. "We were going up that last quarter, and the whole building collapsed." Some of the men on this job shared a similar belief as to the cause of this destruction. Their boss, on the other hand, had a different and slightly more scientific theory about the building collapse. With several jobs underway in various locations, he had hired extra workers and had ordered extra crib blocks. For the first time in memory and contrary to specifications, his supplier had shipped one "unclear" block; it contained a knot in its grain. One of the inexperienced new hires unwittingly inserted this substandard piece into the mix, and the rest was history. Pete described it this way: "The knotty block broke at its very end, and when it broke, the jack there collapsed, and the base of the jack beside it broke in half. Then it was just a matter of watching the building come down."

"Okay, boys, there is nothing more we can do here today," called the boss. "Let's gather up our gear and head home. We've got another job near there." By the time Pete got back to his West Chicago office, almost everyone at AMC was referring to his favorite beams as the "Unlucky Fifties."

"Golly, gee whiz!" (or some such thing) lamented his employees, almost in unison. "Boss, don't you see? Those Unlucky Fifties are jinxing us. You should bury those beams before they bury all of us."

"Easy, boys, easy. That's just superstition," assuaged Pete. "I don't believe in any of that stuff. These are just pieces of steel, and they're not going to get me down." Undaunted by superstition or fears of mutiny, our hero bravely loaded up his cherished beams and led his men to their next assignment, the relocation of a large older home less than ten miles from their home base. After helping his crew get started on the necessary preliminaries, Pete departed to take care of some administrative business north of Chicago. While he would never admit to worrying about the Unlucky Fifties, they may have been on his mind. As he drove through a northwestern suburb, he remembered a previous moving job there involving these now-notorious load beams. Although he had been preoccupied by another project at the time and had not been present at this particular one, he now recalled that it must have gone well, unlucky beams or not. There had been no adverse reports, and his company had been paid in full for the job.

"That's right, the client was active in the Church ... a Bible school or something," Pete remembered. "He was obviously a true believer," Pete chuckled aloud. "The Unlucky Fifties didn't get him!" Pete then recalled that this client was a barber in the very town he was now driving through. With a quick look in his rearview mirror, our hero decided he needed a haircut, and he steered toward Main Street. Once in the chair, he and the barber soon established their previous business connection. On the subject of his own business, Pete made reference to a particular pair of load beams considered ornery or even unlucky by some of his workers; they had been coincidentally involved in moving complications that had cost considerable time and money. "Boy, oh boy!" chortled Pete. "It's good to know your job survived the so-called jinx of the Unlucky Fifties."

"I wouldn't be so sure, if I were you," said the barber, with a quick snip beside Pete's right ear. "See that guy over there, the one who just came in?" asked the barber, with a point of his scissors. "He used to be mayor here. When your boys moved my building … well, there was such an uproar in town about so many trees being cut down during the move. Well, he got turfed out of the mayor's job and almost run out of town."

Somewhat daunted by the implied reference to cut-and-run house movers, Pete paid for his haircut and quietly left town. He had people to see elsewhere and was behind schedule. Driving back toward West Chicago after completing his business, he remained preoccupied by administrative matters of the day, and he had little inkling of the big trouble looming on the horizon. His first hint came on his return to the new jobsite, where things were getting off to a slow start.

The concrete foundation under the large old house was resisting all attempts at penetration. The manual concrete-breaker could barely punch a hole through and was incapable of knocking out pieces large enough for the load beams. Undaunted, Pete hired a heavy-duty power concrete-breaker, as well as an operator purported to have the special skills required to operate it. Just as soon as it was unloaded from its transport vehicle, the heavy-duty power concrete breaker went sideways on its operator and smashed into the building. "No damage!" laughed Pete, as many of his employees exchanged knowing glances.

Although powerful enough, the heavy-duty concrete breaker proved to be somewhat temperamental. Every so often it would take off on the operator and crunch into the building's wooden structure. While this erratic behavior was funny to watch, it did little to humor the boss who was footing the bill. Perplexed, Pete took the rogue machine to another jobsite for some scientific research. "There, it behaved perfectly normal. It poked those holes oh so smoothly," Pete recalled. "But when we brought it back to this job, it just jumped straight into the side of the building."

Eventually, perseverance prevailed on the foundation, and the beam slots were successfully opened up. However, by this point, many of Pete's men were in a state of nervous distraction. The entire operation had acquired the twitches. During excavation around the building, every now and then the front-end loader would rear up and hammer into the roof overhang. Every time it came near, the loader's bucket would slap sideways into an air-conditioning unit that projected from one end of the structure. More than once, a load of beams in transit slid off and speared the house. On one occasion, the beams slid sideways and crunched the boss's automobile—not a good omen.

While taking time out to examine the damage to his beloved old Buick, Pete was approached by a neighbor who had a story to tell. Apparently, several years ago, the wealthy couple that owned the home had befriended him. The three became good friends and occasionally socialized together. Once, returning from a Cubs game in the big city, the woman, who was seated in the center, began to get cuddly with the neighbor while her husband drove the vehicle. The neighbor was able to successfully and tactfully deflect the woman's inappropriate advances, according to his story. However, the next day, he was shocked to learn the husband had committed suicide during the night.

About two years later, the widow asked the neighbor to accompany her to another baseball game. He agreed, thinking such an outing might help her with getting over her husband's passing. On the drive home, the woman again became very friendly toward the neighbor, inviting him into her home. Once again, according to the neighbor, he was able to successfully deflect the woman's advances, however less inappropriate they may have seemed. The next day, she was found dead in her home. Then the property was sold, and the house was now being moved. Pete certainly knew there was much more to this story than he had been told. At the same time, our hero could not allow himself to imagine that he might be trying to move a haunted house with his own jinxed main load beams.

The house itself presented no special problems for the experienced house mover. Containing a concrete-floored addition, it was a simple one-story ranch-style home over a full basement. Because of its L-shaped design, Pete decided to move the building in three sections: the first was the multi-car garage, the second was the 30' by 90' main section supported by Pete's favorite fifty-foot beams welded to a set of forty-five-foot extension beams. The third and last part was a reasonably open section measuring about 30' by 40'. Crib piles had been constructed; jacks were placed and then connected to the unified jacking machine. When hydraulic pressure was applied, Pete was surprised to see his gauges indicate a total weight of 105 tons for their load. His prior calculations had suggested a maximum weight of ninety-five tons. Although this 10 percent differential was within his own tolerance, Pete was perplexed by the apparent miscalculation.

Undaunted, Pete and his crew began jacking this section of the house, a process that would take two days or more. Returning from lunch on the next day, the boss was startled to see the readings on his jacking unit. "They were totally wrong," Pete recalled. "The jacks had been set in just such a way ... the panel had been marked beside the readings and the previous weights were recorded. Now some of them were reversed ... some that had been 6,000 psi were now reading 3,000 psi, and some that were originally 3,000 were now showing 6,000." Initially, Pete thought his crewmembers were having him on by changing some of the hose connections while he was at lunch—just for the fun of it.

"Not so!" his stalwarts protested, avoiding any reference to a certain pair of load beams. Being careful not to look over at the Unlucky Fifties, they dutifully followed their leader back under the load, checking jack positions and hose layouts.

"Lo and behold," recalled Pete, "everything was exactly as it was before, exactly as we had left it before lunch." All jacks, valves, connections, and controls were as they should have been. There was no other possible source of trouble. Pete had no choice but to block the load in place and release the hydraulic pressure from every jack circuit before making a fresh start. The reloading procedure worked, in a sense. When hydraulic pressure was re-applied, gauge readings were unlike anything previous, before or after lunch. "Oh well," Pete sighed, "there was nothing we could do but record the new readings, re-mark the panel, and resume jacking."

Based on his proven method for determining building weights, Pete had estimated this section of the house to weigh 95 tons. He calculated hydraulic pressure of 7,000 psi from his jacking unit being applied to six fifteen-ton jacks, operating slightly below their rated maximum of seventeen and a half tons, would be sufficient to lift the house. However, feedback from his jacking-unit pressure gauges suggested a rare miscalculation. This supposition was reinforced by the fact it took the maximum pressurization of all six jacks to barely raise this section of the building high enough to accept the dollies.

When it came time to load this section for transport, Pete once again used his tried and true teeter-totter model to determine its center of gravity. This simple and effective method would determine dolly placement in keeping with his three-zone loading. As was his custom, Pete checked and rechecked his center of gravity calculations several times. Needless to say, he was startled and astonished when the load was transferred to the dollies. One corner sagged badly out of level. It sagged so badly that the boss called a halt to the operation and told his men to take the rest of the day off while he went home to think it through. Pete visualized the process backward and forward. The answer always looked the same—he had not miscalculated. No matter how he worked it through, the center of gravity for this building remained exactly where he had first found it.

Although he was unable to establish a "better" position for this particular center of gravity, in the process of trying to find one, Pete discovered shortcuts and alternatives in his usual method, so much so that he would soon be inspired to write a computer program utilizing those very same principles. In the same way an unforeseen problem on the Sumas Mountain Road almost four decades before had inspired creation of his teeter-totter principle, this driveway problem in West Chicago would motivate Pete to bring his method for finding center of gravity into the electronic age.

Meanwhile, back at the ranch, little had changed. Pete was in a bit of a pickle: after pushing his own limits regarding safety margins by using only six jacks, he was now looking at one section of one house weighing more than it was supposed to weigh. It was sagging badly out of level before it was even moved. While the boss took yet another look under his load for any possible clue to this dilemma, his workers made busy wherever they could while avoiding eye contact with the two load beams resting beneath an adjacent house section. "What could I do?"

questioned Pete in retrospect. "My calculations were correct. All I could do was make some major adjustments to the loading and jack pressures and allow this building to live the way it wanted to live."

Then, as Pete describes it: "We loaded it and started driving off. The farther we drove, the flatter the tires went. We decided to put in another set of dollies because the tires were going so flat. We put the jacks back in to lift it, and now we couldn't raise it at all with the six jacks … so we put in another six jacks and they were just about to capacity. We barely got it high enough to get the dollies in place. The road we had to travel on was not a particularly good road, although it was good enough for trucks that were hauling full loads of gravel on it. No matter what kind of matting we put underneath, everything went down and kept going down … the tires kept getting flatter and sinking in. Before we got off the property, the rear end of the pull-truck tore itself out. We had to jack the building to repair the truck; but now, for some reason, the twelve jacks couldn't raise it and we had to put in several more. As crazy as it sounds, my pressure gauges were now saying this section of the house weighed 180 tons!"

A perfect example of three-zone loading this was not. A finely tuned operation running like a Swiss watch, this was not. If little else, this would prove to be a classic example of one very determined leader and his company battling through conflict after conflict until the job was done. Pete Friesen and his company of loyal, if superstitious, co-workers eventually completed their assigned task, albeit far behind schedule and way over budget. Although insurance coverage would ameliorate the costs of damage to the home, and his car, and his truck, Pete was entirely on the hook for the budget overage and costs from excessive delays. While his heretofore-favorite fifty-foot beams could not be held directly responsible for his financial downturn, even Pete could not help noting the Unlucky Fifties were used on less than 10 percent of his jobs, but were present at almost every jobsite where damages, accidents, and serious difficulties had occurred during a fifteen-year period.

Pete Friesen offered his last words on the subject: "I don't know. It was just one thing after another. I lost thousands upon thousands. I lost well over $200,000 on this one job. Now whether there is a connection to the infamous fifty-foot beams, I do not know, and I am not prepared to guess. I was broke, and I sold the company."

# 10

# San Antonio

Three hundred years before a particular set of American-made steel beams made life difficult for a certain Russian-born structural mover, Spanish authorities set out to locate and destroy a French settlement at the mouth of the Mississippi River, between the Spanish colonies in Florida and Mexico. Finding no French settlement and barely any sign of La Salle's ill-fated 1684 expedition to colonize Louisiana, the Spanish planted their own flag. In 1718, at a river crossing near the midpoint of their fledgling east-west trade route, Spanish colonials established a small settlement at a mission site known to Coahuitecan people as *Yanaguana*—Place of Restful Waters. The river and this new community were named San Antonio, honoring the same saint who was also recognized thirty-eight years before in the naming of Saint Anthony Falls, a thousand miles north on the Mississippi River. In 1773, with almost two thousand inhabitants and five missions established nearby, San Antonio became the seat of Spanish government in their Texas territory. Twenty years later, Mission San Antonio was removed from Church control and became a military barracks; by turn of the century, it was manned by a cavalry troop from the Mexican post of San José y Santiago del Alamo de Parras. This cavalry unit became known as the "Alamo Troop," and their new headquarters became known as the Alamo—a Spanish word referring to cottonwood trees.

Incorporated as a city in 1809, San Antonio became part of Mexico after that country's successful war of independence from Spain in 1821. Fifteen years later, disgruntled Mexican and American settlers in Texas began their own war of independence from Mexico and immediately occupied the old Alamo mission. Forty-six days after the legendary fall of the Alamo in March 1836, the Texans rallied behind Sam Houston to defeat Santa Anna's Mexican forces at San Jacinto, and the Republic of Texas came into being. In 1845, the new republic joined the United States of America as the twenty-eighth state in the Union. Sixteen years later, Texas was one of the first states to secede from the Union in the beginnings of the Civil War.

Largely because of its remote location on the southwestern frontier, San Antonio survived the Civil War relatively unscathed and continued to prosper as a distribution center on an ancient trade route. For its fifteen thousand citizens, any sense of isolation disappeared with arrival of the first railways in 1877. Along with a dramatic increase in commercial trade came the first voice to publicly advocate historic preservation in San Antonio. Colonel Thomas W. Pierce of Boston, president of the Galveston, Harrisburg and San Antonio Railroad, suggested restricting modern business growth in the old part of the city, so as to maintain that quarter's "ancient quaintness." Already, "old" San Antonio was recognized for its colonial-era charm. Having thus far resisted conversion to more modern rectangular grid lines, the downtown core featured narrow streets meandering alongside the river and its canals and boasted a mix of cosmopolitan architecture. Several waves of European immigration had brought new ideas and new materials; multi-storied structures of steel and glass blended harmoniously with the traditional single-story adobe and limestone construction. More and more visitors were extolling the virtues of this quaint and colorful city. Almost everyone agreed: San Antonio had big-time character.

It probably came as little surprise to Pierce that his comments would strike a chord with certain San Antonians. Two years after his call for preservation, the ten-year old Alamo Literary Society became the Alamo Monument Association (AMA) and adopted a mandate to preserve the Alamo and mark its place in history. The Association's twenty-six charter members elected a pioneer San Antonian, Mary Adams Maverick, as their first president. Coincidentally, Mrs. Maverick's late husband had been one of two delegates dispatched from the Alamo fortification to sign the Texas Declaration of Independence only a few days before the old mission fell. (Maverick's name entered the English lexicon as a noun after he allowed some of his cattle to wander about unbranded.)

In 1883, encouraged by the AMA and other similar-minded citizens, the Texas Legislature became the first public body west of the Mississippi River to purchase a historic landmark—the Alamo—solely for preservation. This peerless symbol of Texan independence became state property with the payment of $20,000 to the Catholic Church. While enduring decades of neglect and inappropriate use, the Alamo had nevertheless remained etched into the Texas psyche ever since 1836, when almost two hundred freedom fighters perished within its walls. Although it would endure many more decades of delay before restoration, the Alamo purchase signaled the outbreak of historic preservation in San Antonio and west of the Mississippi.

By 1900, citizens of San Antonio had organized several heritage-minded groups and took the issue of historic preservation beyond the walls of the Alamo. As dictated by the era's social norms, most of the preservationists were well-educated women with time on their hands. Notable among these groups were the Daughters of the Republic of Texas (DRT), who pursued recognition of "true history," as well as preservation of the Alamo. Notable among the activists were Adina Emilia De Zavala, an energetic granddaughter of the first vice-president of the Republic of Texas, and Clara Driscoll, a woman of means who would eventually re-purchase the Alamo property on behalf of the DRT.

In 1906, another San Antonio woman left her mark on the city. Widowed three years earlier, Veronica Felix followed through on her late husband's plan to build a hotel in downtown San Antonio. The Fairmount Hotel, a modest three-story, thirty-room "salesmen's hotel," was erected on busy Commerce Street between Alamo Plaza and the Southern Pacific rail depot. For the following six decades, the Fairmount would participate in the comings and goings of San Antonio life while bearing witness to dynamic change around its sturdy brick walls.

By the turn of the twentieth century, San Antonio had become the largest city in the largest U.S. state. By 1920, its population had leapt to one hundred and fifty thousand, as post-World War I growth carried into the following decade. Along with the need for an incredible number of new buildings came the need for new infrastructure to accommodate the arrival of the automobile. Along with the automobile came the suburbs and the need for even more infrastructure. A rising tide of tourism created the need for large hotels, while skyscraper bank buildings managed the city's newfound wealth. Bolstered by $10 million of construction in the downtown core alone, San Antonio embarked on another exuberant period of growth in the mid-1920s. While many San Antonians championed this enthusiastic development scheme, some citizens were concerned about the potential loss of historic buildings and classic architecture.

Rena Maverick Green, granddaughter of pioneer preservationist Mary Adams Maverick, was actively engaged in many social issues while also serving as Missions Committee chairperson for her chapter of the DRT. In early 1924, after reading a newspaper article about the impending demise of the state's finest example of Greek Revival architecture, she immediately went to examine the old Market House in downtown San Antonio. While admiring the 1859 structure's columned façade, she chanced to meet another person who had come there for the same reasons. Emily Edwards, a schoolteacher and social worker, had been intrigued by the same newspaper article describing plans for demolition of this classic architecture to make room for a wider street. Within weeks of their fateful meeting, Rena Green and Emily Edwards hosted a gathering of like-minded women who immediately organized around their common interest. On March 22, 1924, Emily Edwards became the first president of the San Antonio Conservation Society (SACS), a fledgling organization with high hopes.

With vigor and imagination, the creative ladies of SACS campaigned to preserve the old Market House, and in the process they literally invented San Antonio's public advocacy machine: city officials were invited out for bus rides through the city and rowboat rides on the river, as well as lobbied by very persuasive puppet shows. Although some of their events could never be duplicated, the methods initiated by SACS established a template for public advocacy that would guide generations of similarly concerned citizens. The very next year, notwithstanding innovative and impassioned advocacy by upstart preservationists, the city razed the Market House in accordance with its extensive urban redevelopment plan.

Although unsuccessful in its first campaign, SACS continued to grow with the city and in due course became a durable and respected voice in virtually every urban planning issue. Meanwhile, in 1925, Emily Edwards and Rena Green led their colleagues back into the streets to continue the fight for heritage preservation, house-by-house, slogging shoulder-to-shoulder with Adina De Zavala, Clara Driscoll, and hundreds of others who hoped to save the soul of their city. Although personalities often clashed, their common purpose was never in doubt. For a more comprehensive and entertaining review of historic preservation in this fair city, readers are encouraged to consult Lewis Fisher's excellent volume *Saving San Antonio: The Precarious Preservation of a Heritage.*

Influenced by SACS and other civic-minded organizations, the city of San Antonio preserved many fine examples of classic architecture while incorporating elements of its history into burgeoning growth. In 1931, on the two-hundredth anniversary of Spanish settlement, the Spanish Governor's Palace was fully restored and dedicated by city and state officials. Almost in time for the one-hundredth anniversary of the Battle of the Alamo, a sixty-foot-high monument to Texas liberty was erected on the Alamo grounds. By 1941, the original La Villita residential area was being transformed into a charming historic district while pedestrian walkways and annual festivals became popular along the downtown riverfront. After another period of intense construction, the HemisFair exposition of 1968 introduced a new convention center, a new skyscraper hotel, and a 750-foot-high revolving restaurant.

Nearby, at the corner of Commerce and Bowie Streets, the Fairmount Hotel of 1906 was faring less well. In fact, the sixty-two-year-old hotel was now vacant, having become just another old building in a newer and taller neighborhood. However, it had long been on the city's list of historically significant structures for its typical Italianate Victorian design. Although the hotel was of sound construction and in reasonable shape, no one had offered to give it a second life. By 1980, the old Fairmount Hotel was in double trouble: on one side was a proposed widening of Bowie Street; on the other was a proposed $250 million hotel and shopping complex. Both projects wanted the Fairmount out of the way.

Joanna Parrish, president of SACS, approached the mall developer to discuss the possibility of incorporating the heritage structure into plans for the complex. She came away with an agreement, backed by a potential $100,000 default bond, to prevent demolition of the old building before the new project had final approval. The agreement also stipulated that, once financial arrangements were completed and final approval was given, developer Edward J. DeBartolo would have a ten-day grace period before declaring his position regarding possible inclusion of the Fairmount. If he chose not to include the old building, he would donate $50,000 to SACS who would then be responsible for moving the Fairmount off the property within sixty days, after which the society would assume ownership of the building.

The Conservation Society was not intimidated by such a prospect. Seventy years before, the five-story Alamo National Bank building had been raised and rolled back—while business continued inside—for the widening of Commerce Street downtown. Society directors were well aware of even more complex building relocations undertaken elsewhere in the country. A study commissioned by the DeBartolo Company found the Fairmount building quite capable of being moved: its thick brick exteriors were augmented by load-bearing, cast-iron columns on the first floor and by load-bearing corridor walls on the upper two.

Suddenly, it was 1984. After years of waiting and wondering, financing was finally in place, and the new hotel and shopping center megaproject had final approval. Having declined his option of incorporating the old hotel into his project plans, DeBartolo asked SACS to remove the building by April 1, 1985. The original plan of moving the hotel to a nearby municipal property fell through almost immediately, and the society was forced to find another site (and additional financing) for a more comprehensive relocation. With the support of Mayor Henry Cisneros, three local entrepreneurs—Thomas Wright, a downtown developer; Virginia Van Steenberg, an attorney; and Belton K. Johnson, a King Ranch heir and part owner of San Antonio's new Hyatt Regency Hotel—formed a consortium to get the job done. Once ownership of the Fairmount Hotel was transferred to their consortium from the Conservation Society, these local developers would invest $3 million to transform the building into the city's first small luxury hotel. In January 1985, the city council offered a lease on the closest site that could be found—a city-owned parking lot at the southwest corner of South Alamo and Nueva Streets—six blocks from the original site, on the edge of La Villita Historic District.

Emmert International, a structural moving company in Clackamas (near Portland), Oregon, was contracted to move the Fairmount and soon had men and equipment on site. Owner Terry Emmert had recently reached an agreement-in-principle to purchase Pete Friesen's Advance Moving Contractors—with the proviso that Pete would help Terry move the Fairmount Hotel. Donning the official title of "consultant," Pete joined Emmert's crew at the corner of Commerce and Bowie. "Well, if it was built by humans," Pete chuckled, in a slight alteration of his credo, "then we beings should be able to move it."

But the move wouldn't be easy. Forecast to weigh about 1,600 tons, the three-story Fairmount building and its support steel were 60 percent heavier than the Brown-Ryan Livery Stable, and similar to that old Minneapolis stable, this seventy-nine-year-old building would require ample support, inside and out. The six-block route to the new site would also be demanding: the route contained three ninety-degree turns on relatively narrow streets, one of which had a center median, and would also require crossing a river bridge of questionable strength. As far as anyone knew, no one had tried moving a 1,600-ton building on rubber-tired dollies before. No, this move wouldn't be easy.

While Emmert's crew prepared the Fairmount for its road trip, a crew from the University of Texas at San Antonio's Center for Archaeological Research began digging up dirt at the destination site. Eureka! Just below the surface, they uncovered artifacts from another time. A quickly assembled team of sixty-three archaeologists—staff, students, and volunteers—was soon working in twelve-hour shifts, shielded from winter rains by a large tent. Their discoveries were numerous and archaeologically significant. As a result, their dig was granted a time extension, slightly delaying site preparations for the incoming hotel and postponing the move itself.

Meanwhile, at the corner of Bowie and Commerce, the old Fairmount had acquired vertical and horizontal bands of tubular steel on all exterior walls, while every one of its doors and windows received a sturdy wooden cross-bracing. All around the foundation, rough-cut square holes framed the H-shaped ends of wide-flange steel beams that pierced the old building across its length and width. The basement was now littered with rubber hoses, wooden blocks, and heavy metal jacks—an arrangement that made some sense to somebody. A screaming concrete saw had girdled the entire structure with a decisive horizontal line of separation. It was time for liftoff.

On March 20, 1985, the jacking machine control lever was selected downward, and thirty-six seventy-ton hydraulic jacks began pushing upwards against the huge steel beams. Joining the large crew to witness this most crucial of moments were the project developers, members of SACS, and representatives from many city departments. More than a few jaws dropped amid murmurs of amazement when a jagged four-inch gap appeared in the foundation walls. Seeing nary a brick fall out of place, the workers all nodded in relief. Below one particular hardhat, a broad smile emerged. "Looking good," whispered Pete, "just like she should." Eight full days of hucking blocks and resetting jacks, at the rate of one vertical foot per day, finally saw the old building raised high enough to accommodate rocker beams and transport dollies.

The dollies used on this job were items of technical beauty, designed and built by Emmert International. Originally manufactured for use in the mining industry, these units were very strong, very low-profile, and steerable. Featuring eight fifteen-inch pneumatic tires, each dolly carried a seventy-ton hydraulic jack and came with disc brakes and a $30,000 price tag. In due course, with generous help from seven thousand crib blocks, thirty-six of Emmert's good-looking dollies were maneuvered into position beneath the Fairmount where, one at a time, each took on its share of the load. In the final configuration, nine rows of dollies four abreast were aligned under nine rocker beams beneath two main load beams carrying nineteen cross beams. Placed across each complete row of jack rams, the rocker beams stabilized each row while distributing weight from the main beams down to the dollies. Shimmed tight and level above the two main load beams, nineteen cross-steel beams spread the underlying support across the entire base area. For additional support of the end walls, thirty small "needle" beams spanned both outside pairs of cross-steel. With 280 tons of steel under the floor and 144 pairs of low-profile tires ready to roll, the 1906-model 1,600-ton hotel was looking pretty good. Obviously, Emmert had invested a few tons of overhead underneath the old Fairmount before driving it off the lot.

While the Fairmount was made roadworthy, excavations were completed and preparations made for a new foundation at the destination site. Approximately halfway between old and new sites, the San Antonio Department of Public Works established a command post in the Convention Center from which to supervise necessary adjustments to municipal services while the large heritage building was in transit on city streets. This unique relocation scenario was carefully monitored by an ad hoc committee that included representatives from the Conservation Society and the development consortium as well as from the architects, the insurers, the moving company, and from all relevant city departments. Out in the trenches, two hundred civic workers took direction from three platoon leaders: the Control Team oversaw the public portion of the move, directing any repairs or adjustments; the Operations Team supervised relocation and protection of public facilities while managing for traffic and crowd control; the Assessment Team inspected the route before and after the move, recording any damage in field notes and photographs. The local development consortium, soon-to-be hotel owners, agreed to reimburse the city for any repair costs associated with the relocation.

Meantime, as the generous but firm relocation deadline proffered by DeBartolo rapidly approached, the Fairmount project was at risk of further delay and possible cancellation. From the outset of the proposed project, owners of the Plaza Nacional Four Seasons Hotel had tried to prevent the Fairmount's relocation by claiming the destination corner parking lot as their own property. One week before the move was scheduled to begin, the Four Seasons owners made good on their threat of legal action. Although the city prevailed in court, injunctions and other legal proceedings created minor delays and shrouded the entire project in a pallor of disharmony and mistrust. As well as legal, weather, and excavation delays, the Fairmount project developers and new owners also had to contend with slower-than-anticipated progress on the jobsite. They were confronted by the very real prospect of not making the first day of April deadline for removing the building. After years of planning and months of preparation, the old Fairmount might be demolished along with their considerable investment. They were in dire straits.

Facing desperate circumstances, the Fairmount investors approached consultant Pete and asked if he could get the building moved on time if he were project supervisor. With his affirmative reply, the hotel investors took steps to have Pete replace Emmert's foreman as overall project supervisor. As one might expect, such action did not sit well with the former foreman or his troops. In protest, all but one Emmert International employee walked off the Fairmount jobsite. The consortium of leaders now faced dissension in the ranks as well as legal wrangling on the periphery. There was no other option—they quickly assembled a small company of local laborers and gave Pete his marching orders: "You move it, or we lose it!"

Saturday, March 30, 1985, was a day unlike any other day in downtown San Antonio. At 0400 hours, the relevant streets were closed; many street signs and all traffic signals were removed. At 0530, the three Public Works teams convened for a last-minute briefing prior to the anticipated 0600 mission launch. With a signal from the project supervisor, the driver of the large tow truck engaged his winch while scores of gathering spectators looked on. Nothing happened. The Fairmount Hotel refused to move. Within a few short hours, a second large crane truck was hooked up to the load. With a thumbs-up from the project supervisor, both drivers engaged their winches while hundreds of gathering spectators looked on. Nothing happened. The Fairmount Hotel refused to move. Within a few short hours, a third crane truck was hooked up to the load. With outstretched arms and a palms-upward shrug of his shoulders, the project supervisor signaled all three drivers to engage their winches while thousands of gathered spectators looked on. The Fairmount moved. Resistant to the end, the old Italianate Victorian structure finally inched forward toward the street, greeted with loud applause from the spectators and the obvious joy of those tasked with moving it.

The forces of nature had made their presence known, seriously testing the wisdom of an experienced structural mover who had never moved a building this heavy on rubber-tired wheels before. As Pete and other heavyweight movers were learning, a pulling force of one ton is required for every seven tons being moved on rubber tires, and radial tires are 15 percent more efficient than hard-walled tires. Having finally overcome compression and inertia and its own reluctance, the 1,600-ton load was soon rolling comfortably on 288 tires across Commerce Street and south down Bowie.

In light of decreased friction, the additional two crane trucks were released from duty. However, to maintain sufficient mass of pulling force, seven dump trucks filled with sand were attached to the tow-cable network. Although these heavy trucks were not actually tow vehicles, they served as counterweights to the load, adding ballast to the one large crane truck that was now "heavy" enough to winch the building forward fifty feet at a time before driving forward and re-extending the winch cable. Throughout this tedious stop-and-go process, the humungous hotel was easily carried by Terry Emmert's dollies and thirty-six seventy-ton jacks in accordance with Pete's three-zone loading system. Having beaten the deadline for vacating DeBartolo's property by one day, everyone breathed a little easier. The Fairmount had escaped demolition and, pending successful completion of its journey, now represented the possibility of a return-on-investment for SACS and the development consortium. All was well in San Antonio. However, the late afternoon departure meant the expedition was quickly running out of daylight. A halt was called approaching the ninety-degree turn onto Market Street, expected to occupy half of the next day.

To everyone's delight, Sunday morning's turn onto Market Street proceeded much better than forecast. Although turning was a tedious and repetitive process—realigning every dolly's steerable front axle between numerous brief forward pulls—it was completed in four hours, half the anticipated time. On Market Street, the outermost dolly wheels were only two feet inside the street's curb margins, while the sides of the lumbering structure overhung both sidewalks by five feet. Of major concern on this section of the route was a bridge spanning a channel of the San Antonio River. While extra support measures were rapidly completed there, the Fairmount expedition stopped short of this Market Street Bridge. A morning crossing with ample daylight and a rested crew was the preferred option.

At 0900 on Monday, inspectors made a final check of the maze of steel supports installed beneath the bridge and signaled "All clear!" Thick steel plating laid across the road surface was expected to transfer the weight of the heavy load directly to the bridge structure and its temporary supports. Like coal mine canaries, two long-necked Lone Star beer bottles placed between supporting timbers and bridge walls would give warning of anything amiss. A large crowd of spectators held its collective breath as the Fairmount Hotel was pulled slowly onto the Market Street Bridge. Nine minutes later, the 3.2-million-pound building was safely across. As the crowd burst into applause, Cosmo and Tom Guido, owners of the construction company responsible for bracing the bridge, slipped into nearby St. Joseph's Catholic Church for a little prayer of thanks.

Once over the bridge, several more short pulls brought the creeping ensemble to the corner of South Alamo where the street's center median complicated a necessary ninety-degree left turn. After the street had been filled with sand and covered with heavy steel plates, the increasingly competent moving crew completed the turn in two hours. Under cloudy skies and ensuing rain, the old hotel crept past the much newer and taller Hilton Palacio Del Rio before coming to rest in the middle of South Alamo Street. Monday's thirteen-hour duty day ended at 1900 hours. At that afternoon's press briefing, the Control Team had reported the day's only damage to be several broken tree limbs and some squashed traffic buttons—road-surface markers. As reported by one interested party, Las Vegas bookmakers had lowered the odds—now listed at 7 to 3—for successful move of the Fairmount.

*Riding on four layers of steel beams and 36 eight-wheeled transport dollies, the 1,600-ton Fairmount Hotel load being pulled along South Alamo Street.*

Pete felt good about the project. His crew of workers, with barely a trace of structural-moving experience among them, had finished preparing the Fairmount building and moved it off the lot in time to save it from demolition. Despite their relative inexperience, they had maneuvered an awkward load over the Market Street Bridge and around some tough corners, becoming more proficient as they went along. Unfortunately, as Pete soon found out, several men on the crew had something other than structural moving on their minds. On that evening of Monday, April 1, while walking around the load parked in the middle of South Alamo Street and thinking things through, he discovered one of his crewmen unhitching a dolly bridle—an act of obviously malicious intent.

Confronting the would-be saboteur, Pete suggested a discussion over a cup of coffee. In the course of a three-cup conversation, the treasonous crewman admitted to several acts of attempted sabotage by him and several others. Pete learned they had purposely misconstructed a dozen strategic crib piles in the destination site basement: with one outside block removed from the same side of each crib, these piles would collapse when the building was pulled onto them. "Never have I been so happy to hear bad news," Pete reflected. "Again, I felt embraced by the everlasting arms from above that have so often protected me. The man repented totally. From then on, he was a loyal and trusted worker. I can't say for absolutely certain," Pete concluded, "but I'm pretty sure his problem had something to do with the Las Vegas odds." Whatever his reason may have been, the crewman's confession saved the Fairmount Hotel.

Tuesday dawned clear and cool. Although standing in front of its new home, the road-weary hotel had to spend another night in the street while hundreds of timbers and crib blocks were completely reassembled in its new basement. For the first time in many weeks, most of these weary structural movers enjoyed a workday of less than twelve hours.

Bright and early Wednesday morning, the moving crew successfully undertook a feat never before accomplished: they rotated a 1,600-ton load ninety degrees in one place—as in, on the spot, without forward movement. Although perilously close to the buildings of HemisFair Plaza and under the critical scrutiny of visiting structural movers, the Fairmount Hotel, riding on thirty-six dollies with 288 rubber tires, was successfully rotated ninety degrees in a tortuous five-hour pivot. The moving crew supervisor had been correct in his prediction of literally "turning it on a dime." The city's director of Public Works and other engineering types found this rotation to be the most fascinating aspect of the entire move. Other city officials were less impressed, as preparations for receiving the Fairmount onto its new site had still not been completed, and the humungous old hotel would be spending yet another night parked in the middle of a major thoroughfare with a busy Easter weekend just around the corner.

On Thursday morning, more than one set of eyeballs rolled skyward when a series of "minor" incidents visited South Alamo Street. First, a broken pulley support caused a delay. When forward movement eventually resumed, the old Fairmount suddenly bucked backward while being pulled across the street median—a tow cable had snapped; fortunately, there were no injuries. Soon thereafter, a dolly got loose from the herd and reared onto its hind legs in defiance; again, there was a delay, but no damage. However, it was mid-afternoon before forward movement could resume. By sunset on Thursday, April 4, the epic six-day, six-block relocation was finally completed. The Fairmount Hotel was home at last.

While the building movers took a well-deserved rest, city crews hastily replaced street signs and signal lights prior to Good Friday's holiday traffic. "It was incredible to see how various city departments worked so well together," remarked SACS president Bebe Inkley. "It is easy to think, especially in our work, that nobody in the city cooperates with anybody else … but this was a wonderful example of everybody working together to attain a major goal."

While plaudits flew far and wide, those closest to the action knew that relocation of the Fairmount had been far more difficult than it appeared. In fact, it came very close to not happening at all. While this job could not have been attempted without Terry Emmert's resources, it would never have been completed without Pete Friesen's leadership and expertise. Both men were deservedly commended for getting this job done under very trying circumstances. The 1986 *Guinness Book of World Records* would list the Fairmount Hotel as the heaviest building ever moved on pneumatic tires.

*With a new entrance and an addition, the completely refurbished Fairmount Hotel continues to serve the traveling public in downtown San Antonio—Dos Kiwis Studio.*

After the $1.2 million move and a $3.1 million refurbishment that included a three-story addition, the "new" Fairmount Hotel joined the ranks of San Antonio's finest hostelries. Located near the Convention Center and La Villita Historic District, it is well situated to participate in the comings and goings of San Antonio. To the south, a walking and cycling trail is connected with four restored and active Spanish missions within a national historical park. To the north, San Antonio's now famous *Paseo del Rio*—River Walk—connects many parts of downtown, while connecting the city to its river with more than two miles of waterside promenade. Immediately beyond, a recently constructed extension channel brings the river into the heart of the large shopping mall and hotel complex where the Fairmount Hotel once stood. Nearby and easily accessible, the well-preserved Alamo historic site colors the bustling downtown core with shades of antiquity and authenticity.

With due credit to the foresight of De Zavala, Driscoll, Green, Edwards, and their cohorts, the historic preservation community in San Antonio has created a level of civic planning and cultural integration unique in the nation. By preserving elements of their past, they have helped define their city's future. Today, San Antonio's $3 billion annual tourism industry is second only to the military sector in annual revenue. In relentless pursuit of century-old ideals, SACS continues to play an instrumental role in the preservation of values that enrich the entire community. Custodians of the Alamo since 1905, the DRT now have a larger complex to maintain, but still operate without charging an entry fee.

Catholic mission, military fort, and historic shrine, the Alamo has always been at the center of San Antonio. As a symbol of courage and independence, it is probably unparalleled, at least in the United States. Casual tourists and history buffs alike find the building irresistible. The name is inescapable in the city, found on streets, plazas, schools, banks, and cement companies. So pervasive is the Alamo, its history sometimes pops out of the ground, as it did in 1985. Considered one of the most important digs in local history, the archaeological exploration conducted in the parking lot at the corner of South Alamo and Nueva uncovered a mother lode of Mexican weaponry and artifacts dating back to 1836. Because of the courageous relocation of the Fairmount Hotel, SACS had inadvertently discovered a post used by Santa Anna's army during the siege of the Alamo.

As Lewis Fisher so aptly summarized in *Saving San Antonio*: "The sort of sophisticated deal-making which accomplished the move had been filtered through the prism of the city's historic preservation movement, polished by the growing appeal of an ambiance so precariously preserved during the previous hundred years. Moreover, as the Fairmount crept across a bridge of the uniquely preserved river and captured the imaginations of nearby convention-goers, it headed toward a site not only dating from the birth of the city, but newly discovered as a key location in the legendary battle which first made San Antonio known to the world."

The local champions of historic preservation had hit the jackpot.

# 11

## The Association

Bill Lee entered the world of structural moving at a very early age. In 1954, his parents upgraded the chicken house on their semi-rural property in the village of Vulcan, Missouri, where they operated a grocery store and tavern. Ten-year-old Billy Lee inherited the old chicken coop. Of solid oak-frame construction with four windows and a good roof, this 5' x 6' "fort" was an ideal retreat for human beings negotiating their second decade of existence. With the installation of a bed and a small wood stove, Bill soon had the best clubhouse in town. While it was a thing of beauty to its sole occupant, the old chicken coop was an eyesore for his mother. It had to be moved! Using a strong metal bar, Bill's father slipped several two-by-fours beneath the floor and several steel pipe rollers under those. With Dad on the pry bar and young Billy pushing with all his might, the old clubhouse was relocated to an alternate site behind the new chicken house, where it was out of sight from the kitchen window. Thus young master Lee was introduced to structural moving and historic preservation.

Although he outgrew the clubhouse, Bill would never forget the lessons of its relocation. As a twenty-year-old attending Southwest Missouri State University at Springfield, he was soon intrigued by the number of homes in his rooming-house neighborhood being bought up and auctioned off in conjunction with campus expansion. Seeing multi-thousand dollar homes purchased for less than $100 by people who could move them elsewhere, Bill was motivated to investigate building relocation as a means of securing a proper home for himself.

Though he could find precious little information on the subject, he recognized the need for seed capital and was soon employed on a construction site where he carried mortar hods for bricklayers. On rainy days when there was no work, Bill continued his house-moving research at the public library in St. Louis, where he discovered a few brief industry reports of two or three pages each. At the same time, he became excited to see that airport expansion and highway construction around St. Louis would put five hundred more "surplus" homes on the market at very reasonable prices. While recuperating from a job-related broken leg, Bill cut and pasted together an overview of the development area from photographed municipal documents and began comparing roof sizes and available lots. After getting back on the construction-industry payroll, Bill pursued his need for house-purchase seed money with maximum effort while temporarily assigning lower priority to his desire for further education.

In 1972, for the incredible sum of $1,500, the twenty-eight-year-old construction worker purchased a surplus three-bedroom bungalow in the town of Arnold, about twenty miles south of downtown St. Louis. After paying Cooper Brothers of Salem, Missouri, $3,500 to move his new residence a half-mile onto his newly purchased $5,000 lot, Bill installed municipal services and began renovations. Four years later, after selling this home at a handsome profit, he bought another surplus house in need of relocation. Moved five miles through Arnold in three easy pieces, this would be Bill's "clubhouse" for the next thirty years. Sonny Johnson and company managed the move and would relocate three more houses for Lee over the next few years. These others were truly surplus homes that Bill rented out for a time before selling. Ten years after his first house purchase, Bill was able to resume his formal education on a full-time basis.

In January 1982, Bill enrolled at Southeast Missouri State University at Cape Girardeau to complete his general-studies degree. For the previous ten years, he had researched the business of structural moving, and while studying at this university, Bill continued extracurricular research about his favorite subject. Frequenting libraries on campus and beyond, Bill soon realized that relocation of historic buildings remained a mostly neglected option for saving architectural treasures which themselves contribute to preservation of cultural values. With sound reasoning and great passion, the thirty-eight-year-old student was able to convince a professor that he should pursue this particular line of reasoning as a subject for independent study within his undergraduate curriculum. With a nod from his teacher, Bill headed north to Iowa for some independent research, at his own independent expense.

The 1982 convention of the Iowa House Movers Association took place on February 20 in Clear Lake. Organized by Doug Alysworth of Wadena and Ron Holland of Forest City, the one-day symposium gathered together two dozen Iowa house movers and a dozen others from outside the state—from as far away as Florida and Rhode Island—to share their experiences and ideas while comparing equipment and techniques. The featured guest presenter was Pete Friesen of Advance Moving Contractors, speaking about his 1980 rubber-tired relocation of a one-thousand-ton livery stable in Minneapolis.

Conducting diligent research among all present, Bill Lee was soon introduced to two house movers from outside Iowa: Jim Kabrick, from Indiana, and Allen Cansler, from Georgia. Having just met each other at the convention, Kabrick and Cansler were already engaged in discussions regarding the desirability of a national house movers association. Later that day, when the Iowa association declined their request to take on such a cause, these two individuals committed themselves to "jacking up" the idea. For the next seven months, when not moving buildings, Kabrick and Cansler were busy writing letters and making telephone calls—hardly the two favorite activities of a house mover.

Kabrick, from Otwell, Indiana, had fallen in love with house moving in 1954, when he had fallen in love with and married the local house mover's daughter. "Back in those early days at Elmer Buchta House Moving," Jim recalls, "the best we could do was raise a building twelve inches per hour with ten-ton screw jacks before we would all need a bit of a rest. Then in 1957, along comes this guy with a machine that he says will raise the same building fourteen inches in five minutes with fifteen-ton hydraulic jacks. Of course, we were skeptical. We set the jacks, and he hooked up the hose and gave it a shot. Sure enough, it worked just like he said it should. That was our introduction to the machine Pete Friesen had designed and built in Canada. It's what every house mover had ever dreamed of. It took some time, but we finally convinced Elmer to buy us one of those new unified hydraulic jacking systems."

"What are you doing?" was the immediate reaction from Jim's friend and chief competitor, Kenny Adair. "You'll never move enough houses to pay for that machine!" Not so, as it turned out. The expansion of the 1960s gave the nation's structural movers more than enough to do, removing buildings in advance of ever-widening highways and never-ending airport expansions. During one such project, using its new jacking system, the Buchta company moved houses at three times the rate of its "non-unified" competitors. Buchta's newfangled moving machine paid for itself within two years. Before long, most serious structural movers in the United States used later editions of Pete's invention manufactured by his former partner Robin Renshaw at Modern Hydraulics Incorporated.

"While his hydraulic jacking machine soon became popular with structural movers, some of the principles and techniques Pete used in conjunction with it were much harder to come by," Kabrick recalls. "In fact, one day in late 1980, I had to fly to Minneapolis just to check out the 'three-point loading' idea that we heard Pete was using to move an old stone livery stable. We house movers were all busy in our own areas and had little time, and often little desire, to share information with our competitors. There were only three or four good associations in the country, and one of them was in Iowa. In February of '82, I had decided it was time to go west again and see what else was going on."

In late February 1982, having recently returned from the Iowa convention, Jim Kabrick was already writing letters to other movers, inviting their participation in a national association as recently discussed with Allen Cansler. Kabrick's commitment can be readily seen in his letter to old friend Kenny Adair, now living in Florida. Dated two days after the Iowa gathering, this letter invites Adair to be the guest speaker at the first national convention, already scheduled for January of 1983, eleven months hence—if they managed to form the association by then.

Back in early 1963, Allen Cansler was behind the counter at Mom's and Pop's grocery store and gas station in eastern Tennessee when the two big trucks pulled up to the pumps. The trucks belonged to house movers who had come to remove buildings from the right-of-way for new highway construction. Upgrading of Interstate 81 would bring dramatic upheaval to the rural village Cansler had always known as home. After showing the movers a good location for their office trailer, eighteen-year-old Cansler began working for them as an agent, arranging and setting up acceptable deals with his neighbors who were about to be relocated. Well-trained by his father in the buying and selling of commodities, young Cansler was quick to recognize "surplus" houses as lucrative merchandise. Investing a good portion of his retail earnings, he purchased a small home in line for relocation and later sold it for considerable profit. When this profit was similarly reinvested, Cansler's enterprise began a rapid expansion; he was very good at this sort of thing, and there were few other distractions in eastern Tennessee. "After watching the movers for a time, I knew I could improve my circumstances by moving my own buildings," recalls Cansler. "So I gathered together a small outfit and starting moving houses. That's when I learned I knew nothing. But I stayed with it, and the more I learned, the more I knew there was more to learn. As well as moving a bunch of local houses, I managed to move our small train station off its pad in 1966."

To complement his expanding house-moving business, Cansler also became a demolition contractor whose very first job was the tearing down of his family's grocery store and gas station. By then, plans for significant expansion of the international airport at Atlanta, Georgia, were shifting into gear. In April 1968, the twenty-two-year-old entrepreneur arrived in Atlanta with his compounded grocery store earnings and purchased 122 surplus houses in one fell swoop. Within a year, he acquired 178 homes designated for relocation or demolition. With so many houses now for sale, Cansler had to organize them in a huge parking lot—like a herd of recreational vehicles—where buyers could shop and compare before having their dream house delivered. With so many houses to move, and with moves of usually more than forty miles, Cansler could not long tolerate all the required fees and procedures—especially, the constant need for over-height permits. He cleverly reconfigured the roof on all of his houses: the eave end of every rafter was severed and reconnected to its joist with a hinge before each roof was sliced in half along its ridgeline. "Presto! Cut away the gable ends, secure them beneath the folding roof, and you are good to go!"

exclaims Cansler. "For the most part, we stayed under the eighteen-foot height restriction, and we could move almost at will without having to worry about moving a lot of overhead wires and the like."

Cansler continues: "In those days, we were pretty much into quantity, not weight. Although we always used hydraulic jacks, I didn't see a unified jacking system until about 1970 when New-Way Transportation Company came through from Kentucky on an unrelated project. When I asked, they said they got their machine in Chicago and that almost every mover north of Louisville had one. Again, I learned there was a lot I didn't know. We were extremely busy with one thing and another right through the '70s. By 1980, I was a member of the National Association of Demolition Contractors, based in Chicago, and had become accustomed to information-sharing and technical support among my peers in that business. By comparison, house movers seemed to be an unorganized and sometimes fractious bunch that worked mostly in isolation, hardly speaking with each other unless looking for information to undercut someone else's bid. It seemed to me that house movers and their industry would all benefit from some sort of professional association ... and I got to thinking."

This kind of thinking had encouraged Cansler to attend the February 1982 convention in Iowa, having already moved twenty-five of his own houses that month. Now, barely thirty days after arriving home from Clear Lake, this same thinking was taking him back west again. The ninth annual Mid-States House Movers Convention in Norfolk, Nebraska, was another opportunity to compare notes with fellow house movers while also beating the bushes for interest in the national idea. To help promote their now-common cause, Cansler's new ally Jim Kabrick had invested $75 in advertising space on the Nebraska conference's agenda sheet, with which all movers and equipment manufacturers in attendance were invited to express any interest they might have in a January 1983 national convention in Atlanta.

Impressed by the energy of a student he had met in Iowa, Cansler invited Bill Lee to join him in Nebraska. Eagerly accepting the invitation, Bill Lee flew off to do more independent research on his favorite subject, meeting Cansler at the Sioux City airport, where they rented a car and drove to Norfolk. No doubt, during their days on the road together, Cansler heard much about the history and merits of preserving old buildings, while Lee got an earful regarding the potential benefits of a national house movers association. Each being far better at telling good stories than reading maps, they were both a day late for their return flights.

Back on campus, Bill submitted his structural moving research and presented a hands-on demonstration aided by some of Sonny Johnson's equipment. Bill's semester had just ended with a perfect A+ grade in his favorite subject when he received an invitation from another house mover. Kabrick was on his way to Portland, Oregon, to observe a heavy move by Emmert Industrial, while also evaluating their seventy-ton dollies with regard to an upcoming heavy move by his own company. While in Oregon, the pair watched one of America's most successful structural-moving companies maneuver a large and heavy railway station through the narrow streets of Corvallis. Having committed to purchasing ten of Emmert's dollies, Kabrick returned home to plan for the August relocation of the historic Huffman house in Dayton, Ohio.

Bill Lee, while back earning construction income to help offset university expenses, could not resist an opportunity for more historical research. In August, he traveled to Dayton where he watched Kabrick's crew use two unified jacking machines, ten seventy-ton dollies, and 125 tons of steel to relocate and thus preserve the 650-ton Huffman house, built in 1863. Soon thereafter, accepting another invitation from Cansler, Lee joined an interim committee to organize an initial planning session for a national house movers association scheduled for October in West Chicago. "It was a pleasant surprise," remembers Bill, "to be included in this group of industry professionals. While I could humorously claim the most youthful beginning to any of our structural-moving careers, my sole claim to fame was pretty weak—I was living in a larger relocated house than anyone else. While I had organized a grand total of five house moves in my lifetime, these guys had personally relocated thousands of buildings. In all practical terms, I was barely a 'wannabe.' However, my enthusiasm and my academic approach must have counted for something in their eyes. I felt very honored."

On October 9, 1982, Lee joined Cansler and Kabrick in West Chicago, where he was introduced to seven other similarly dedicated individuals: Pete Friesen, Robin Renshaw, Carl Tuxill, a graduate engineer and experienced house mover from upstate New York who had worked on several projects with Pete, James Drake, a fourth-generation house mover from Houston, Terry Emmert of Emmert International, Roy Emmert, a moving force in his brother's business, and Dave Pizur, proprietor of a Milwaukee insurance firm specializing in coverage for structural movers. Everyone was there with the same purpose in mind, and they soon agreed on the name and aim of a professional organization to be run for the benefit of its members while improving the public image of house movers—the National Association of Structural Movers (NASM) was born.

By all reports, the meeting was a convivial eight-hour exercise in consensus making. It was agreed that their newly formed organization would be governed by twelve or more directors, half of them coming from each side of the Mississippi River. While planning further representation from a number of regional associations, seven of those present volunteered to serve as first-term directors. An interim executive board was elected and charged with organizing the association's first national convention to be held in Atlanta, Georgia, on January 15 and 16, 1983: Jim Kabrick was to be chairman, Allen Cansler co-chair, Terry Emmert treasurer, and Bill Lee secretary.

Unable to obtain the mailing list from any existing trade magazines, Cansler had already purchased a Yellow Pages listing of 1,100 structural movers who would be informed posthaste of the NASM's existence and upcoming national convention. Contributing to the same cause, Renshaw and Pizur both volunteered their company's mailing lists. In order to maximize exposure, the interim board also authorized its first expenditure, allocating $75 to advertise in Bill Edward's publication *House and Building Mover*. Fresh from his first two classes on magazine design, Lee dared to suggest the idea of an association-specific magazine. In response, his most supportive colleagues unanimously directed him to get on with it: "Have it out by mid-December, and be sure to mention Atlanta!"

The first and only issue of the magazine came off the presses on December 19, 1982. Entitled *NA of SM: National Association of Structural Movers*, its front cover featured type in a bold, red, mechanical-styled font. Inside, the feature article by Everett Boerhave outlined the seven-hundred-mile move of a nineteenth-century farmhouse from North Dakota to Iowa by Badger Movers of Minneapolis in 1980. An article by Renshaw described how one of Modern Hydraulic's latest jacking machines had taken structural moving to another level in New Zealand by helping Warwick Johnson move a 360-ton church. An article by Kabrick summarized the recent Huffman house move in Dayton, and another described the disassembly method utilized by students at Southeast Missouri State University to move an 1850s-era two-story log house. Modern Hydraulics, Emmert Industrial, and Dave Pizur Insurance were three of the six advertisers on board. The inside back cover presented a full-page invitation and membership application for potential NASM members while the front cover beckoned: "See you in Atlanta."

On the eve of the new association's first national convention, the situation in Atlanta was pretty bleak. "I was somewhere between terrified and distraught," remembers Cansler. "Despite all our best efforts, despite a thousand or more telephone calls and hundreds of mail-outs, we only had thirty people registered for a two-day event that began the very next day. My lawyers had drawn up a draft constitution and a set of bylaws, and I had committed $15,000 to the Marriott Hotel for catering fees. We were jacked up as high as we could go, and we were suddenly out of fluid … I can't begin to describe my feelings of relief to see three hundred people come through those doors and register the next morning."

The first and only convention of the NASM was an overwhelming success: 302 people, representing 121 companies from forty states and three countries, mingled and convened around ten trade exhibits at the Airport Marriott in Atlanta. Guest speaker Chip Belding entertained and informed during Saturday's dinner, followed by a dance with live music. One of the first items of business for Sunday's administrative session was a name change. Given that house movers from as far away as New Zealand were in attendance at this inaugural convention, a motion was passed to rename the organization accordingly: the International Association of Structural Movers (IASM) came into existence.

After approving the constitution and bylaws, the membership then formally elected the seven interim directors and the four interim executives to an official term before voting in five additional directors.

The first directors of the IASM were Kabrick, Cansler, Terry Emmert, Lee, Friesen, Drake, and Tuxill, along with Charlie Blake of North Carolina, Dave Scribner of Nebraska, Ron Holland of Iowa, Lee Wetzell of California, and Richard Knapp of Florida. At its inaugural convention, the IASM also awarded lifetime memberships to three industry pioneers: Chip Belding, Robin Renshaw, and Elmer Buchta.

*Head table guests at the 1983 National Association of Structural Movers convention where the International (IASM) designation was adopted. Seated from left: Terry Emmert, Chip Belding (Guest Speaker), Pete Friesen, Carl Tuxill, and Charlie Blake. Standing: Allen Cansler, Jim Kabrick, Bill Lee, Dave Scribner, James Drake, and Lee Wetzell—International Association of Structural Movers.*

Before adjourning with 148 members signed up, the assembly directed Terry Emmert and his planning committee to begin organizing the 1984 convention and directed Bill Lee to get busy producing another magazine. In closing, Cansler expressed his gratitude: "We appreciate the opportunity to have hosted this first convention, and we thank all of the members who have contributed to making the IASM a reality rather than just a dream. We consider it long overdue and believe we will all benefit greatly by formation of this association."

How true it was! Cansler's dream had indeed been realized, and the new organization would soon prove to be of far more benefit than any of its members could have predicted. Suddenly, scores of disparate and isolated building movers had united under one umbrella organization with international reach. The IASM's membership list soon included hundreds of structural movers and scores of industry affiliates from across the United States, throughout North America, and beyond. While enjoying broad technical support, constructive dialogue, and many other benefits, every member of the IASM can thank two men for its creation. Their vision inspired an idea and their determination brought together a group of founding directors who embraced the concept and brought it to life. The fact that the IASM came into being less than eleven months after these two first met in Iowa is ample testimony to the energies and abilities of Allen Cansler and Jim Kabrick.

Soon after the inaugural convention, the first issue of the international association's magazine came off the presses; in green mechanical-style type on a black background, its cover boldly introduced *IA of SM: International Association of Structural Movers.*

Unfortunately, late that year, inclement weather and uncooperative hotel scheduling forced a change in venue for the IASM's forthcoming 1984 convention. At the eleventh hour, the host city was changed from Portland, Oregon, to Houston, Texas. Disappointed but still actively involved, almost-host Terry Emmert handed the reins over to James Drake in the latter city. On very short notice, Drake organized his friends, family, and colleagues into a mini-task force that secured the Houston Airport Hilton for three days in early February. By their combined efforts, the IASM's second "national" convention was a well-organized and well-documented event attended by three hundred people. In his opening remarks, IASM President Kabrick warmed at least one heart with an impassioned plea on behalf of historic preservation: "It seems to me that we Americans are getting into an era where it is easier to throw things away rather than fix them. Federal, state, and city governments are all guilty of doing this. They tear down buildings, bridges, and houses to build something that won't last as long as what they tore down. Why? Usually, because they claim it saves time and money ... and we all know where governments get their money. And while there is never enough time to do the job properly, there is always enough time to do it over again."

While rallying his troops, Kabrick also clearly defined a major obstacle confronting his industry: "Isn't it remarkable that almost every new law and regulation on the subject seems to be against the house mover? I am afraid it's getting worse instead of better. Right now, in some states, it takes as much time to get all the bonds, permits, and utilities lined up as it does to actually move the building. While we are busy making a living, we seldom notice new laws being passed in favor of other organizations that have the time and money to lobby the politicians. There are so few movers in most cities that it is hard for them to be heard, and in the larger cities where there are several movers, they seldom stand up for one another … in fact, most don't even talk to each other. By working together, we may be able to influence some changes so that everyone comes out a winner, and I think *you* are all winners, or you would not have come to this convention."

In closing, Kabrick touched upon the kind of information-sharing that would soon become a hallmark of the IASM: "Have you ever stopped to look at yourselves? You are a unique group of people engaged in an exacting profession—moving buildings. There is no school to teach you how to do it better, and there are very few books on the subject. Only in meetings like this one can we band together and exchange ideas, resolve our differences, and work toward our common goals. If you are ever in need of help about anything, talk to any one of your directors; you will be glad you did, and so will they. Meantime, enjoy the seminars being offered, and ask all the questions you want."

Without further ado, the president introduced the chairmen of the nine committees that would henceforth give operational direction to the association. Also instituted at this meeting was a series of twelve awards in recognition of member accomplishments during the previous year, in categories ranging everywhere from "Oldest Mover" to "Tallest Move." These presentations would become a feature of all future conventions. On the business side, the association membership re-elected the entire executive slate for a second term—for the sake of continuity with interpretation of the original bylaws—while voting in favor of one-year terms for all subsequent officers. Thus, James A. Kabrick of Otwell, Indiana, became the one and only consecutive-term President of the IASM.

In retrospect, this second IASM convention proved pivotal to the eventual success of the organization. That it happened at all after a last-minute, cross-country change of venue attests to the ingenuity and determination of all concerned. If this gathering had not happened, it may have been extremely difficult for IASM leaders to regenerate the necessary momentum among a loose collection of very busy and ever-skeptical structural movers. Without this second convention, the programs and benefits initiated there may have never happened. The IASM had also acquired a first sense of itself—it was real, and it had a right to exist. Collectively, members were coming to understand the benefits of association and recognize a purpose to their organization. The IASM was beginning to project an aura of success.

When Cansler became the IASM's second president at its third convention in Tampa, Florida, in early 1985, he inherited a functioning organization largely of his own design. Though there were more growing pains to come, the operation was up and running. More importantly, most of its membership was catching onto the spirit of the thing. "It was very satisfying to see the changing attitude," Cansler recalls. "Where there was once only isolation and suspicion, there was now growing trust and cooperation. It was far from perfect, greed and insecurity being what they are ... but, for the first time in some cases, competitors were helping out on each other's jobsite instead of just sneaking around at night looking to take or break something. The old cut-throat, almost sinister, image of your average house mover was slowly giving way to a more open and friendlier form of competition that was better for everyone.

"The conventions are vital to this process. There is nothing like a good meal and some live music for bringing people together. Once they all see they are all people, they usually figure out ways to make things better for themselves. For a structural mover, what could be better than rubbing shoulders with friends and competitors while learning from veterans and leaders in their industry? Most movers would agree that the IASM is one of the best things that ever happened. In fact," Cansler concludes, "the IASM has probably done as much to unify the movers as Pete's unified machine did for the business end of moving."

Pete Friesen was present at this third convention, as he had been at the previous two. Of similar mind with Cansler and Kabrick, Pete had been quick to embrace the national idea. Although he never served on the executive, Pete was one of the IASM originals: a founding director, he continued to serve the association while happily sharing everything he had ever learned about moving equipment and moving buildings. As Chairman of the Methods and Procedures Committee, Pete wrote magazine articles and presented seminars about many on-the-job issues, usually with a strong emphasis on safety. At the 1985 convention, Pete facilitated a workshop examining the technology and operating principles of the UHJU, now known in industry parlance as a jacking machine. At the conclusion of this third convention, Pete departed Tampa and returned to his consulting work in San Antonio, where one of these same jacking machines would help move the 1,600-ton Fairmount Hotel.

The IASM would continue to grow and improve. Third, fourth, and fifth generation house movers would soon follow their parents' footsteps into annual assemblies of like-minded professionals who shared their love for a very challenging craft. Through their conventions, magazines, and newsletters, members would keep up to date with the latest techniques and the newest developments. Often working together, they would learn to complete ever more complex relocations of larger and heavier buildings.

# 12

## The Consultant

As far back as Pete could remember, his father Dietrich always referred to him as a *dummkopf,* a dumbhead who would never amount to very much. Pete's older living relatives remember the prevailing paternal attitude around the Friesens' prairie farmhouse: little Pete, the hardworking servant son, had no smarts and was not deemed capable of any significant accomplishment; he wouldn't go very far in life ... according to his father. Of course, Pete had learned to forgive his parents, and in doing so, he had learned to believe in himself and to trust his instincts. Being open to new opportunities and using his God-given talents, Pete had eclipsed his father's expectations many times over.

Never one to shy away from innovation or technology, Pete recognized the onset of the electronic age. He knew the plastic boxes called computers were here to stay, in one form or another. He realized that one of these machines could greatly simplify filing, accounting, and other everyday procedures around the office of Advance Moving Contractors. His secretary would love it, thought Pete, if she understood what it could do. He began making inquiries.

"Why bother?" one of Pete's brothers had asked. "Why get distracted by something that will take you the rest of your life to learn?"

"That's for sure!" Pete's son-in-law had exclaimed. "It would be impossible for you."

"I agree," Pete's lawyer said. "I am having a terrible time with my own operating system ... they are far too difficult."

In 1984, motivated by comprehensive research and long accustomed to being told his plans were impossible, sixty-two-year-old Pete Friesen went shopping for his first computer. Of course, the youthful computer salesman who attended to Pete knew nothing about him or his accomplishments. While resting his hands on an Apple, the sales agent politely suggested Pete was probably too old to grasp this new technology that was difficult even for younger people. After thanking the young man for his time, Pete Friesen walked across the street to another store and purchased the most powerful IBM computer in stock. "After all, it's just another machine," mused Pete, "and I've already built a couple of those in my short life." Indeed he had. In fact, he was on the very short list of people who had designed and manufactured their own beanpole digger as well as their own unified hydraulic jacking system.

Of course, at Pete's subsequent stop, the sales manager of the computer software store knew about neither of these inventions. Without direct reference to his customer's apparent age, the young salesman politely suggested Pete would be unable to fully understand and successfully operate an AutoCAD design package. "Then, obviously, I won't be able get it from you," thought Pete, before heading off to the competition, where he purchased the DesignCAD program. Never one to shy away from technological innovation, Pete wanted the latest and greatest computer-assisted-design program available. He was busy thinking through another idea.

Pete credits his son-in-law, Wayne Rhoads, for introducing him to computer operation. Although initially a detractor of Pete's "cybergeriatrics," Wayne had since taken an introductory course and become excited about a computer's capabilities. Motivated to further study and active use, he was soon passing along massive amounts of newfound information regarding its operation to Pete. In no time at all, Pete and Wayne had the IBM machine up and running. Thereafter, Pete taught himself word processing, PowerPoint, CAD, and spreadsheets. Once familiar with e-mail and connected to the Internet, Pete's repertoire grew by leaps and bounds. With his ability to decipher technical jargon and his natural tendency toward visualization, he was soon away to the races. The computer became a fixture in the front office of AMC, where Pete introduced it to his secretary, Karen Snyder.

Karen Snyder had this to say: "During the seven years I worked as his office secretary, Pete Friesen 'made' me do some things I really didn't want to do. Although I had enjoyed driving the company pull-truck once and had learned a lot by going into Chicago for relocation permits, I didn't care about computers. What was I ever going to use a computer for? Well, Pete insisted and 'made' me learn. How will I ever thank him enough? The computer did a marvelous job cleaning up our office paperwork, and knowing how to use it gave me a head start with my subsequent career in the legal system. Working for Pete was truly an honor. He is the most trusting and genuine person I have ever met. His gentle philosophy of learning things by doing things has been a part of my life ever since."

The AMC computer soon replaced the water cooler as the preferred place to hang out, and whenever the machine was available, Pete would hop into the driver's seat to do a few laps with his new CAD programs. Pete was soon spending more time at the office than had previously been his custom. After almost forty years of hucking blocks and pumping jacks, he was now more excited by the challenges and possibilities of electronic design. Pete was moving inside. Using the same hands-on approach that made him a leader in his field, he engaged in creative expression of the principles that move his industry. From application to theory, this elder statesman of the structural-moving industry put his experience to good use: he was creating computer programs to more easily determine a building's weight and locate its center of gravity.

After four decades of sketching on paper napkins, Pete Friesen was now drawing on computer screens. During the next several years, Pete committed himself to transferring his knowledge about building materials and balanced loading to computer memory, writing easy-to-use formulae for application by any structural mover on any conceivable job. His efforts resulted in two programs—Building Weights and Finding Center of Gravity—that have since become industry standards. By entering data into Pete's programs and following their prompts, a user will soon find answers to the most basic and pressing of concerns: How much pressure is exerted by each building section? Where is this building's exact point of balance? Pete Friesen's computer programs took guesswork out of determining numbers and placement of jacks, dollies, and beams. "Nothing to it, really," said Pete. "The programs are just explaining what we already knew in a different format. The computer just sped up a process that many of us house movers were already using."

In the same way his 1948 hydraulic crib jack design had contributed to the industry arsenal, Pete Friesen's Building Weights computer program expanded the industry toolkit electronically, forty years later. In the same way his 1955 UHJS had revolutionized house moving mechanically, his Finding Center of Gravity computer program pushed the industry envelope electronically, thirty years later.

One hundred years before a certain Russian-born house mover purchased his first computer, another house mover had received his first job offer on the other side of Lake Michigan. In 1884, having migrated from eastern Canada to eastern Michigan where he homesteaded a large farm while working as a general contractor, James Wellington Davis began his structural-moving business by helping relocate a neighbor's farm building. Of Davis's many children, four sons were raised as structural movers, and each of them subsequently owned his own business. From these four sons of James W. Davis came eight grandsons who also became structural movers. In 1952, one of these grandsons opened Delmar B. Davis & Sons House Moving Company. With Delmar's passing in 1964, the company was taken over by his son James E. Davis, a great-grandson of J. W. Davis. Soon at work in this family business was the eldest of James's three children, J. W.'s great-great-grandson, Delmar B. Davis II, known to his friends as Dell.

In 1986, half a dozen regional house movers from five companies with the surname of Davis registered at a statewide gathering of structural movers in Lansing, Michigan. Twenty-three-year-old Dell Davis was particularly excited to be there, because he knew the house mover he had been reading about in magazines was expected to attend—Pete Friesen. At the conclusion of the day's business agenda, Dell had an opportunity to meet Pete Friesen, and the two of them were soon engaged in lively discussion about personal experiences and perceived directions for the structural-moving industry. A tentative deal for the sale of AMC had recently fallen through. Now heavily committed to the development of his computer programs, Pete was on the lookout for prospective site supervisors and crew foremen for his company. Impressed by the younger man's gentle nature and eagerness to learn, Pete asked Dell for his telephone number. "No way!" Dell replied instantly. "I am nowhere near qualified to be in any position of responsibility on the caliber of jobs you are doing."

"I wouldn't be so sure about that, Dell." Pete responded. "If the door of opportunity opens, be sure you walk through it."

"I was overwhelmed," Dell still remembers. Dell was even more overwhelmed a year later, when he received a telephone call from Pete inviting him to run a job in St. Paul, Minnesota. Already concerned about his own family's business prospects, Dell feared his father might freak out over the idea; Dell broached the subject cautiously. While the Davis family example is exceptional in its size and longevity, many structural movers learn their trade by working in the family business. Dell credits his father with being the best possible teacher for many family members, including himself. Indeed, the company's great progenitor James W. Davis would have issued a happy sigh from on high to witness the manner in which his great-grandson carried on the family tradition with a fine bit of mentoring for his great-great-grandson Dell.

"Son," said James E. Davis, "you're crazy if you don't accept an opportunity like this one ... especially from that man!"

"Man, oh man! You never saw this guy pack a bag that fast in his life!" remembers Dell. "I was in St. Paul twenty-four hours later, bug-eyed and ready for work." One week later, as Dell was getting a handle on his new role of foreman, the large moving job was unfortunately shut down because of the building owner's financial problems. While paying Dell the agreed-upon amount for the job, Pete suggested there was lots of work to be had around Chicago, if Dell wanted to come take a look. Dell was back home in Michigan for only a few days when he received another invitation from Pete. In the process of selling his company to a gentleman with minimal experience in the field, Pete asked Dell to consider signing on as field manager while he (Pete) remained on board doing sales and engineering for the new owner. Soon after reaching an acceptable employment agreement with Dennis Fruin, the new owner of AMC, Dell moved to Chicago with his wife and their two young children. Working together, Pete and Dell would make the company go.

Unfortunately, after only eighteen months of ownership, Fruin realized structural moving was not for him, and he began planning to sell the business or shut it down. Having relocated his family to join AMC, Dell was not particularly happy. He sought out Pete's advice. Pete confessed he had been thinking the situation through, and he forthrightly suggested Dell should buy AMC. "No way!" Dell instantly replied. "I'm in no financial position to consider that kind of investment."

"You have more borrowing power than you think, Dell," encouraged Pete, "and if the door of opportunity opens wide enough, you should walk through."

With Pete agreeing to oversee sales and engineering aspects for the company, twenty-five-year-old Dell Davis became the proud new owner of Advance Moving Contractors in September 1988. "I never realized what Pete meant about high-volume production until then," Dell recalls. "He sold more moving and raising jobs than I could keep up with. Before I really knew what was going on, we were moving a 650-ton shopping mall in downtown Chicago!"

Built in 1903 and measuring 270' by 55', Armitage Plaza was a single-story shopping mall with solid brick walls three layers thick. The owners of the mall wanted it moved sixty-six feet to the rear of their property, where a rear parking lot had become prone to nighttime robberies. As well as improving customer appeal with front parking, this would also please the tenants with an increase in available retail space. By elevating the structure an extra two feet above ground level, each retail unit would have higher ceilings and many more square feet of display or storage space. Any idea of razing the old building in favor of a new one had been rejected because of current zoning bylaws: new shopping centers had more restrictive setback conditions limiting the size of stores and parking-lot footprints. Having accepted this challenge, the young owner of AMC and his sixty-seven-year-old consultant were on the job.

Because all 14,850 square feet of the shopping center had been built on grade, there was no basement foundation to permit the insertion of load beams. All required beams would have to be inserted through openings in the triple-brick walls, above the concrete floor. In order to stabilize these eighty-six-year-old walls, scores of vertical steel straps were inserted around each wall's lowermost courses of bricks, squeezing the bricks tightly together by forcing pairs of opposing wedges under the straps. With their lower courses held together in this manner, the old brick walls could withstand the necessary drilling and cutting as well as their relocation. While one crew was busy digging up the rear parking lot in preparation for the new concrete pad and two-foot-high foundation walls, Dell and his men began cutting carefully into the triple-brick walls.

The first beams inserted were nine sixty-six-foot slide-beam sections placed across the building's width on thirty-foot centers. Each slide-beam section consisted of two beams: one U-shaped slide-channel welded open-side-up on top of one twenty-one-inch-deep, wide-flanged support-beam. Resting on grade, these twenty-one-inch support-beams, weighing seventy-six pounds per linear foot (21WF76), would take the weight of the load while their eight-inch-wide slide-channels, welded on top, provided a trough for six-inch-wide shoe beams that would slide the load "effortlessly" along. Each 4' by 6" by 6" shoe beam came with a hard plastic slide-plate attached to its six-inch bottom surface. Four of these shoe beams would be sliding in each of the nine slide-beam channels: one shoe beam would be under each of the four twenty-one-inch-deep main load beams to be inserted parallel to the structure's long axis. According to the consultant's plan, nine fifteen-ton hydraulic rams pinned to the slide beams would push the 650-ton mall backward on four 280-foot main load beams, resting on thirty-six slide-plated shoe beams guided by nine slide-channels, welded atop nine support-beams. *Visualize.*

In due course, all nine slide-beam sections received sixty-six-foot extensions toward the back of the parking lot; sloping upwards on supportive cribbing, the slide-beam extensions reached over the forward stub wall to the back wall of the newly poured pad. With the destination ends of the slide beams resting four feet above grade, it looked like an uphill battle all the way. To reduce friction enroute, the consultant's preferred and proven lubricant, Ivory soap, would grease the tracks. Behind the load, nine fifteen-ton-capacity push-ram cylinders were attached to the rearmost main load beam at the front of the building. Their ram ends were pinned to heavy steel brackets, known as push blocks, firmly bolted to each of the slide beams. For ease of operation, both flanges of each support beam were pre-drilled at fourteen-inch intervals adjacent to the slide-track, thus facilitating rapid and secure forward positioning of the heavy push blocks.

The nine push-rams would be powered by pressurized hydraulic fluid from a jacking machine. However, because of space limitations, the movers had to make do with a smaller-than-ideal machine. They opted for a state-of-the-art, six-circuit UHJU, a scaled down version of Pete's original nine-circuit jacking unit.

The jacking unit's six slave circuits would supply unified pressure to six of the push-rams; its three supply-side outlets would power the other three with common pressure. Of course, the three push-rams powered by the higher amount of common pressure would extend more quickly than the other six and thereby threaten the load's structural integrity by application of unequal force. Therefore, to maintain push-force harmony, the three common-pressure rams were each installed between unified rams then physically connected to those unified rams with metal rods. In this manner, the three common-pressure rams were physically limited to the same rate of movement as the adjacent unified ones. Always a practical man and never one to shy away from new ideas, Pete Friesen had just resolved another complex problem by simple means. Hardly classified as one of his inventions, this innovative method would see Armitage Plaza hydraulically pushed to its new place of business with "mechanically unified pressure"—*Derch denche!*

After four months of preparation, everything was in place and ready to go. With no small degree of apprehension, Dell selected the jacking machine control lever downwards. Highly pressurized hydraulic fluid suddenly surged through nine circuits of reinforced rubber hose and forcefully extended nine piston-rams from their cylinders. Reluctantly at first, the eighty-six-year-old building slid backward several inches. "Lo and behold!" declared the consultant. "She moved real smooth, just like she should." After a brief equipment check and a nod from their boss, Dell's crew repositioned the nine push blocks while he recharged the jacking machine in preparation for a full fourteen-inch push cycle. This fourteen-inch push cycle was followed by another and another. The workers soon fell into a rhythm with their machinery.

Then it began to rain. Soon, nine torrents of very soft water were gushing down the four-foot inclines of nine very sturdy sixty-six-foot gutters. Below, the nine shoe beams in the first rank were soon immersed in a white frothy wash of Ivory soap. With freshly cleansed slide-tracks exhibiting a refreshed coefficient of friction, Dell and his consultant faced an interesting new conundrum: their load wouldn't slide without lubricated tracks, and their lubricant was washing away. Recognizing an opportunity when they saw it, Dell and Pete walked through the door of a nearby automotive supply store and emerged with numerous lubricants. Their experiment was simple and conclusive. Applying different substances to different slide-tracks before cycling the push-rams, they were able to determine the relative merits of several leading products by simply recording hydraulic backpressures on their jacking machine gauges. The eventual winner proved to be a synthetic lubricant made from paraffin wax, with Vaseline a close second. The rails were soon re-greased with this "new goo," and several more push cycles were completed before darkness set in.

When attempting to get underway next morning, the 650-ton load seemed reluctant to move, and pressure readings on the jacking machine gauges were much higher than expected. Investigation of the slide-track channels soon revealed cause of the problem: an abrasive foreign substance—brick dust—now coated one of the previously lubricated tracks.

"Obviously it hadn't grown there, and conditions were such that it couldn't have blown there. It was deliberately sprinkled into the channeled track!" Dell recounts.

Fortunately, other than delaying the proceedings and creating some mistrust for its proponents, this malicious act by a person or persons unknown did nothing to adversely affect outcome of the move. Fortunately, there were no injuries to personnel and no damage caused to the structure. Three days and countless cycles after first pushing off, the shopping mall was successfully coaxed backward up a greased 3 percent incline to the awaiting pad. Enabled by hundreds of crib blocks, all of the steelwork was gradually removed. After the completion of masonry work around base of its exterior walls, the Armitage Plaza shopping mall was soon open for business again, slightly taller and much better positioned than before.

This particular move was an opportunity for Dell to meet Carl Tuxill, an engineer and house mover of considerable renown. An old friend of Pete's, Carl was also a founding member of the IASM, and he was now in Chicago to report on the Armitage Plaza project as a feature story; Carl was now editor and publisher of the association's *Structural Mover* magazine. More through osmosis than by persuasion, Dell Davis soon became a full-fledged member of the association Pete and Carl had helped to create seven years prior. "Joining the IASM was one of the best things I have ever done," Dell now relates. "Over the years, I have come to know a majority of its members and have made many good friends there. I have also learned a lot, including tricks of the trade, through the association, and I look forward to many more years of membership."

The name Advance Moving Contractors was retired to the annals of history when Dell Davis renamed his company the Dell-Mar Corporation. A short time after seeing Armitage Plaza safely into position, Dell and his consultant eyeballed another historic building in need of salvation. In order to avoid demolition, a 175' by 42' masonry structure, now housing a successful pizzeria, required relocation to another site two miles distant. The only available route was one of Chicago's busiest expressways, which presented an overpass too low for passage of a dolly-borne load underneath. Not to worry. The project consultant soon acquired permission to bypass the overpass by hauling the three-hundred-ton pizzeria up the near-side exit ramp and down the far-side entry ramp back onto the highway. Looking at his long load and the tight curves of the exit ramp ahead, Dell was scratching his head when he heard Pete shout, "It looks good to me, Dell. Let's go!"

"These words from Pete were very motivational," Dell recalls. "They encouraged me to trust my instincts and reminded me not to be intimidated by the size of a building or by the size of a problem. Nothing ventured, nothing gained, as they say. Not only that, but looking back, these words pretty much summed up this five-year period. We moved 120 homes that year and raised seventy-eight more. We were even busier the next year."

Along with another hundred or so small residential jobs, Dell-Mar undertook three major projects in 1991, the first of which was the

Kuppenheimer house. In 1937, the recently married Mr. & Mrs. Louis B. Kuppenheimer Jr. commissioned architect David Adler to design a new home for their six-acre property in Winnetka, a northern suburb of Chicago. Wanting something more manageable than the sprawling mansion of Louis's childhood, they downsized to a modest three-storied structure of French-Georgian derivation with fourteen rooms on three levels.

Featuring concrete floors and a copper-plated mansard roof above whitewashed brick walls with French doors leading to flagstone patios, this mini-mansion had first been sold after Jane Kuppenheimer's passing in 1985. Having changed hands again in 1990, the current owners planned to replace it with a new home better designed for their special-needs family. However, their application for a demolition permit caught the attention of the Landmark Preservation Council of Illinois. The council facilitated a more preservation-friendly option: the house was offered *free* to anyone willing to move it from the property. After establishing a shortlist of forty-five applicants from around the world, the new owners of the Kuppenheimer house graciously donated it to nearby neighbors whose own home had been heavily damaged by fire. "Wow! What a beautiful story and what a beautiful *big* house!" declared Dell, looking at the 105' by 48' home he had bravely contracted to move.

"It looks good to me, Dell, about seven hundred tons," said Pete. "Let's get on with it!" With no fuss and a minimum of muss, Dell and company cut eighteen holes through the fifty-four-year-old foundation, inserted beams, and jacked 730 tons onto fourteen hydraulic dollies for a 1,400-foot journey down an 8 percent grade from atop one twelve-foot basement to another. The 1991 relocation of the Kuppenheimer house was then believed to be the heaviest private residence ever moved.

While Pete was carefully monitoring holdback vehicles on this downhill house move in Winnetka, Dell was attending to an overlapping project in the nearby suburb of River Forest. Here, Dell-Mar was hired to elevate that community's historic library building to enable a planned expansion. Constructed in 1929, the iconic 585-ton brick structure was being raised five vertical feet to accommodate the addition of a full second floor. This fairly straightforward yet time-intensive task was accomplished to the great satisfaction of all concerned. Dell and Pete then confronted their third major project of 1991.

Farther to the south, in the village of Frankfort, Illinois, there sat a very old and fragile historic building known as the Creamery. If not moved from its current site, the Creamery would be demolished to make way for two additional lanes on an adjacent highway. This was one of many jobs during Pete's career that was described as impossible. Not for the first time, his detractors and other industry pundits were wagering heavily against the move's completion. While photojournalists commissioned by the state of Illinois recorded the process, Dell Davis and his crew labored intensively for many weeks, under the guidance of project consultant Pete Friesen, to adequately prepare the 650-ton "pile of bricks" for a two-mile journey on sixteen rubber-tired dollies.

"I would qualify this job as one of the toughest," Pete recalled. "This old brick building had hand-wide cracks in it, and one wall was bowed-in six inches. To keep the building low enough to get under high-tension wires, we had to band it at an elevation lower than our dolly system. It wasn't an easy move in many ways. We were lucky and careful, but we made it."

After beginning with another burst of activity, 1992 ended on a sour note for Dell Davis and his Dell-Mar Corporation. While most structural movers are surprisingly comfortable with the daily threat to life and limb, they must also adjust to the razor-thin financial reality. Voluminous inventories, simultaneous projects, scattered jobsites, a seasonal work force, and very competitive bidding are some of the weighty issues bearing down on an enterprise that, by nature, is high in overhead. With unexpected difficulties like equipment failure or delinquent payment thrown into the mix, disaster often results. "A wonderful five-year run came to a sudden halt in late 1992, and we were suddenly in a very tough financial crisis," recalls Dell. "After our heavy expenditures on the big jobs of the previous two years, several of our major contractors and clients seemed to find every excuse in the book for not paying their bills. In short order, we were broke. By August of 1993, Dell-Mar Corporation was no more."

Although this turn of events was temporarily devastating, it was not the end of Dell Davis as a fifth-generation house mover. Dell and Pete would work together again in the not-so-distant future. Far from being out of work, Pete had been invited to participate in a very large and very complex project now getting underway on the east coast. In a telephone call from Rhode Island, Pete offered encouragement to his good friend Dell. "This kind of setback is hard for an honest and hard-working man like you, Dell … but try not to look on it as defeat, and don't be discouraged," said Pete. "Speaking with considerable experience about financial loss, I think you should just be patient and watch for another door of opportunity to open for you."

# ———— 13 ————

# Block Island

Giovanni da Verrazzano, an Italian navigator in the service of France, represented that country's entry into the race for empire and riches in the New World. Preceded to the south by fellow Italian Columbus in the service of Spain, and to the north by another Italian, Cabot, sailing for England, Verrazzano is credited as the first European to visit the mainland shores of what would become the United States. Sailing north from Cape Fear in 1524, Verrazzano briefly explored a broad northern inlet that would later be known as Lower New York Bay. While following the east-trending coastline toward home, the expedition "discovered" a small island, which Verrazzano described as similar in shape and size to the Mediterranean island of Rhodes. Without setting foot on it, he named the island *Luisa* for the queen mother of France.

Unaware of the new name, the undiscovered Narragansett people who inhabited the island continued to call it *Manisses*—Little God. The oral history of these Manisseans recounts a battle with invading Mohegan warriors, forty of whom fell to their deaths from the 150-foot cliffs at the island's southeast corner—known ever after as Mohegan Bluff. In 1609, an Englishman named Henry Hudson sailing on behalf of the Dutch East India Company also passed by without coming ashore, but his expedition presaged irrevocable change in the region. Five years later, a Dutchman named Adriaen Block, sailing out of Fort Amsterdam at the mouth of Hudson's River, landed on the island and initiated trade with its inhabitants. In reference to its auburn-colored cliff faces, Block called it *Roode Eylant*—Red Island. In 1672, two years before New Amsterdam became permanently known as New York, an influx of English pioneers and exiles from the Massachusetts Bay Colony to the north joined with their countrymen who had settled in and around the town Providence on the mainland to form a new colony—Rhode Island and Providence Plantations.

After decades of plague and several years of violent bloodshed, the newcomers finally gained firm control of all land and resources around Narragansett Bay and subjugated the scant remains of a once-flourishing aboriginal population. Thereafter, the colony prospered and engaged in agriculture, fishing, and shipbuilding. Very progressive for its time, the colony passed laws to abolish witchcraft trials, imprisonment for debt, and chattel slavery of both blacks and whites. By this time, Roode Eylant had become known as Block's Island. On May 4, 1776, the colony of Rhode Island became the first of the thirteen colonies to renounce its allegiance to the British Crown. Fiercely independent, it was also the last of thirteen colonies to ratify the U.S. Constitution, doing so only when threatened with "foreign nation" taxation on its exports.

With advent of the Industrial Revolution and exponential increases in maritime trade, the sea-lanes off the northeastern United States became very busy and hosted their full share of shipwrecks and sinkings. Surrounded by dangerous shoals and ledges, Block Island (the possessive was dropped eventually) was often referred to as the stumbling block of the New England coast, and this island of seven thousand acres was identified as a desirable place for the installation of lighthouses. The first, erected in 1829 at the island's north end, washed out to sea and was replaced eight years later. The ocean also claimed the replacement lighthouse. The third rendition of Block Island's North Light was constructed in 1867, and it remains there to this day. Approval for a lighthouse at the island's south end was much later in coming. Finally, in 1872, a petition circulated by local merchants inspired a $75,000 appropriation from Congress, and the sum of $1,350 purchased a ten-acre site at Mohegan Bluff on the southeast coast. Despite concerns expressed by local farmers regarding the rate of cliff erosion at the intended building site, construction of the lighthouse began the very next year.

The building, as approved by the United States Lighthouse Board, was an architectural showcase, melding Italianate and Gothic styles into a brick structure featuring extensive use of granite blocks for its foundation and corner accents. A sixteen-sided cast-iron lantern platform capped a five-story octagonal light tower attached by an indoor walkway to a three-story keepers' residence. Accommodating two families with different lighthouse schedules, the house featured two independent kitchen wings of two stories each. Designated as a primary seacoast aid to navigation, the stylish new lighthouse was outfitted with the most powerful lighting apparatus then available. Illuminated by the burning of lard oil, a $10,000 handcrafted Fresnel lens of the first order pushed the project slightly over budget before casting its broad, white beam as far as twenty miles out to sea.

Soon after becoming operational in February 1875, Block Island's Southeast Light hosted a series of experiments, conducted by the Lighthouse Board and the Smithsonian Institution, designed to measure the effects of weather conditions and air currents on the range of the light's steam-driven fog whistle. In 1906, the Southeast Light received a new compressed-air fog signal powered by a kerosene engine. In 1929, new flash panels were added to the lens, giving the Southeast Light a flashing green signal to differentiate it from many white lights in the region. At the same time, the lens rotation assembly was upgraded with a mercury floatation device. The hurricane of September 21, 1938, New England's worst ever, did tremendous damage to the light, knocking down the radio beacon, demolishing the oil house, blowing out windows, and cutting off power. As a result, the keepers had to turn the lens by hand for several days.

By 1993, 120 years of erosion had left the Southeast Light on precarious footing. Originally constructed three hundred feet back from the cliff edge, the stylish old structure was now only fifty-five feet away from the same fate that befell Mohegan invaders four centuries before. The U.S. Coast Guard deactivated the light station and replaced it with a steel tower and electronic beam. The National Trust for Historic Preservation had listed the Southeast Light as one of America's eleven most endangered structures of historic significance. For many Block Island residents, this lighthouse was a thing of beauty, a local landmark they could not bear the thought of losing. Ten years prior, a dedicated group of volunteers, inspired by the Block Island Historical Society, formed the Southeast Lighthouse Foundation and had immediately started searching for money and ideas for preserving their beloved structure. By 1993, the Lighthouse Foundation had raised $2 million in support of a plan to move the historic lighthouse back from the edge of doom. "If we had stood by and done nothing while it fell into the sea, we would have felt remiss and irresponsible," stated Dr. Gerry Abbott, chairman of the Southeast Lighthouse Foundation. "Finally, after three Acts of Congress, many generous donations, and ten years of hard work, we had a plan that might work."

The plan was simple enough: pick up the lighthouse and move it another three hundred feet back from the cliff edge. Putting the plan into operation was not so simple. Responsibility for the task fell on the shoulders of the New England District of the North Atlantic Division of the U.S. Army Corps of Engineers (USACE). This job would require experienced operators and people of considerable imagination. While lighthouses had been moved before, no one had ever attempted to move one as heavy or as complex as this one. Study after study had been completed; idea after idea had been investigated; proposal upon proposal had been reviewed. Bids had been entertained and the candidates interviewed. The Corps of Engineers selected a consortium of three major players for the moving team: International Chimney Corporation of Williamsville, New York; Expert House Movers of Sharptown, Maryland; and Friesen Consulting of Lynden, Washington.

As their name implied, International Chimney Corporation (ICC) had extensive experience with tall vertical structures. In existence since 1927, the company specialized in the design, construction, and repair of chimneys and other tall vertical structures. By the 1990s, the company's range of equipment included the latest machinery for cutting through thick masonry walls like those of the Southeast Light.

Expert House Movers was a family business started by "Big John" Matyiko in the 1950s. Since then, four sons and half a dozen grandsons have kept the operation going and growing from bases in Maryland, Virginia, and Missouri. Jerry Matyiko of the Maryland office had met up with Pete Friesen in the 1980s through the IASM; he was one of those who came to observe Pete's 1985 move of the Fairmount Hotel. Jerry invited Pete onboard as project consultant for his bid on the Block Island lighthouse move.

Pete had relocated to the small city of Lynden, way out west in Washington State, where he attempted semi-retirement by playing golf more often while consulting on various moving projects throughout the country. Having convinced his new teammates that moving the building in one piece—light tower and living quarters together—was the best way of maintaining structural integrity, Pete set to work on the detailed computer-generated drawings that would secure the contract. As history would prove, Pete Friesen accepted the Block Island lighthouse job more for the technical challenge it presented than for the financial reward it offered.

The project's supervising engineer, James A. Morocco of USACE's New England District, describes his team this way: "International Chimney was the general contractor; they had the engineering background and did the shop drawings; they were the money guys. Expert House Movers were the hands-on people; they supplied most of the men and equipment; they did most of the physical work. Pete Friesen was the man who had the original idea of how to move the building; on site, he was the symphony conductor who knew the music best and who brought everyone together to make it happen."

The task of relocating Southeast Light officially began on April 12, 1993, with a formal groundbreaking ceremony to initiate foundation construction at the new site. Joining representatives of the Lighthouse Foundation, the U.S. Coast Guard, and many island dignitaries, Governor Bruce Sundlun and Senator John Chafee both offered tributes to the people who had made the project possible. An attending throng of newspaper and television reporters recorded local school children participating in a traditional shovel ceremony. After such an auspicious introduction, the pressure was now on the players to get the job done.

As is often the case, the finest of drawings and the best-laid plans could not anticipate every problem. Although ferry service between Block Island and the mainland operated frequently, the small vessels in use could only carry automobiles and smaller trucks; both locals and tourists alike often left their vehicles onshore. Obviously, many of the larger pieces of moving equipment would prove problematic. Although the seventy-foot steel beams coming by barge from Expert's Maryland yard could easily be handled at Chesapeake Bay loading facilities, they posed a great difficulty to the island town of New Shoreham's small ferry terminal. However, in typical house mover fashion, the problem was quickly overcome with a couple of boom-trucks and a front-end loader.

Meanwhile, the old lighthouse was readied for action. The floating mercury base was removed from beneath the fragile Fresnel lens, which was then taped and braced into position; the sixteen-pane glass lantern atop the light tower was also taped and secured. All four chimneys were braced with wooden harnesses; basement windows were temporarily bricked in, while all other door and window openings were braced with wooden supports. For good measure, a single band of strong steel cable was girdled tight around the entire structure. Amid widespread speculation from experienced engineers and would-be structural movers who maintained the impossibility of moving the old structure in one piece, a betting pool was established. Far from the first or the last of such relocation gambling games, the pool allowed selection of a day when the building would collapse—winner takes all.

The move did not start well. Initial excavation revealed the light tower to be resting on a circular foundation of unconsolidated rubble. The original construction had been based on a collection of random boulders poured into a perimeter ditch fifteen feet wide and about thirty-five feet in diameter. This stumbling block was overcome with Gunite—air-sprayed concrete—to seal and bind the supporting rock base. While the sprayed concrete dried, the four main load beams were assembled on site. Each of the four mains was a welded pair of 70' by 24" wide-flanged steel beams weighing 162 pounds per linear foot (24WF162). Once the Gunite had hardened, the sprayed concrete rubble was stable enough to permit core drills as well as the big hydraulic chain and cable saws to do their work. To accommodate the two innermost main load beams, two 3' by 5' slots were cut through fifteen feet of stone foundation on both opposing arcs of the tower base. In careful alignment with these slots, identical openings were cut through exterior and interior foundation walls beneath the house section to receive the innermost main beams parallel to the structure's long axis. While the two outermost main load beams would use similar openings beneath the house section, their southern ends would rest outside opposite arcs of the light tower circumference.

Proceeding in accordance with Pete's plan, the entire moving team developed intense *esprit de corps* while confronting unprecedented challenges. While so-called experts from far and wide were betting against their success, Expert House Movers and all others on the job became committed to a common cause. Everyone did their utmost to achieve the impossible; they wanted to move the two buildings together without knocking a brick out of place. While his company's crew and equipment were preparing the structure for separation from its foundation, ICC's chief engineer, George Gardner, had this to say: "Like many other old buildings, these lighthouses are all unique. They all have their own quirks about them, and you need somebody on site with experience, someone who knows how they are going to act. To my mind, there's no one better in this regard than Pete Friesen."

Pete's Building Weights program had determined a total weight of 1,650 tons for Southeast Light and its supporting steel, the heaviest structure he had yet tried to move. Although scarcely heavier than the 1,600-ton Fairmount Hotel load in San Antonio, the lighthouse was a building of far greater complexity. This job would demand refined calculation and great care to lift the structure in a balanced manner. Careful planning and some good luck were needed to move this building without damage. Unlike the Fairmount, which was transported on dollies, the Block Island lighthouse would be moved on rails and rollers, similar to the 1976 Highland Park fire station project. However, unlike the fire station, which was pulled along, the lighthouse would be pushed along by large hydraulic rams attached to the roll-track. In contrast to the fire station's diagonal direct route, the lighthouse would undergo two ninety-degree direction changes on a three-leg zig-zag route.

Similar to other aged structures, this building's mode of construction was also a legitimate concern. In this case, the entire light station—house and tower connected by a short walkway—was an unsupported masonry structure. It was a pile of bricks, albeit a fine looking and obviously functional pile of bricks. Well-crafted with the finest of bonding mortar, the double-walled brick building had no need for a wooden framework or steel reinforcement. It had long withstood hurricanes and was now the last surviving lighthouse of its architectural genre. It is highly unlikely, however, that any of the designers or expert craftsmen who worked on the light ever envisioned a day when someone would want to lift their building off the ground and carry it away. The heavy brick lighthouse was beginning to look a bit fragile.

*Southeast Light being prepared for relocation with chimney bracing, lantern glass taping, and a weight-distribution beam inserted through the tower's east-west windows.*

While investigating the possibility of picking up the building and carrying it away, the project consultant had determined the light tower and house sections to be of similar weight, slightly more than 800 tons each. However, their two footprints were vastly different. Calculating the building's center of gravity, Pete saw a small, round, concentrated load at one end of his teeter-totter model and a large, square, spread-out load at the other. Thirty feet in diameter at its base, the tower occupied about seven hundred square feet, while the fifty-foot square house occupied 2,500 square feet. Although the building's ultimate point of balance would easily be determined by Pete's Finding Center of Gravity computer program, the disparate size and shape of the two component footprints would be a challenge for determining a balanced arrangement of jacks and beams.

Further complicating the move, the walkway connecting the house and light tower was not simply a pile of bricks—it was a freestanding pile of bricks! Constructed without being horizontally tied to the two main sections, the walkway offered no rigidity to the total structure and was more liability than asset. Furthermore, any inherent strength in the walkway itself was greatly reduced by generous window and door openings built into its sidewalls. In practical terms, relocating the old light station would amount to moving three buildings at the same time with the same equipment.

A more positive factor in Pete's planning dynamic was the symmetrical design of the keepers' house, especially the two north-end kitchen wings. As such, the centerline of the overall structure's long axis divided the house section into two balanced zones. In keeping with Pete's three-zone loading principle, the two house sections became Zone Two and Zone Three while the light tower was designated Zone One. Inserted on the overall structure's long axis, four feet on either side of centerline, the two innermost main load beams were centered beneath the light tower and lay slightly inside exterior walls of the connecting walkway before underlying their respective zones in the house section. Twelve feet outside these beams, the two outermost main load beams lay beyond the light tower and walkway walls while underlying their respective house section zones. Each main load beam was a welded pair of 24WF162s. Near the base of the light tower, a convenient pair of windows permitted insertion of a thirty-six-inch-deep beam on an east-west orientation, above and horizontally perpendicular to the main beams. When firmly secured to the outermost main load beams, this "window" beam would transfer a share of the tower's weight to the outermost jacks of Zone One. Pete Friesen had been *thinking it through*.

*The 36"-deep distribution beam is inserted through
tower windows and attached to the outermost main beams.*

Before insertion, the four main load beams were outfitted with thirty-eight fifty-ton jacks, all arranged in a carefully measured pattern to not only balance the load, but also to align with horizontally perpendicular roll-tracks for the planned ninety-degree change in direction of travel. With jack bases firmly bolted to the underside of the main beams in the same manner as the Highland Park project, the inverted jack rams would extend downwards onto creeper-dollies riding along the hardened steel surface of the roll-tracks. Above and perpendicular to the four main beams, eleven equally spaced cross-steel beams each provided load distribution under the house section. For distribution of the light tower's load, four short radial beams were inserted above the main beams, with two placed across each pair of inner and outer main beams at forty-five degree angles.

After all this cross-steel had been pre-loaded and shimmed, four thirty-six-inch-deep beams were installed around the base of the building: two resting across exposed ends of the cross-steel and two resting across exposed ends of the main load beams. Welded together at their corners and secured to their respective support beams, these four "strong-backs" formed an external steel frame to help counter any small stresses during movement. Back down below, a horizontally perpendicular series of eleven reset beams was clamped to the underside of the main beams. When supported by carefully placed crib piles, these reset beams would accept the load during jack resetting and roll-track changes. When not in service, all eleven reset beams would travel with the load. In the meantime, between the reset beams and directly beneath the four main load beams, hundreds of crib blocks were assembled into scores of carefully planned crib piles supporting the ten fifty-ton jacks inverted under each outer main beam and nine fifty-ton jacks inverted under each inner main beam. *Visualize.*

With a nod from his consultant, Jerry Matyiko depressed the jacking unit control lever downward. Hydraulic pressure at 5,000 psi immediately pushed through nineteen slave circuits and three splitter-manifolds to all thirty-eight fifty-ton jacks—sixteen in Zone One, eleven in Zone Two, and eleven in Zone Three. As the large crew of hard-hatted humans looked on in excited silence, Block Island's Southeast Light lifted from its foundation "just like she should." Operating at approximately 85 percent capacity, the thirty-eight jacks easily raised the old structure aloft while onlookers scanned in vain for falling masonry. When nary a brick was seen out of place, the project consultant allowed himself a happy smile. The latest model of Pete's original jacking unit invention was a marvelous machine. Built by Modern Hydraulics and later modified by Jahns Structure Jacking Systems, this particular UHJU featured "double-length" master-and-slave cylinders capable of pushing sufficient fluid to adequately supply thirty-eight jacks through nineteen split hydraulic circuits at pressures approaching 10,000 psi. Although a number of his original units were still in service, Pete's old nine-circuit UHJU of 1955 was not up to a task of this magnitude.

Even the latest machines had difficulty keeping up with jack design innovation: fifty-ton, sixty-ton, and even seventy-ton hydraulic jacks were now available. While remaining consistent with Pete's original design for at least fourteen inches of ram extension, the larger bore of the newer jacks caused them to draw much more fluid. Manufactured with inferior internal tolerances, new jacks also failed more frequently than Pete's original quick-change hydraulic crib jacks. Fortunately, on this job, there was only one jack failure, and it was a non-event owing to the inherent redundancies in Pete's zone-loading method. On this large-scale layout, the amount of hydraulic fluid being supplied was also noteworthy. The five-inch bore of the thirty-eight jacks was twice the diameter of the jacking unit's nineteen slave cylinders. Because the slave circuits each supplied two jacks through their splitters, a 4:1 relationship existed. Thus, four complete pressurization cycles of the jacking unit were required for each complete sixteen-inch extension of the jack rams. After several sixteen-inch lifts, each requiring four pumps from the jacking machine, the old lighthouse was finally deemed high enough to travel.

While reset beams supported the load, jack cribs were dismantled and jack rams were retracted as four 14WF145 roll-tracks, each topped with hardened T-1 steel, were placed immediately below and parallel to the four main load beams. Once the four roll-tracks were in position underneath, pressure was reapplied, and the inverted jack rams extended downwards against creeper-dollies riding on the hardened steel surface of the track. The 1,650-ton load was soon removed from the reset beams and transferred through the jacks and dollies to the roll-tracks. Valves were then closed on each of the splitter manifolds to block the fluid supply in place, thus isolating all jack circuits downstream. Having been raised on unified pressure, the old lighthouse now floated on three zones of common pressure. After three days of this track preparation, it was time to get the show on the road. It was time for a push.

At the south end of the building, rearward extensions of the four roll-tracks now protruded from beneath the light tower. To each roll-track extension, Expert personnel had firmly secured a heavy steel bracket, also known as a push block. Pinned and locked to each track bracket, the business end of a hydraulic ram extended from a cylinder firmly attached to its respective main load beam. Rated at thirty tons each, these four push-rams were more than capable of propelling the 1,650-ton load forward along the smooth and hardened roll-track. Having ridden the rails several times before, the consultant knew that one ton of push-ram pressure would move thirty-five tons of load along beams plated with T-1 steel. Through a combining manifold, four circuits from the jacking unit's double-length cylinders would power each push-ram. After every pressurized extension and push by the rams, the load would be blocked and hydraulic pressure reduced before all four track brackets were repositioned farther forward. In this manner, the fragile old lighthouse would appear to be pushed along the track by four inchworms flexing their way home.

*Behind the lighthouse load, four push-rams are attached to the roll-tracks and to ends of the main load beams situated between reset beams below and strong-back beams above.*

While the expert movers applied bars of Ivory soap to the roll-tracks—primarily to reduce friction on the creeper-dolly guide bars—the Corps of Engineers engineered another media event. Organized by the Public Affairs Office of USACE's New England District, the gathering of media and dignitaries on August 13, 1993 also attracted hundreds of summer tourists. Once again, island ferry service was stretched to the maximum. A large fishing boat was chartered to transport the dozens of media personnel, and a military helicopter brought in Senators John Chafee and Claiborne Pell along with Congressman Jack Reed. After a round of remarks from the dignitaries, Jerry Matyiko depressed the control lever, and to the delight of all in attendance, the 120-year-old lighthouse slid smoothly forward for a distance of sixty-four inches. While Lighthouse Foundation and Coast Guard representatives were thrilled to see their dream finally in motion, Pete Friesen and other moving team members were happy about not seeing any loose pieces of masonry in motion. After congratulatory handshakes, the celebrants dispersed via helicopters, ferries, and fishing boats while the working folk returned their attentions to the work at hand.

Having once again been the subject of intense media attention, the players really felt the pressure. One day does not a season make, and you're only as good as your next song, as the old adages go. Having successfully lifted their house of bricks, the Expert Movers still had to get it home in one piece or lose their newly established, fan-inflated reputations; having bathed in a bit of fame, it was back to the dirty work at hand. Hardly glamorous, the work certainly was repetitive—the old and almost funny joke about playing golf with a heart-attack victim comes to mind: tighten fifty-six bolts, push the load sixty-four inches, loosen fifty-six bolts, move the brackets sixty-four inches, tighten fifty-six bolts, push the load sixty-four inches. Over the low whine of the hydraulic pressure pump and the constant murmur of its power source came the "chanking" rhythm of pneumatic drill sockets and the occasional "chunk" of tossed wooden blocks. From underneath came a counter-rhythm of deep moaning—like whales in the ocean—as creeper-dolly guide bars rubbed up against edges of the roll-track. From out front came the throaty rattle of diesel engines in vehicles grading and compacting soil before laying new sections of roll-track.

After a two-day run, the first verse was done. In two very long days of repetitive toil, old Southeast Light had moved 126 feet in a northerly direction, straight back from the edge of Mohegan Bluff. A three-day interlude now followed in preparation for the second verse—a lateral move of 135 feet to the east. After raising their load another half-lift, workers hucked blocks under the building, assembling a comprehensive array of crib piles beneath eleven reset beams. Avoiding all existing roll-track, this network of reset cribbing was designed to remain clear of those horizontally perpendicular avenues reserved for installation of new eastbound roll-track. As with many other such details, the locations of reset beams and their dependent cribbing had been determined long ago, during the project consultant's visualization phase. Now it was time to lower the 1,650-ton load onto the reset cribbing while removing all thirty-eight creeper-dollies from beneath the depressurized jack rams. Once cleared, all north-south roll-track sections were removed and re-installed on an east-west axis.

Lo and behold, it worked. Within the vast array of reset cribs, each of the ten newly placed east-west roll-tracks lay perfectly aligned beneath a row of four jack rams, one on each main beam. As soon as the creeper-dollies were in place and pointing east, the jack rams were re-energized downward against them. The load, including reset beams, was raised off the cribbing. While all this action occurred underneath, another crew repositioned the trailing-end roll-track and the four push-rams to the building's west side. Here, arranged in a balanced pattern along the load's west face, four trailing track extensions were joined to the back ends of four eastbound tracks. After the four push-ram cylinders were attached to the lower edge of the westernmost main beam, their actuator arms were re-pinned to the heavy brackets bolted to the track extensions. The hydraulic hoses were hooked back up, and all ten lines of roll-track received a rub of Ivory soap. After a last look underneath, the crew foreman yelled, "All clear!"

The second verse sounded pretty much the same as the first and featured the same players playing the same instruments. After two more long days of repetitive toil, their fragile house of bricks stood 135 feet farther east, and the time had come for another interlude. This second three-day interlude was much like the first, but with reversed direction. The load was raised half a lift before being lowered onto carefully constructed reset cribbing; thirty-eight heavy creeper-dollies were removed from beneath depressurized jack rams. All ten lines of used east-west roll-track were removed and re-assembled, amidst a vast array of reset cribbing, into four lines of new north-south track. The heavy creeper-dollies, all pointing north again, were placed back on the roll-track and directly below the re-pressurizing jack rams. By this time, the four trailing-end track extensions had been removed from the west side and were rejoined to the south end of the four northbound lines of track; with their cylinders re-attached to ends of respective main beams, the four ram actuators were re-pinned to the heavy brackets bolted to the four trailing track extensions. Hydraulic lines were reconnected, and track rails were greased. After a last look underneath, the foreman raised his right thumb to the sky. "Hit it!" yelled the conductor.

*Viewed from northwest, the lighthouse load is being pushed north along four roll-tracks while stabilized by 36"-deep strong-back beams.*

The third verse sounded pretty much the same as the previous two and featured the same players playing the same instruments. After two more long days of repetitive toil and some last minute "jigging and jiving" toward a perfect conclusion, Block Island's Southeast Light was maneuvered gently over the concrete slab that marked its new home. The 120-year-old lighthouse had survived a three-legged, 350-

foot odyssey without so much as a crack or a whimper. After years of organization, months of preparation, and two weeks on the road, the show was over, and the curtain came down. In due course, the relocated light station was jacked gently down to rest on new foundation walls built up to meet it. Perched three hundred feet farther back from the ocean's cliff, the old lighthouse sat at precisely the same elevation and exactly the same aspect it always had. After being pushed around by heavy equipment for months, the stylish old pile of bricks now rested comfortably, within one quarter-inch of where the project consultant said it would. *Derch denche!*

As Pete would later summarize: "The zig-zag method was the natural way to move it. If we had tried to move it on the diagonal, some parts of the building would not have been supported as well as some other parts ... the placement of the beams and tracks would have been a problem. We wanted to create no damage to the building, so we moved it in the safest way possible. They [project organizers] were very happy with the way we moved that lighthouse."

The Army Corps of Engineers was very happy. Its New England District had just organized the heaviest lighthouse relocation in the nation's history—the first ever with lens in place. In so doing, they had preserved an architectural icon. By employing experienced operators and imaginative people, the well-organized project had come off without a hitch. Even better, the project's $1.93 million cost did not damage any Army budget. The state and the Lighthouse Foundation had contributed $970,000 while the federal government provided the remainder. The happy people at USACE HQ recognized the Southeast Light move with their award for the top engineering job of 1993.

The U.S. Coast Guard was very happy. With a minimum of expense and hassle, they now had the makings of a rejuvenated light station on the southeast coast of Block Island. The Southeast Light's original lens was replaced with another first-order Fresnel lens salvaged from Cape Lookout Lighthouse in North Carolina. On August 27, 1994, a relighting ceremony marked the Southeast Light's return to service. If geophysicists are correct and erosion rates remain steady, it will be another hundred years before the children of the children who helped officially inaugurate this relocation need to be concerned about another move. Meanwhile, at Mohegan Bluff, there is once again a fully functioning Class I maritime navigation aid flashing a green light every 3.7 seconds and counting.

Gerry Abbott and his foundation members were certainly very happy, having felt the weight of the world lift from their shoulders when their dream project finally touched down on its new foundation. Yesterday's dream had become today's reality. This monumental feat of engineering could never have happened without this handful of very dedicated people who knew very little about hydraulic jacks and steel beams. Thanks to these people, the Southeast Light survives as a stylish example of historic preservation while remaining in service as a prime aid to coastal navigation. In addition, this classic old lighthouse now serves the public with a museum, gift shop, and bed-and-breakfast.

The people in the trenches were also very happy. ICC had officially and very successfully entered the realm of structural moving; Jerry Matyiko of Expert House Movers had moved his first "heavy," a structure weighing more than 1,000 tons; Pete Friesen had stretched the limits of his industry's technical envelope one more time.

Although this consortium of structural movers—ICC, Expert House Movers, and Friesen Consulting—would work together on many more projects, some even larger than this one, the Southeast Light on Block Island would always represent something special. Coming from different directions and bringing task-specific skills, three men—George Gardner, Jerry Matyiko, and Pete Friesen—soon acquired mutual respect for each other's talents. In the wind and rain atop Mohegan Bluff, they first learned to work together. This was where they attained the high level of professional camaraderie that would carry them forth to even greater achievements.

Forever destined to attempt "impossible" performances, maestro Friesen had found two perfect friends with whom to play moving music.

# 14

## Cape Cod

When North America's great Laurentide ice sheet melted about eighteen thousand years ago, it left behind a large, curving terminal moraine at its southeastern edge. From the forty-mile arc of this broad ridge, myriad braided rivulets washed down a gravel apron into a multitude of shallow streams merging into rivers that traversed a vast coastal plain enroute to an ocean a hundred or more miles away. Paleo-Indians and other beings that came to inhabit this exposed continental shelf were soon migrating toward the northwest into ever-greening landscapes at the foot of melting ice, pursued by an ocean that was rising fifty feet every one thousand years. By six thousand years ago, ocean waves were lashing at the base of the arcing moraine, carving steep cliffs into unconsolidated headlands and creating long sandbars, spits, and islands.

On the way home after charting Block Island in 1524, Giovanni da Verrazzano sailed past the southern elbow of this broad, arm-shaped peninsula which would soon become well-known to fleets of European fishermen harvesting the prolific fishing grounds off its northeast tip. In 1602, Englishman Bartholomew Gosnold landed on the peninsula and named it Cape Cod. Samuel de Champlain charted its waters in 1606, and Henry Hudson came ashore briefly in 1609. Cape Cod was clearly identified on Captain John Smith's 1614 map of New England. Arriving late in the sailing season of 1620, a lone ship bound for the mouth of Hudson's River found the ocean off Cape Cod impossible to contend with. Unable to negotiate the shoals while facing contrary currents and winter winds, the *Mayflower* retreated behind the cape's northern tip and dropped anchor in a sheltered bay, now called Provincetown Harbor. The religious refugees and would-be colonists who came onshore received a less-than-warm welcome.

For decades, the aboriginal inhabitants of Cape Cod had been badly mistreated by European explorers, fishermen, and traders. Having already seen a large number of their loved ones murdered or abducted or both, this semi-isolated tribe of fishers and farmers was now experiencing a rapid decline in population due to an imported smallpox epidemic. Although now few in number, these Nauset people mustered enough resistance to drive off this latest invasion of the pale, smelly beings who came ashore and stole maize from their ancestors' gravesites. The newcomers weighed anchor and sailed west to the mainland coast, where they found an abandoned village at the head of a small, sheltered inlet. Recently eradicated by disease, the former inhabitants had left behind a managed forest, cleared agricultural lands, and several lodge houses inhabited by unburied skeletons. There was no resistance to immigration here.

Life in the New World did not begin well for the Pilgrims of Plymouth Colony. Suffering from scurvy and other diseases, 47 percent of the new arrivals perished during that first dreadful winter. Early the next spring, survivors signed a peace treaty with Massasoit, chief of the remaining Wampanoag population who had greatly contributed to their survival. Massasoit's spirit was subsequently celebrated in the naming of Massachusetts Bay Colony in 1629. On February 6, 1788, most Nausets, many Wampanoags, and much of their original territories were absorbed into the state of Massachusetts when it became the sixth former colony to join the United States of America.

By 1800, trade and commerce was already flourishing among the coastal states and was particularly brisk between the cities of Boston and New York. Intense marine traffic between the two often fell afoul of numerous hazards along the irregular coastline; shipping companies and other commercial interests were soon lobbying hard for installation of navigational aids. In 1796, the nation's first president, George Washington, authorized construction of the country's twentieth light station. The following year, near the town of Truro, Massachusetts, a forty-five-foot wooden tower was erected five hundred feet back from the edge of a high bluff on Cape Cod's east coast. Forever known to many locals as Truro Light, this first lighthouse on Cape Cod was officially named Highland Light.

Within a few years of Highland Light's appearance, a pair of light-towers was erected near the town of Chatham to provide navigational reference at the cape's southeastern elbow, while an 1816 lighthouse at Race Point identified the cape's most northern tip. By the middle of the nineteenth century, a set of twelve lighthouses completed an outline of Cape Cod's inner and outer shores.

Highland Light was constructed on ten acres of cliff-top land purchased for the grand sum of $110 from a farmer who coincidentally became its first keeper. Whatever his daytime chores might have been, this local agrarian was well occupied during the hours of darkness, lugging cans of whale oil up forty vertical feet and tending fifteen single-wick, Argand-style lamps burning within a glass lantern. To differentiate it from Boston Light, a rotating eclipser was added to Highland's white light, making it the first flashing light in the nation, crude and erratic though it was. The eclipser was removed in 1812 when the lighthouse was reduced in height by seventeen feet to accommodate a new system of lamps and reflectors. In 1833, a new brick tower and keeper's house replaced the aging wooden structure. However, both new buildings were found to be of very shoddy construction and were soon declared unsafe. The keeper's house and light tower were both replaced in 1857.

Topped with the latest and greatest Fresnel lens, this new $15,000 sixty-six-foot Highland Light became the highest on the New England mainland and one of the most powerful on the east coast. By then, lard oil had supplanted expensive whale oil as fuel for the lamp. Also included in this major upgrade were a coal-burning fog signal and a telegraph line for reporting ships' progress. A fully equipped modern light station, Highland Light was now manned by two assistants as well as a keeper, working in shifts to ensure a constant light all night, every night. During daylight hours, the keeper was required to count and sometimes report on ships passing by his light station. In an eleven-day period of July 1853, the keeper counted 1,200 vessels passing by Highland Light. During one summer day in 1867, six hundred ships were counted! Meantime, a naturalist and writer named Henry David

Thoreau visited several times during the 1850s, and while "standing with his back to all of America," he recorded forty feet of cliff erosion at Highland Light during the course of one winter. Wild weather has always been a frequent visitor to this coast. One of the worst storms in New England history was the Portland Gale, so named for the steamer *Portland* that went down in Massachusetts Bay with almost two hundred souls. At about ten o'clock on that night of November 26, 1898, the wind indicator at Highland Light was demolished by wind speeds of more than one hundred miles per hour: the lantern windows were ripped apart and the light was blown out.

In 1901, Highland Light was equipped with a larger, first-order Fresnel lens and a newfangled, floating-on-mercury rotational device. By then, kerosene had replaced lard oil as the fuel of choice for firing the lamp. In 1932, electricity replaced kerosene with the installation of a four-million-candlepower electric lightbulb that could be seen more than forty miles away. In the 1950s, this 1,000-watt bulb was replaced by higher-efficiency flashing aerobeacons. In the 1980s, as with most other lighthouses, Highland Light became an automated facility; although the U.S. Coast Guard continued using their buildings, the role of lighthouse keeper became a thing of the past.

Less than two hundred years after its erection, the light tower originally located 500 feet away from the ocean was now within one hundred feet of a cliff eroding at an average rate of three feet per year. The original ten acres had been reduced to barely two. In the winter of 1990, the Atlantic took another forty-foot bite from the escarpment in front of Highland Light. After nearly two centuries of faithful service, Cape Cod's very first lighthouse now appeared destined for the very fate it was built to prevent. It too could be swallowed by the sea.

In the early 1990s, the Truro Historical Society had created a Save the Light Committee dedicated to preserving this favorite local landmark. Gordon Russell, president of both the society and the committee, spearheaded a campaign that distributed 30,000 brochures and collected a petition of 140,000 names. Selling T-shirts and other souvenirs, the society raised more than $150,000 toward the cost of relocating their cherished lighthouse. In 1996, the federal government contributed $1 million, and the Massachusetts state government added another $500,000 to the cause. Under the watchful aegis of the Army

Corps of Engineers, the Highland Light would be moved 450 feet back from its present position by the same consortium that had successfully relocated Block Island's Southeast Light three years prior. By June 1996, International Chimney Corporation, Expert House Movers, and Friesen Consulting were on task in Cape Cod. Now known colloquially as "the Three Houseketeers," George Gardner, Jerry Matyiko, and Pete Friesen slipped comfortably into their familiar structural-moving roles. At the jobsite, a large sign welcomed tourists and residential spectators to the mid-summer moving experience with its declaration: *On The Move!*

*Before being moved, Highland Light is close to the edge of an eroding cliff on Cape Cod's eastern shore—Brian Tague.*

Though of different design and construction, the overall layout of the Highland Light complex was similar to the Southeast Light on Block Island, with the brick light tower connected by a walkway to the keeper's residence. In this case, however, the keeper's house was a much smaller wood-frame structure of only one and a half stories, without a basement. Much longer than the corridor at Southeast Light, this walkway connection doubled as a service building, providing additional space for communications equipment and other tower-related activity.

Cylindrical in shape, the Highland tower was only fifteen feet in diameter, whereas the octagonal foundation walls of the Southeast tower were fifteen feet thick. While only one foot less in height, the sixty-six-foot Highland tower was far lighter than its counterpart. In fact, at 525 tons, the entire three-part Highland Light complex weighed less than one-third as much as the Block Island structure. Although these professional movers could have relocated the Highland Light as one piece—house, tower, and walkway—they decided in favor of simplicity. Rather than import extra men and equipment to support a complex "all-together" relocation of this relatively light and fragile structure, the movers decided in favor of a quick and easy move using readily available resources. The keeper's wooden house would be separated from the walkway and moved independently, while the two brick sections would move as one unit. A major factor in this decision was the significant weight differential between ends of a load that had to descend 9.3 vertical feet during its 450-foot journey. Pete Friesen had been *thinking it through*.

While moving the house section would be a no-brainer for such experienced house movers, the combined tower-walkway would give their minds a few new things to chew on. For one thing, there was no basement foundation to facilitate beam placement. For another, there was no solid concrete footing under base of the walls. Working on loose sandy soil and with few options available, the original contractors had simply dug a four-foot-wide and four-foot-deep trench around the outline of their walls and filled it with multiple layers of clay-fired bricks and mortar; they built up from there ... with more bricks, of course. For a tall lighthouse on a windy shore, a mortared-brick footing is obviously better than no footing at all. Walkway walls were two bricks thick with airspace between, and the tower walls were three bricks thick with ventilation space between each layer. Thinning very slightly with elevation, the tower wall was forty-two inches thick at its base. Naturally, there was no rebar reinforcement anywhere and barely a scrap of metal in the entire structure. The closest thing to concrete was the mortar holding the triple-walled, sixty-six-foot-high tower of clay-fired bricks together. Given that the brick lighthouse had survived a century and a half of wild weather, the brick footing underneath it seems to have been adequate.

As the 40' by 20' house section was prepared for separation from its northern end, the thirty-foot walkway and the light tower at its southern end were also readied for action. Per normal procedure, all door and window openings were bricked in or filled with wooden supports, chimneys were braced with harnesses, and all glass was taped over for safety. The electronic light was secured in position within the glass lantern gallery atop the 149-year-old tower. To improve rigidity at the tower base, great amounts of grout were pumped into the ventilation spaces between all layers of brick, binding the three-layered wall to a height of three feet above its base. To improve stability, a multitude of two-by-fours were strapped, end-to-end in twenty-four vertical columns, to the tower's exterior wall. Buffered by interior bracing, the tower was then slightly compressed by a half-dozen steel cables wrapped horizontally around it. With the old tower properly girdled in this manner, it was hoped that no bricks would fall out of place.

After being separated from the north end of the walkway, the seventy-five-ton house section was expertly jacked up with two main load beams and six pieces of cross-steel, loaded onto three dollies, and rolled quickly out of harm's way. Then the real fun began.

Given the narrow profile of the fifteen-foot-diameter tower and the twelve-foot-wide walkway, Pete planned for placement of his main load beams completely outside the footprint of this two-section load and parallel with its long north-south axis. To accommodate these two exterior main beams, excavation began on a wide trench along each side of the tower-walkway section. However, these excavations posed a considerable threat to the stability of the mortared-brick footing and everything resting on it. As a precaution during trench excavation, cross-steel beams resting on dedicated cribbing were inserted across the width of the walkway to support a portion of the structure's weight.

As the existing ground floor contributed very little to structural integrity, the plan called for removal of the walkway floor and placement of the cross-steel beams at the ground-floor level, above and horizontally perpendicular to the exterior main beams. Joe Jakubik and his International Chimney crew cut precise slots through the walkway and tower walls for eight cross-steel beams. Four fourteen-inch-deep beams weighing 120 pounds per linear foot (14WF120) were inserted through the walkway walls; two beams of the same type were inserted, twenty-four inches apart and on the same east-west axis, under the center point of the light tower. Two more beams were placed on the same east-west axis slightly outside the north and south arcs of the light tower wall. Above and horizontally perpendicular to this tower cross-steel, a duplex needle beam—a welded pair of 14WF120s—was inserted on a north-south axis through the tower center point. Inserted on the same plane and angled at thirty degrees from each end of this duplex needle beam came four short-length, fourteen-inch-deep radial beams. Allocated two per side, these short radial beams spanned the respective inner and outer cross-steel beams below. Occupying the same horizontal plane, the duplex needle beam and the four radial beams would distribute the tower's weight evenly to the four cross-steel beams that transferred the load to the two exterior main load beams. *Visualize.*

Meanwhile, down in the trenches, modern structural movers took a page from the original contractor's 1857 handbook, placing a mat of layered crib blocks on the sandy trench bottoms to improve the footing for all subsequent crib-pile construction. In each of the two trenches, seven crib piles each supported a sixty-ton hydraulic jack inverted against the lower surface of a main load beam. Shimmed tight against eight cross-steel beams, each of these two mains was a welded pair of thirty-six-inch-deep beams weighing 160 pounds per linear foot (2X36WF160). The technique Pete had been forced to develop for moving the Highland Park fire station twenty years prior was now his industry's accepted normal procedure for short-distance relocation of large and heavy structures: turn the jacks upside down under a duplex beam and skate to destination with creeper-dollies riding on roll-tracks. Nothing to it! So it might seem.

"Each job is different, and you learn to expect the unexpected on every one," said Pete the consultant. "There was nothing too difficult to overcome on this job, but what with some loose bricks underneath and other little problems that came up as we went along, this move was more difficult than some others. I always describe the Block Island lighthouse as a gentle old woman," Pete Friesen explained "while this lady [Highland Light] is a little bit cantankerous sometimes … nothing serious, but this one needs more attention."

Having calculated his total load at 450 tons, Pete arranged fourteen sixty-ton jacks into three zones around the center of gravity—slightly north of the light tower center point. Pete's three-zone loading system dictated four jacks in Zone One under the connector walkway and ten jacks beneath the light tower, five each in Zones Two and Three. Supplied with unified pressure at 6,000 psi from the jacking machine, these fourteen jacks were operating at slightly more than 50 percent capacity when they separated Highland Light from its moorings. After raising their load seven feet during two days of jacking, the experts began preparing for horizontal movement. Between multiple sets of jack cribbing, another series of crib piles was built beneath the main beams in order to support the load while the roll-tracks and creeper-dollies were installed. So far, "Lady Lighthouse" exhibited no bulging bricks or fallen arches.

To reach her new home, the old lighthouse would have to travel 450 feet in a westerly direction and then 12 feet south, while losing a total of 9.3 feet in elevation. Almost the entire journey would be made sideways, perpendicular to the long north-south axis of the main beams and load. For this sideways travel, seven roll-tracks would be required underneath seven pairs of jacks, one jack of each pair under each main beam. Given the amount of track required for such a relatively light load, it was considered unnecessary to manufacture boxed-beam roll-track. Instead, seven fourteen-inch-deep wide-flange steel beams weighing 145 pounds per foot (14WF145) were top-plated with T-1 and placed on cribbing, immediately beneath and in alignment with the seven pairs of carefully aligned jacks. After several days of concentrated activity, fourteen inverted jack rams were pressurized downward against fourteen creeper-dollies pointing west along seven sets of roll-track beneath and horizontally perpendicular to the main beams. With subsequent closing of control valves on the jacking machine, hydraulic fluid was blocked in place, isolating each jack circuit downstream. Raised on unified pressure, Lady Lighthouse would float home on three zones of common pressure.

While now-redundant crib piles and other obstructions were cleared away underneath the load, each of the seven roll-tracks received a forty-foot western extension out front, in the direction of travel. In a balanced arrangement behind the load, four roll-tracks received a rearward extension for the acceptance of push-rams. As installed at

Armitage Plaza and Southeast Light, the bases of push-ram cylinders were fastened to beams beneath the load while their business ends were pinned to heavy steel brackets bolted to the roll-track. Given the sideways direction of travel and the relative uniformity of this lighthouse route, reset beams were not included in the moving package. Pete, the mild-mannered consultant, had another plan.

*Braced with columns of lumber and bands of steel cable, the light tower is ready to travel on seven roll-tracks while the previously detached keeper's house looks on.*

*Behind the load, a crewman adjusts the push-rams attached to the roll-tracks and a main load beam.*

While some crewmembers waxed the roll-tracks with bars of Ivory soap, the person who had long ago introduced his industry to unified jacking machines and hydraulic three-zone loading systems had another idea to present. Given the very short distance the load needed to travel in a southerly direction and the excessive amount of time and labor required to change direction ninety degrees, the project consultant suggested it would be much easier to simply bend the roll-tracks and push the load to its destination in a gentle S-shaped route. At first, there was silence. Well, why not? Pete had moved the Highland Park firehouse on a direct diagonal line, and he had moved Southeast Light with a zig-zag route. Why not try a curve or two here on old Cape Cod? *Derch denche?*

With varying degrees of skepticism, Pete's colleagues went along with the idea. First the load was push-rammed forward until it occupied the near end of the forty-foot westward roll-track extensions. Hooking a chain to his faithful and multi-talented front-end loader, Matyiko began applying gradual southern pressure to the western end of the southernmost roll-track beam, which was held firmly in place by more than one-seventh of a 450-ton load. It worked. The free end of the 40-foot extension beam bent almost a foot south; this was enough to satisfy Pete Friesen's imagination and any calculations he may or may not have made. Seeing another invention in the making, Pete's less dubious colleagues quickly bolted telescopic tubing between the seven roll-track extensions; these spacer-bars would keep all seven roll-tracks aligned in a semi-rigid network during Highland Light's highly anticipated first southerly bend.

With whale-like moaning from the creeper-dolly guide bars grating along roll-track flanges, the ancient lighthouse rolled slowly forward, one sixty-four-inch push cycle followed by another. The men and their equipment settled into rhythmic routine, dancing to a chorus of air-wrenched bolts "chanking" in and out between verses of screeching incantation from the "whales" below. All the while, the faithful front-end loader strained at its chain, keeping constant southern pressure on the network of roll-track beams and spacer-bars. It did not exactly conjure up the image of a train chugging around a bend, but the lighthouse did keep rolling ahead, and yes, it did start turning south, ever so slightly.

Once the load and push-rams had passed, the original set of seven roll-track sections was leapfrogged forward and bolted to the western ends of the forty-foot sections currently in use, bent as they were. After the load had traveled far enough to weight down their near ends, these "new" track extensions were given spacer-bars and their fair share of chain-induced southern persuasion. So it went, day after day: pushing the load and pulling the track with some "time off" to step down the track every now and then. The step-down procedure, incrementally adjusting the load to the lower destination elevation, was time-consuming and labor-intensive in itself: building up crib piles for blocking the load while the jacks were depressurized; removing creeper-dollies and retracting jack rams; chaining roll-track up to the main beams while track cribs were deconstructed and reconstructed. After putting everything back into place a couple of feet lower, the lighthouse movers then added new track extensions on new crib-piles out front and reinstalled the push-rams out back.

Finally, after more than a week of creeping along this slightly curving path, the project consultant, in accordance with recent habit, extended his arm full-length to the west and squinted over his poked-up thumb. "Okay, boys!" Pete declared. "Let's start bending back to the north." And so it went for another week: pushing the load in sixty-four-inch strides while holding the forward track ends to the north; leapfrogging the used track forward and stopping twice more for stepping down the load. Eighteen days after beginning this innovative exercise, these envelope-pushing, track-bending structural movers finally approached their mission's end. The old lighthouse was inching slowly into place over its new concrete footing, while poised ten feet above ground on radial beams, needle beams, cross beams, and main beams—all riding on upside-down jacks head-standing on creeper-dollies rolling on bending track beams.

Pete remembered the last few minutes of this incredible move very clearly: "Jerry was at the jacking machine, and I was eyeballing the load. We were busy trying to tweak the angle of rotation by changing the speed of some of the rollers on different tracks by changing the pressure in their jacks. We got our signals crossed at the last minute and were busy wondering what to do next when all of a sudden the guy watching the plumb bob yelled at us to "Stop!" We stopped and found ourselves within one-eighth inch of his rough indication. So, then we called in the surveyor who had the final say. He checked the alignment and reported that our rotation angle was perfect. He then checked the tower plumb—how straight it was up and down—and he said it was perfect east-to-west ... not a hair off. When he measured north-to-south and said it was perfect too ... within a hair, I suggested he check again, because no one can move a building this size this far and be absolutely accurate in every which way. He did, and then he let me look through the lens. Lo and behold, we were dead-on. We were perfect!"

That evening when he called home, Pete was deeply saddened to hear about the death of his best friend, Karsten Vegsund, back in British Columbia. "He helped me with the design of my first dollies, and he had a real heart for me and my work," Pete stated solemnly. "You know, I got the strangest feeling when I looked through that surveyor's lens ... somehow, I think the good luck we had that day was a gift from Karsten ... an act of kindness coming from beyond."

On Sunday, November 3, 1996, the Highland Light Bagpipe Band and hundreds of lighthouse devotees participated in an official lighting ceremony marking Highland Light's return to active Coast Guard service. Officially known as Cape Cod Light on navigational charts since 1976, this veteran tower of white-painted bricks remains on duty, flashing its strong, white light deep into the North Atlantic night every five seconds. Down below in the keeper's house, a spin-off company of early volunteers from the Save The Light Committee operates an interpretive center and gift shop open to the public for six months every summer. Among the maritime artifacts and lighthouse memorabilia on display in their adjacent museum are a segment of the original first-order Fresnel lens and a section of the legendary mortared-brick footing that held Cape Cod's first lighthouse upright for so many years.

*Officially known as Cape Cod Lighthouse, the reunited Highland Light tower and keeper's house continue to serve the public—Jeremy D'Entremont.*

✳   ✳   ✳   ✳

In March 1837, a $10,000 appropriation from Congress appeased the residents of Eastham Town on Cape Cod who, motivated by an endless series of shipwrecks at Nauset Bars off their stretch of coast, had petitioned the authorities for a lighthouse. To distinguish their new light station from the single beam at Highland Light to the north and the double beams at Chatham to the south, it was decided to build three light towers on the cliffs above Nauset Beach. Each fifteen-foot-high conical tower was fifteen feet across at the base and nine feet across at the lantern deck. They were situated one hundred and fifty feet apart and aligned on a bearing within ten degrees of true north. Each octagonal lantern held ten oil-burning lamps and thirteen reflectors producing a steady white light. Looking like demure ladies in white dresses and black hats, this trio of light towers became known as the Three Sisters of Nauset.

Beginning in the 1850s, the Nauset Sisters were twice upgraded with the latest Fresnel lenses as they became available. Threatened by shoreline erosion, these Fresnel lenses were transferred to three portable twenty-two-foot wooden towers in 1892, just in time to witness the demise of the original Three Sisters, who soon tumbled down the eroding cliff into the sea. By 1911, thirty more feet of cliff had been consumed, and one of the new wooden Sisters was within eight feet of the edge. Having finally decided in favor of a single light, the Bureau of Lighthouses moved the center tower inland, attached it to the thirty-year-old keeper's house, and gave it a solitary white light that flashed, in tribute to the original trio, three times every ten seconds. The two surplus wood-shingled Sisters were sold for $3.50 each and incorporated into the construction of a nearby cottage.

By 1923, the lone surviving Sister was in poor shape and barely able to hold up its light. Around the same time, Cape Cod's second-oldest lighthouse, Chatham Light, was downsized from a double tower to a single tower. The forty-six-year-old surplus Chatham tower was dismantled and transported to the Eastham site, where it was reassembled on a concrete foundation two hundred feet back from the cliff's edge. Soon thereafter, the much older keeper's house was separated from the ailing wooden tower and moved beside this "new" brick-lined, iron-plated beacon from Chatham. The last wooden tower of the second-generation Three Sisters, after passing its kerosene-fired "torch" and a fourth-order Fresnel lens to this forty-eight-foot-high replacement, took a $10 buyout and also retired to a life of leisure as part of a nearby summer home.

In the early 1940s, the top half of this solitary Nauset lighthouse was painted red to distinguish it from other white towers along the coastline during daylight. In 1955, when the Coast Guard automated the Nauset light, the keeper's house was sold and became a private residence. With the creation of Cape Cod National Seashore by President John F. Kennedy in 1961, the market in used lighthouse parts was reversed. For an unknown sum, the National Park Service purchased back all three of the second-generation Sisters and returned them to their original configuration—150 feet apart and aligned 8.5 degrees off true north; although back in their old neighborhood, they were placed a far more conservative 1,800 feet from the shoreline. While north and south towers were only partly refurbished, the center Sister was fully restored to her original condition, complete with lantern-light. Their days of active service long past, the Three Sisters of Nauset continued to serve the public as an attraction in one of the country's most popular national parks.

In 1981, the fourth-order Fresnel lens was replaced by modern electronic aerobeacons in the lantern cage atop the red-and-white operational light; at the same time, its characteristic signal was changed to alternating red and white flashes every five seconds. Unimpressed by such technological advances, the ocean relentlessly gnawed away at the Cape Cod coastline. The "Perfect Storm" of October 1991 chewed enormous chunks from the cliffs of Nauset and made kindling out of a well-constructed stairway to the beach. Another thirty feet of cliff face disappeared during the next three years. When the resident owner of the old keeper's house began seeing too much ocean from her kitchen window, she donated the home and property to the National Park Service in exchange for a rent-free, twenty-five-year lease. The ocean continued to eat away at the base of Nauset Bluff.

*Before being moved inland, Nauset Light is perilously close to the edge of Cape Cod's receding shoreline—Brian Tague.*

When the Coast Guard proposed decommissioning Nauset Light, their regional headquarters in Boston received a seemingly endless stream of letters requesting relocation and preservation of the historic beacon. Responding to the bell first rung by Harold Jennings, a former lighthouse keeper, Eastham Historical Society members and scores of like-minded citizens organized the Nauset Light Preservation Society (NLPS). When the Coast Guard granted them a five-year lease on the lighthouse property, the NLPS immediately shifted into high gear with fundraising and feasibility studies. By the time a new site was decided upon in April 1996, only forty-three feet of cliff-top remained between the ocean and the tower. By selling T-shirts to the tourists and soliciting memberships and donations everywhere, the society raised an initial $80,000 that attracted $250,000 more from Congress—enough to complete the move. When the approved moving contractor arrived on site, there was only thirty-six feet of remaining bank to support a relocation task requiring a good thirty feet of operating room.

Having returned to Cape Cod from the successful relocation of an 82' by 72', 640-ton school gymnasium complex in Providence, Rhode

Island, that familiar team of experienced relocation specialists was now on the Nauset Light job—International Chimney Corporation, Expert House Movers, and Friesen Consulting. Led by project engineer Valerie Dumont, International Chimney was the overall contractor and primarily responsible for most of the masonry and foundation work; Jerry Matyiko and his Expert Movers again provided most of the equipment and labor; as per usual, project consultant Pete Friesen brought along many years of experience and a new bag of tricks. Although not as "impossible" as other missions they had accepted, the Nauset Lighthouse move was becoming more daunting every day. In October 1996, seeing their grounds for success rapidly disappearing into the ocean, the Three Houseketeers sharpened their tools and entered the fray.

By the fifth day of November, an access road had been cleared and graded to the new site; new footings had been poured for the lighthouse and for an oil-storage house that was also being moved. The twelve-inch-thick concrete floor had been removed from the base of the old tower; excavation was in progress both inside and out. As soon as excavation activities permitted, the big concrete saws went to work cutting beam slots through the walls of the tower foundation that was later cut horizontally into upper and lower halves. The ninety-ton Nauset Light tower and the top half of its foundation soon rested on four cross-steel beams which sat on two horizontally perpendicular main load beams resting on ten hydraulic jacks atop dedicated crib piles.

On November 16, 1996, the forty-eight-foot-high, red-and-white tower was nonchalantly chauffeured 336 feet home; all 105 tons were pulled along by a good old-fashioned truck tractor. After crossing his arms above his head to end the move, Pete Friesen, the smiling project consultant, gave his head a gentle shake while remembering a much steeper curve of narrow road from forty-eight years before. The loads were now larger and the equipment was now better, but the basic principles for relocating man-made structures were still the same as what he and Arthur Dyck had discovered on the Sumas Mountain Road in 1948.

*The three buildings of Nauset perched demurely on a knoll 300 feet back from the bluff—Shirley Sabin.*

When they arrived at Cape Cod almost four hundred years ago, occupants of the *Mayflower* had no idea how much of this newfound shore was disappearing every year. Later, even the people of Eastham were surprised by the short lifespan of their first Three Sisters of Nauset. It must have been alarming to see their second set of triplets sitting on the edge of impending doom only twenty years after they were built thirty feet inland. Erected a more conservative two hundred feet from the edge in 1923, the current tower had to be rescued in 1996 and is now expected to stand still for several more centuries. Perched demurely on a gentle knoll three hundred feet from the sea, Nauset Light is a fitting symbol of mankind's eternal struggle with the elements surrounding us. This black-capped, red-and-white tower is also a Cape Cod icon, appearing on countless calendars, postcards, license plates, and potato chip bags. Property of the National Parks Service and included within Cape Cod National Seashore, Nauset Light is leased to the Nauset Light Preservation Society that is now responsible for keeping the light on.

While the Pilgrims of 1620 would no doubt be shocked to see

horseless carriages racing up and down the sandy beaches for no apparent purpose, they might also be heartened to see their descendants paying tribute to the past while contributing financially to their national system of parks and recreation areas. Recently saved from the sea, Nauset Light and Highland Light are two major components of a booming regional tourism industry. While guided tours and museums provide hands-on history for visitors, the very presence of these two lighthouses speaks a lifetime about the place and its people.

"There's a lot to history," Pete reflected. "When I was younger, I used to say 'away with the old, bring on the new.' Today, I feel a bit different, maybe because I'm older. When I first came here, I drove along the shore and watched the waves crashing in … I thought about the Pilgrims way back then and I was totally overwhelmed." Pete concluded, with moisture welling in his eyes, "So I'm grateful to have been able to be on these jobs."

# 15

## Detroit

*Those who shall be so happy as to inhabit that noble country cannot but remember with gratitude those who have discovered the way by venturing to sail upon an unknown lake for above one hundred leagues.*

These words by Father Louis Hennepin, penned in 1679, came from the deck of Sieur de La Salle's vessel *Griffon,* the first European sailing ship on the Great Lakes. On his way to becoming a volunteer explorer of the upper Mississippi River and a well-traveled Ojibwe captive before naming Saint Anthony Falls at modern-day Minneapolis, Hennepin was referring to hospitable-looking terrain bordering the narrow strait—*l'etroit*—connecting Lake Erie to Lake St. Clair. Thirty years after the entire Great Lakes country had been claimed for King Louis XIV, the authorities of New France finally approved settlement at this very strategic location. In 1701, Antoine de Lamothe, Sieur du Cadillac, erected a small fort and fur-trading post on the northwestern bank of the strait. In honor of M. Pontchartrain, his country's minister of marine affairs who had generously supported this western enterprise, Sieur du Cadillac named the new settlement Fort Pontchartrain d'etroit.

When it came under control of England after the fall of Quebec in 1759, this sixty-year-old settlement and its river frontage became known more simply as Detroit. With the 1783 Treaty of Paris formally ending the American Revolutionary War, the former fur-trading post became property of the newly formed United States. Incorporated as a city in 1815, Detroit was an administrative center for the Michigan Territory created in 1805. In two major treaties, the Ojibwe, Ottawa, and Potawatomi tribes transferred most of their territories to the United States by 1821. A few years later, opening of the Erie Canal across upstate New York brought a significant increase in trade and commerce as well as wave after wave of new settlers to the western territories. At the same time, completion of the "Chicago Road" extended the land route west from Detroit. By the time Michigan became the twenty-sixth state admitted to the Union in 1837, the strategically situated fur-trading post had evolved into a thriving commercial center and transportation hub. In the first thirty years after incorporation, the population of Detroit increased twenty-fold to more than twenty thousand souls. Accelerated growth of population and industry came with the railways during mid-century and was followed by an unprecedented period of expansion after the Civil War. Numbering 285,000 at the turn of the twentieth century, the population of Detroit had increased a hundred-fold in fifty years.

By 1900, in a mix of classical and avant-garde commercial architecture, many corporate princes and prosperous merchants inhabited tree-lined residential neighborhoods. With some downtown streets recently wired with electric lights by Thomas Edison, Detroit was then described as the "Paris of the West." Then along came Henry Ford, Walter Chrysler, and the Dodge brothers to initiate an even headier wave of economic expansion evolving from the city's carriage manufacturing industry. While never again compared to Paris, the old French fur-trading post had become center of the world's automobile industry. As well as a host of automotive related enterprises, Detroit was also a powerhouse in the sports and entertainment industries. By the middle of the twentieth century, "Motor City" hosted 1,850,000 residents, many of whom knew it better as "Hockey Town" or "Motown."

With the outstanding growth of its business sector and explosion of its population, Detroit constantly scrambled to keep pace with ever-increasing demand for physical infrastructure while respecting, to varying degrees, less tangible qualities such as arts and culture. Similar to San Antonio and other preservation-minded communities, responsibility for nurturing arts and culture in Detroit defaulted to a substantial degree onto the shoulders of its female citizens. Whereas the womenfolk of San Antonio were in an early-century struggle to prevent destruction of historic buildings, their equally dedicated contemporaries in Detroit were conspiring to create their own significant architecture.

Having organized as the Women's Twentieth Century Association, a group of civic-minded females of social prominence needed a clubhouse where they could meet for music and sewing lessons while planning their next philanthropic event. With a $35,000 bank loan in 1903, they built their own: a solid, two-story Mission-style structure of red brick and white limestone adorned by stone carvings and copper cornices. With great halls accommodating formal dances and other social gatherings, the newly created Women's Century Club was no doubt a happening place. Twenty-five years later, having recognized a shortage of live stage venues in the city, the Women's Association engaged a noted architect, George D. Mason, to build the complementary and complimentary-looking two-story Little Theatre on an adjoining property. Unfortunately, the year was 1928, and the Association's $40,000 construction bond soon floated away with the stock market crash. The first women in Detroit to obtain a bank loan and the first of their gender to issue stocks were soon victims of the Depression. Both the Century Club building and their Little Theatre were foreclosed upon, repossessed, and eventually sold to other interests. The Women's Twentieth Century Association disbanded in 1933.

The Century Club building, adjoining but distinct from the theatre, eventually reopened its doors to the Concordia Singing Society, a group of Civil War veterans of Germanic descent who gathered to celebrate music, until the passing of its last member in the mid-1940s. Later that decade, it became the Russian Bear, a restaurant offering authentic Russian fare and balalaika music. After serving during the 1960s as a student-union center for a campus of the Detroit Institute of Technology Training, the former Women's Century Club headquarters transformed into another restaurant, La Trocadero, serving gourmet Italian food until closing in 1978.

After the Women's Association disbanded in the early 1930s, their former Little Theatre soon reopened as a motion picture venue, offering alternate phases of mainstream and risqué film. While undergoing several name changes before becoming the Cinema, it served for some time as a "saucy" cabaret and as Detroit's first ever foreign-film venue before returning to live theatre in 1959. Known then as the Vanguard Playhouse, it hosted a five-year run by a theatre company headed by George C. Scott, prior to his fame in Hollywood. Another decade of live theatre began in 1967 when the thirty-nine-year-old Little Theatre became an adult burlesque house known as the Gem.

Inspired by their civic conscience and having watched a half-century of cultural change take place in their former buildings, the surviving veterans of the Women's Twentieth Century Association were now, more than many other citizens, very well acquainted with the idea of "social evolution."

After more than a hundred years of unbridled growth, Detroit began the latter half of the twentieth century in anguish. Several decades of intermittent labor unrest combined with race-related rioting and drug-related crime had devastating effects on the city. Many citizens and their employers retreated to affluent suburbs, leaving behind a very depleted tax base and a burgeoning ghetto. By 1980, the population of the city proper had declined thirty-three percent from its peak of thirty years before, while the downtown core was becoming a near-wasteland of abandoned and neglected buildings. The Century Club and the Gem Theatre were left standing side-by-side and long vacant.

Then, along came Forbes, Charles Forbes that is, a white knight in entrepreneurial armor riding a powerful steed of corporate success, a homegrown hero hell-bent on saving his fair city from the jaws of the demolition dragon. Aided by his son James and other family members, Forbes was on a mission: "To recreate the Theatre District that existed in the 1920s and to make Detroit a nationally recognized theatre city." Thus began an incredible act of historic preservation performed on a very large stage. Including the purchase of the Century Club in 1981 and the Gem Theatre in 1983, Forbes Management Company soon had twenty-four buildings and sixteen parking lots in its collection of downtown properties.

Unable to bear the thought of these beautiful old buildings standing around empty until they turned to dust, Charles Forbes got heavily into the renovation business. Among a multitude of projects, Forbes and company began restoration work on the old Gem Theatre.

Any attempt to describe Forbes's obvious passion would only lead to understatement; it might be said without exaggeration that he fell in love with the Gem. Scouring the archives for records and photographs, his restoration team set about to faithfully reproduce the theatre's original décor. Salvaging many fixtures from similar-period buildings nationwide and remanufacturing some items from authentic materials, the dedicated crew returned the 450-seat playhouse to its former glory. Once again, fine oak paneling rose from lushly carpeted floors while warm chandeliers hung from a gilded fresco ceiling. Celebrating years of painstaking labor and considerable investment, the Gem Theatre doors opened for a New Year's Eve gala in 1991.

The Gem's new life was short-lived. Five years after reopening, the Gem Theatre and its adjoining Century Club building were found to be in the way of a megaproject proposed by the city of Detroit and Wayne County as part of a plan for downtown revitalization. The recently refurbished Gem and Century buildings were standing in an otherwise run-down and desolate neighborhood seen as an ideal location for Comerica Park, a new stadium for the Detroit Tigers baseball team. Across the street, a new Ford Field would be home to the Detroit Lions football team. Although now listed on the National Register of Historic Places, the tiny Gem-Century building was powerless against a multi-million dollar offense. Threatened by possible retraction of $55 million in state funding because of undue delay, the Stadium Authority wanted the artsy old building demolished as soon as possible.

Unable to bear thought of a beautiful old building being turned into landfill, and having read a magazine article on the successful 1985 move of the Fairmount Hotel in San Antonio, Forbes was soon on the telephone with Friesen Consulting in Lynden, Washington. After briefly outlining his situation, Mr. Forbes was immediately encouraged by Friesen's stated philosophy regarding man-made buildings. Inspired by Pete's positive approach to the problem, Forbes became another devotee of historic preservation through relocation and soon identified a new site for his cherished building. However, several of his business associates were soon suggesting that perhaps the Forbes should be committed elsewhere. "We may very well be crazy," father and son quipped to the *Detroit Free Press*. "We haven't explained our plan to one person yet who doesn't think it's a crazy idea!"

Pete Friesen was soon on the phone with Rick Lohr, president of ICC, and with Jerry Matyiko at Expert House Movers. This consortium of ICC, Expert Movers, and Pete Friesen had recently finished up a productive year's work featuring four major projects in the northeastern United States. As well as moving two historic lighthouses back from the eroding Atlantic shoreline of Cape Cod, they had relocated the 72' by 82' gymnasium complex in Providence and a five-hundred-ton smoke stack for an industrial firm in State College, Pennsylvania. Among numerous recent awards for their work, this latter 135-foot-high project had been recognized by their colleagues at the IASM as the Tallest Move of 1996. After inspecting the Gem-Century structure and after confirming his trusty wingmen to be interested and available, Pete the consultant began making plans. Keeping him occupied for most of the next year, this new project began with a full month of *thinking it through.*

Obviously, the attached buildings would have to be moved together as one structure. Although the exact weight would not be known until it was on jacks and registering hydraulic pressure, the Gem-Century load was estimated to be about 50 percent heavier than the 1,600-ton Fairmount. Anticipating a significant expansion of his personal operating envelope, Pete Friesen began by refining his self-designed computer program for determining a building's weight. For this project to succeed, he would need extremely accurate calculations.

Of slightly disparate age and material, the adjoined buildings made for a somewhat fragile combined load. While there were loose bricks and a weak foundation under the ninety-four-year-old Century half, Pete's major concern existed at one end of the younger theatre section, where the extra height and weight of its performance stage made for an extremely imbalanced load. Almost one-half of the entire structure's total weight was located in this one corner. Figuring seventy-one steerable dollies with sixty-ton jacks as sufficient to carry the load, Pete was then challenged by the necessity of fitting a disproportionately large number of them into this relatively small area under the performance stage. Compounding this problem was the need for tire-maneuvering space to accomplish the 180-degree rotation required to properly orient the buildings at their destination. Pete was soon working on refinements to his self-designed computer program for determining a building's center of gravity. He had little margin for error on this job.

Entering the structure's measurements and building materials into his program and adding in the amount of supporting steel required, Pete estimated the total load would weigh in the neighborhood of 2,750 tons, or 5.5 million pounds. After inserting a multitude of numbers into his computer and spending some time with his teeter-totter, Pete precisely located the building's center of gravity, as expected, very slightly northeast of the heavy southwest corner. With these two vital pieces of information, Pete defined the size and shape of his problem.

By arranging seventy-one dollies under nine rocker beams beneath three main load beams, he was able to bias sufficient dollies toward the heavy southwest corner, thus satisfying his weight concerns while maintaining his three-zone loading principle. Fitting seventy-one dollies with rotation diameters of eleven feet into place was one thing, but steering them was another matter. Angled off centerline by the rotation of their front axles, the 568 tractor-trailer tires, each measuring 8″ by 15″, would soon take up most of the available space between dollies. Given that large number of tires and the limited space between dollies, the project consultant decided against any attempt at large-scale steering change while the load was in motion. To facilitate the necessary building rotation, dolly tire angles would instead be pre-positioned according to mathematical calculations before any movement. Prior to each stage of movement, the pre-determined angle for each dolly would be referenced to precise markings on the beam directly above its steering tongue. Of course, in order for its tires to be re-angled, each dolly would need to be unweighted, transferring its share of the load unto temporary support. Obviously, with the need to unweight and manually adjust the angles of two axles on each of seventy-one dollies, rotation of the building would be a lengthy and largely stationary procedure.

To accurately guide the load into position at its destination, some means for making small steering adjustments while underway was necessary. Applying his Minneapolis livery stable experience of seventeen years before, Pete utilized the steerable front axle on his dollies by joining all the steering tongues in each row with a length of steel chain attached to come-along winches at each end of the row. By adept toggling and counter-toggling of the come-alongs, an experienced wrangler could herd a heavy load into line, one link at a time.

Also of major concern was hydraulic supply. Although their jacking machine was a late-model unit with double-length piston strokes capable of supplying very high-pressure fluid to a multitude of jacks, Pete did not like the scenario of nineteen slave circuits powering seventy-one sixty-ton jacks through at least one too many splitter-manifolds. Not only would the jacking unit be operating close to both fluid-pressure and quantity limitations, but there would also be myriad weak points in the overall layout. There would be too many hoses and too many connections, too many places where a simple failure could jeopardize a complex system operating near maximum capacity.

Pete, the safety-minded consultant, opted for another idea. Each of the jacking unit's nineteen slave circuits would be split once only, and unified pressure would power thirty-eight jacks divided among the three zones. The other thirty-three jacks, also divided among the three zones on a weight-required basis, would be supplied by three independent hydraulic systems, one for each zone. Each zonal "helper" system would be self-contained with its own fluid supply and with its own pressure-regulating pump supplying common pressure to each of the helper jacks in that zone. By pre-setting each pressure-regulating zonal pump to the same value as the actual or anticipated unified pressure, the thirty-three helper jacks would employ common pressure to help raise the load in a unified manner. With four hydraulic systems operating across three zones and with two independent systems in each zone, Pete's safety margin had grown to a more breathable level. Having engineered a degree of redundancy into the overall system, he then downgraded the dolly jacks from their sixty-ton maximum rating to an operational limit of fifty tons. Even so, Pete's jacks would operate at less than 80 percent of their fifty-ton limit and would demand only moderate output pressures from the jacking machine. *Derch denche.*

Preparations for the move got underway in early summer 1997. After removal of the more decorative items from inside and out, the floors of the buildings were removed to make space for a complex network of steel bracing to support all exterior walls from within. After all door and window openings had been braced or covered in, ICC's big masonry tools went to work on the foundation. Through large openings in the walls, Expert House Movers inserted their heavy steel beams into a basement full of wooden crib blocks. Several weeks later, an extensive network of jack cribs and safety cribs was in place beneath three main load beams. With two of them biased under the stage-heavy theatre section, each of the three duplex main beams was a welded pair of twenty-four-inch-deep beams (2X24WF162). Above and horizontally perpendicular to the mains were twenty-four fourteen-inch-deep cross-steel beams. Above and horizontally perpendicular to the cross-steel came scores of short needle beams distributing weight immediately beneath the heavy exterior walls. For good measure, two thirty-six-inch-deep strong-back beams were added above the cross-steel along both sides of the building. For increased security, a twelve-foot-high A-frame truss braced each end wall.

With the insertion of seventy-one dollies and nine duplex rocker beams, the moving crew would be ready to roll. However, they had no dollies! Therefore, neither did they have any fifty-ton jacks. An unfortunate dolly delivery delay had found the structural movers with a major interruption in their progress while being threatened by a looming deadline. Summer was marching quickly onward, and the Stadium Authority's "You move it or we demolish it" ultimatum carried a date of October 1, 1997. It wasn't looking good.

Hoping to expedite the process as much as possible, the project consultant suggested the idea of raising the building on readily available fifteen-ton and thirty-ton crib jacks. By arranging them into seventy-one groupings, each containing sufficient smaller jacks to approximate the twenty-square-inch ram surface of one planned fifty-ton jack, Pete was able to generate the necessary lifting force while remaining true to his three-zone loading schedule. As in his original concept, almost half the number of jacks in each zone would be common-pressure helpers powered by that zone's independent hydraulic system, while the remainder received unified pressure from the jacking machine. Lo and behold, it worked! Although it took 132 smaller jacks instead of the intended seventy-one large ones, the old Gem-Century building was dutifully released from its moorings. Although it took ten days to lift it instead of three, the 90' by 100' structure was successfully elevated seven feet above its foundation.

*Looking east along the Gem-Century's initial route through
an area designated for stadium construction.*

Finally, the dollies arrived. With a network of safety cribs to block the load in place, another week of arduous toil saw the seventy-one dollies and their fifty-ton jacks properly aligned under nine simultaneously installed duplex rocker beams. When everything was said and done, there were 568 large-diameter rubber tires riding on eighteen thousand crib blocks carefully stacked in the building's basement. Atop the dollies, 550 tons of steel in four layers carried two thousand tons of brick and limestone. As indicated by jacking-machine pressure gauges, the load weighed a total of 2,593 tons. Only 157 tons less than Pete's original estimate, this 6 percent differential was comfortably within safety margins, and such accuracy attests to the utility of Pete's computer program for estimating building weights. On the subject of numbers: the fifty-ton dolly jacks carried an average weight of 36.5 tons each; the 568 pneumatic tires carried an average weight of 4.5 tons each; and at a total cost of $1.5 million, Charles Forbes paid 37.5 cents per pound to relocate his 2,000-ton building. While Forbes and company lobbied the Stadium Authority for an extension of the October deadline, the on-site crew prepared to get underway. Summer had come and gone in downtown Detroit, and the Gem-Century building was still many weeks from home.

Because much of the anticipated three-week journey would traverse recent landfill and other unpacked surface, the ground immediately ahead of the load required a running surface of wood matting under the dolly tires. To that end, five flatbed truckloads of planking were bolted together into portable 5' by 16' mats. After these mats were laid out in the direction of travel, initially to the east, six large tow vehicles were marshaled into place ahead of the load. Two heavy bulldozers (D8 Cats) flanked four heavy excavators (hoes). Running through snatch blocks both on the six tow vehicles and on the load, a two-thousand-foot length of steel cable produced twenty-four segments of strong pulling harness. Similar to the Fairmount Hotel pull, the additional machines gave necessary weight to the tow vehicle assembly while its network of pulleys and steel lacing allowed flexibility and maintained pull-cable tension. Here in Detroit, the load would be pulled forward in short increments by alternating pairs of vehicles while the other four held firm as counterweights. *Visualize.*

*Looking southwest toward downtown Detroit as the Gem-Century building is about to be pulled east from its original site onto wooden mats.*

On Thursday, October 17, 1997, a band of local musicians entertained believers and non-believers alike gathered to witness a first attempt at forward movement. On a signal from one of the hard-hatted workers, the four big yellow hoes turned their backs to the load and dug their heavy steel buckets firmly into the earth. On another signal, the two big yellow cats crunched into gear and chugged slowly forward, straining taut all twenty-four laces of the tow cable. More than one heart fluttered, and several voices rose to join the band in a familiar refrain of "Sentimental Journey" as 5.186 million pounds of brick and steel crept forward on 568 rubber tires. The move was on! By end of that day, the object of their attention had been moved half a city block to the east. After months of speculation, some of the many skeptics finally began to relent, while most of the true believers could only sigh in relief. "Suddenly, we weren't quite so crazy," remembers Forbes. "Now everyone was simply awed by what was happening … it was almost beyond comprehension."

The move went well. Alternating pairs of tow vehicles pulled their burden forward in increments of four to six feet, while city crews hastily removed signposts and lamp standards on the route ahead. During an extended pause every eighty feet or so, five more rows of wooden running mats were leapfrogged forward of the dolly wheels. Meantime, down at the northwest corner of Brush Street and Madison Avenue, a new twenty-foot-deep concrete foundation awaited arrival of the Gem-Century building. The new basement was filled with sand to a depth of fifteen feet, on top of which a solid layer of crib blocks provided stable footing for an emerging network of cribbing to support the load after the dollies were gone. In accordance with drawings provided by the consultant, jack and safety crib positions would exactly duplicate the layout used for raising the structure at its original location. While Pete and his moving crew rotated their load two city blocks to the north, another crew of men transferred thousands of four-foot-long crib blocks to the new site.

Having crept eastward for the better part of a week, the 2,593-ton load approached the west side of Brush Street where it was to head south. Here, while undergoing a change of direction, the recently mobile structure would also experience a change in attitude. Having spent the better part of a century facing north, the Gem-Century building was scheduled to spend its next life looking south. Having thus far been pulled parallel to the rocker beams, the load would execute a clockwise turn before pulling parallel to the main beams and rolling front-side first directly into place. Oh, how easily one short sentence completes a long week of hard toil! Using a post-jack—one jack plus one length of strong steel pipe—workmen began unweighting seventy-one dollies, one at a time, rotating them and further rotating their steerable front axles to precise angles as previously determined by the consultant's mathematical calculations. The amount of angular change varied with the dolly's position in the whole formation.

*Pete's pirouette begins with preset angles on the 568 wheels of 71 dollies beneath three layers of support beams braced by strong-backs on the side walls and by trusses on front and rear walls.*

After each of seventy-one dollies was unweighted, realigned, and re-weighted, the tow vehicles resumed their task of pulling on the eastern ends of the rocker beams below the exterior sidewall of the Century Club section. In accordance with its recent wheel alignment, the massive load immediately entered a right-hand turn centered around a point twenty feet away. After completing a tight 170-degree southern arc, the Century Club's exterior sidewall was facing west. Entrance doors for the club and theatre were now 240 feet closer to home and at the front end of a southbound load. Because space limitations during the turn precluded an arc long enough to complete a full 180-degree reversal of the building, a further ten degrees of rotation was programmed into the initial southbound pull. Another pause of several days—in forward motion, not work—allowed for realignment of dolly angles and forward positioning of the running mats. After each of the seventy-one dollies had been unweighted, realigned, and re-weighted, the tow vehicles commenced pulling on the load's nine-dolly southern row. Lo and behold, it worked just like the consultant said it would. Describing a short arc on a long 314-foot radius, the hulking load roller-skated gently onto centerline while rotating into perfect alignment. After one more complete wheel alignment, it was a straight run home, guided by gentle nudges from Pete Friesen and his come-alongs.

Although the seven-day turn was certainly laborious and time-consuming, it proceeded very smoothly and was far more satisfying in execution than a description of its mechanical process might suggest. Viewed in time-lapse photography, the Brush Street turn and rotation is a graceful half-pirouette, much like a figure skater changing from a forward inside to a backward outside edge. Masterfully done, it was a beautiful thing to behold.

*Four "hoes" and two "cats" pull the Gem-Century south toward*
*its new sand-filled basement being topped-off with crib blocks.*

On November 11, 1997, two hundred people gathered in the rain to see the old building reach her new home. Having undergone many months of preparation, the actual 1,850-foot relocation phase of the Gem-Century move was completed in twenty-five days. For the long-sedentary building, the move was a rather abrupt, life-altering experience. For the many people responsible for its relocation, the building's short journey was just another month-long adventure in a lifetime of hard work. For all of them, there was much work waiting to be done. While Jerry Matyiko and Pete Friesen headed west to check out their next project, Rick Lohr and his ICC crew remained behind to "cement the deal" by bonding the relocated building to its new foundation. During the next several years, James Forbes committed to a magnificent restoration program for the Century Club's interior. Meanwhile, the "crazy" idea of Charles and James Forbes was sitting pretty at the northwest corner of Madison Avenue and Brush Street in downtown Detroit. The 1998 *Guinness Book of World Records* would list the Gem Theatre-Century Club complex in Detroit, Michigan, as the heaviest building ever moved on pneumatic tires.

Down but not out, the recently desolate core of Detroit is rejuvenating itself. Once a cutting-edge metropolis running primarily on automobile manufacture, the city fell into several decades of disarray and disillusionment before finding a road back—downtown Detroit is transforming itself into an entertainment center. It's not quite there yet, but the essentials are in place: new hotels, bold casinos, and old historic theatres complement up-to-date facilities for all major professional sports; a light rapid-transit loop connects all the primary attractions while weaving through canyons of impressive architecture from two centuries. The city has rediscovered its waterfront heritage with the beginnings of a riverfront promenade. While few pedestrians are to be seen, there is hope that the people of Detroit will once again stroll their downtown streets. On the way there, Motor City serves as a regional adult arcade, attracting entertainment-minded suburbanites into a high-rolling center. In addition to well-recognized museums and galleries, arts and culture keep pace with a noticeable number of re-inspired outlets for live theatre and music. A dollar is a dollar, and tourism is an industry. Motown is becoming Showtown.

One of the city's finest new venues sits at 333 Madison Avenue, just a block south of Detroit's two new mega-stadiums. Sporting a renovated orange-tile roof, the old Mission-style Gem-Century offers a warm and solid welcome into an interior of magnificent restoration. In harmony with the previously refurbished Gem, the Century Club has been totally restored to its original grandeur with inclusion of many antique items salvaged from nearby buildings of similar age and less good fortune. Fireplaces, chandeliers, stained glass, and furnishings from the early twentieth century blend authenticity with graceful architecture. The two recently interconnected buildings now boast the 450-seat Gem Theatre and the 192-seat Century Theatre, as well as a one hundred-seat restaurant and a 250-seat banquet facility.

The Women's Twentieth Century Association would no doubt be heartened by the present level of cultural awareness in their city and by the commitment of its current generation of civic-minded residents. Founding members of the organization would be particularly enamored by the efforts of Charles Forbes, who has preserved their century-old clubhouse and brought about the realization of their original dream. Certainly they would be enthralled to know their old headquarters had been transformed into such a charming work of "modern" art. Surely they would be pleased to see their daughters and granddaughters in rollicking good cheer, along with thousands of other daughters, at standing-room-only performances in their seventy-five-year-old Little Theatre. First presented by the little Gem Theatre in 2004, *Menopause: The Musical* is the longest running show in the history of Michigan. Surely the members of the Women's Twentieth Century Association would laugh too, wouldn't they?

# 16

## Minneapolis Encore

*I believe that in a great city, or even in a small city or village, a great theater is the outward and visible sign of an inward and probable culture.*

*Sir Laurence Olivier*

Long accustomed to risqué variety shows and bawdy saloon entertainments, the citizens of Minneapolis were offered formal theater for the first time in 1867, the year of their city's incorporation. This first professional production at the Pence Opera House set the stage for a long tradition of live theater in this rapidly growing community. Early in the 1900s, with more than three hundred thousand residents, this bustling city of sawmills, flourmills, and railways saw construction of new performance spaces to accommodate traditional theater as well as the emerging vaudeville genre. Shubert Brothers of New York, an organization that eventually owned half the performance houses on Broadway and one thousand theaters nationwide, built one of their new theaters in Minneapolis.

Designed by William A. Swasey and constructed at 22 Seventh Street, the $250,000 Minneapolis Shubert Theater presented an exterior façade of Beaux-Arts design with glazed terra-cotta bas-relief columns on a granite base. The interior featured a forty-piece orchestra pit and superior acoustics as well as superb sight lines from three levels of seating. Opening its doors in 1910, the new 1,500-seat house brought Broadway to Minneapolis via the Shubert Theatrical Company and also hosted a resident stock company of actors led by the theater's manager, Alexander "Buzz" Bainbridge. The most successful theater company in Minnesota, the Bainbridge Players disbanded in 1933 when their leader was elected mayor of Minneapolis.

In 1915, the Shubert Theater of Minneapolis hosted its first motion picture presentation. Although the theater and its resident stock company successfully resisted wholesale transition to cinema, the house was eventually wired for sound to accommodate the "talkies" of the late 1920s. After the Great Depression took its toll on attendance and revenues, the Shubert changed ownership and reopened in 1940 as the Alvin, a house of burlesque. In 1953, when nudie-show profits began dropping like table-dancers' tunics, the venerable old house was leased to a gospel preacher who welcomed one and all to his Minneapolis Evangelistic Auditorium. After a four-year period of cleansing and redemption, the house changed ownership again in 1957, finally becoming a full-time motion picture venue. Reduced to one thousand seats, but still sporting that Beaux-Arts façade beneath a new neon sign, the Academy welcomed Minneapolis theatergoers to a premiere presentation of Michael Todd's film *Around the World in Eighty Days*.

When constructed in 1910, the Shubert was situated between the city's business hub and a reasonably affluent residential neighborhood undergoing early stages of commercialization. Within a decade, the Shubert was one of forty playhouses in a thriving downtown theater district. In the following decades, retail outlets and office buildings inexorably supplanted the original mansions and townhouses. By mid-century, the seven-story Shubert was but another wave in a concrete ocean crawling with rubber-tired vehicles. As the automobile pushed the city limits outward, the inner city began to decline in appearance and personality. As major players withdrew to greener pastures, hordes of smaller ones filled the hastily subdivided spaces left behind: retail stores became arcades and fast-food outlets; floors of office space became art studios and casual flophouses. Late-night clubs and other drinking establishments catered to thirsty clientele while other appetites were tempted by storefronts offering sex toys, sexy lingerie, and pornography. The handsome old performance house became a lonely relic of another time, awash in a sea of excess. By the 1970s, the theater's once-stately neighborhood had become known as Block E ... as in Erotica.

As downtown succumbed to urban retreat and suburban growth, the advent of multiplex cinemas took their toll on downtown motion picture venues. The Academy Theater closed in 1983. After twenty-five years in the movie business, the future looked pretty bleak for the house built seventy-three years prior. Its old neighborhood, after decades of transformation, had now deteriorated toward the point of no return. Absentee landlords and transient residents helped turn an area of already undesirable urban decay into an ugly city block of unbearable misuse—so it seemed to a community now committed to aggressive redevelopment of its downtown core. By the time public protest finally reined in fast-charging redevelopers, the city had razed almost 40 percent of its central core, losing much in the way of significant architecture, including all but four of its original forty theaters. Nevertheless, some parts of town really did need improvement. In 1987, the city council voted to completely demolish all the buildings of Block E, except for the old Academy Theater, recently purchased by the city for $1.3 million. By 1990, the old theater was the only building left standing on the entire block, the rest having become parking lot. Although city administrators weren't quite sure what they wanted, they knew exactly what they didn't want on Block E. While future options were examined and discussed, the one-time vaudeville theater and burlesque hall, part-time gospel auditorium and recent movie theater stood empty and alone.

Jackie Cherryhomes remembers the scene. Elected to the Minneapolis City Council in 1990, she represented the Fifth Ward, home to Block E and the long-abandoned Academy. "That theater was part of my childhood. I saw *South Pacific* there!" Jackie recalls. "It was a grand old building with a special place in our hearts ... and most of us knew it only as a movie theater. By the time I came to city council, there was already a 'Save the Shubert' group lobbying for survival of the building, and it was soon protected with heritage designation. We didn't have a plan in place, other than hoping to incorporate it into whatever development was eventually approved for Block E. In the meantime, as everyone became better acquainted or re-acquainted with the building's history, it became known again as *the Shubert*."

Several years later, as council president, Cherryhomes became very well acquainted with many plans for Block E and the Shubert. "Although separate from other redevelopment projects in the city, the Shubert was an item of daily discussion," she continues. "For seven years, we had been looking at proposals of every kind for Block E. Developers offered us everything from 'Las Vegas North' to 'Disneyland Downtown,' but none of them seemed capable, or willing, to incorporate a classic old theater into their sophisticated designs for urban renewal. We were in a bind for a long, long time. Even if we wanted to, we couldn't tear down our own heritage building—it had just been placed on the National Register [of Historic Places]—and we couldn't seem to get Block E developed with it still standing. Finally … it was at a year-end cocktail reception, probably 1995 … a colleague suggested, with the super-lucidity that comes with several refreshments, that we should just pick up the old pile of bricks and move it out of the way. I could find no fault with his logic and, encouraged by refreshment and civic responsibility, I began floating the idea into conversations with other colleagues. By the time the reception wound down, most of us there had decided, in collective wisdom, that moving the Shubert was the only sensible solution. Of course, it was only an idea and one that needed careful study in the bright light of day. For the moment though, most of us connected with city hall were just happy to be thinking we had a plan."

In the late 1970s, when gentrification had commercialized the city's historic Warehouse District beyond the financial means of the artists who had recently reinhabited and revitalized it, Minneapolis created a nonprofit organization—Artspace—dedicated to the creation and preservation of suitable, large, and affordable spaces for artists and arts organizations. Ten years later, under leadership of Kelley Lindquist, Artspace expanded beyond its advocacy role and began developing properties specific to its purpose. With a mandate also recognizing the need to preserve performance spaces, the organization had already conducted three feasibility studies regarding potential restoration of historic downtown theaters, including the Shubert. Although not present at the fateful cocktail reception, Lindquist was soon eagerly sharing the buzz about moving the old Shubert Theater.

While Cherryhomes began rallying the troops at city hall, Lindquist and his Artspace cohorts immediately commissioned another Shubert-related feasibility study for the Minneapolis Community Development

Agency (MCDA). By the time of the next year-end cocktail reception, the idea of moving the Shubert was in full flight. The city council soon voted overwhelmingly in favor of a motion to reposition the historic theater on the 500 block of Hennepin Avenue while making way for a now-approved mega-mall complex on Block E. The city would provide MCDA with a budget of $4 million to oversee the relocation in conjunction with Artspace, who would assume responsibility for the Shubert after its move.

Artspace retained the engineering firm of Bakke Kopp, Ballou, & McFarlin for a 1998 study that confirmed the feasibility of physically moving the fragile and heavy Shubert. Known for its experience with heritage buildings, this firm had participated in the successful relocation of the Brown-Ryan Livery Stable back in 1980. Also commissioned by Artspace in 1998, Miller Dunwiddie, a local architectural firm, submitted conceptual drawings depicting the Shubert as major component of a proposed new arts and education complex on Hennepin Avenue. The theater building was deemed reasonably solid, and everyone liked the drawings. By this time, George Kissinger, project manager for MCDA, had been in regular consultation with Stubbs Building and House Movers, a local third-generation mover. In a short period of time, Kissinger had learned much about the world of structural moving. He would soon meet several heavyweights in the industry.

After two years of municipal planning and meetings too numerous to count, a collection of producers, directors, and players convened in Minneapolis to prepare for taking the Shubert Theater on the road; it was late in the summer of 1998, and it would be a six-month run. Among the cast of characters were several familiar names: George Gardner and ICC, Jerry Matyiko with his merry band of Expert House Movers, and project consultant Pete Friesen. In keeping with the trio's well-proven modus operandi, ICC would be responsible for shop drawings and blueprints as well as masonry cutting and foundation work; Expert Movers would provide most of the men and equipment while doing much of the physical work; Pete would be responsible for the overall plan and would advise on all operational aspects. While the city of Minneapolis was the executive producer and Artspace was the producer, ICC and Expert Movers would be the marquee performers in a drama about "Shubert, the Moving Theater," to be directed by Pete Friesen.

Also starring in a supporting role was Larry Stubbs of Long Lake, Minnesota. The first mover to be consulted when the city began exploring the idea of relocating the Shubert, Stubbs immediately and accurately assessed the magnitude of the job before he recruited moving stars who had more experience with heavier roles. While contributing personal expertise, his company also supplied experienced manpower and essential materials. The production's credit list also includes dozens of unknown actors who labored intensively on-site—hucking crib blocks, resetting jacks, and wrestling endless yards of hydraulic hose. Among the legion of unsung heroes were the municipal workers who made the performance possible by pushing the paperwork, preparing the route, maintaining services, and managing traffic. For Minneapolis theatergoers, it was like having the traveling circus back in town.

Director Friesen had been here before. Back in 1980, as part of the Central Riverfront revitalization project, Pete had orchestrated relocation of the Brown-Ryan Livery Stable in the Saint Anthony area, just across the Mississippi River. The challenge of moving that century-old limestone-block structure contributed to Pete's appreciation for historic buildings and encouraged him to develop and refine techniques for the successful relocation of others. Since coaxing that 1,000-ton livery stable safely into place, Pete had moved a number of similarly fragile buildings and many far heavier. Only a few months before accepting the Shubert job, he had ushered Detroit's 2,750-ton Gem Theatre onto its new foundation by the "come-along" method first developed for the stable move eighteen years prior. Now, fresh from their resounding success in Detroit, the director and his cast of characters were making plans for an encore performance at the Shubert. According to advance billing, the Shubert performance would challenge their previous year's Guinness World Record for heaviest building ever moved on rubber-tired dollies.

Far in advance of the Shubert's opening act, Pete Friesen was busy with his tape measure and calculator. After determining the exact dimensions and the construction materials used throughout the building, Pete entered the data into his Building Weights computer program. Lo and behold! The program showed the combined weight of the building and the steel beams required to move it at 5.816 million pounds. Although the 80' by 80' Shubert had a smaller footprint, this weight of 2,908 tons was 158 tons heavier than the total Gem-Century load. Pete soon determined the feasibility of moving the Shubert with seventy-two fifty-ton jacks mounted on seventy-two rubber-tired dollies, only one more than required at the Gem.

Early planning uncovered other differences between the two theaters. Whereas the Gem-Century complex had an extremely heavy corner under the stage section, the Shubert building presented the opposite concern. By design, its original performance stage section, with heavy support equipment for lights, curtains, and backdrop, had been self-contained in a building extension affixed to the theater's rear wall. Superfluous to the Shubert's post-relocation function, this stage extension had been completely removed. Accordingly, Pete's Finding Center of Gravity program located the building's center of balance toward its front wall, where the load was heavily biased by two large balconies and the granite façade. Designed with exemplary sightlines, the theater's floor sloped measurably from the front lobby wall down to the now-stageless rear wall. Because the Shubert's next life called for a level floor above a two-story basement, this old sloping floor would be left behind with the redundant stage extension. Although some degree of structural rigidity would be lost with removal of the floor, the associated weight loss would be a positive gain for the project by significantly decreasing the number of beams and dollies required.

Similar to many other theaters of its era, the 1910-vintage Shubert had been constructed almost entirely of bricks—gazillions of clay-fired bricks mortared together and unsupported by rebar. As such, despite the theater's renowned history and recent heritage status, nothing could guarantee survival of its Beaux-Arts décor, not even the diligence of the many hard-hatted humans who now scrambled around it. The day had finally arrived. All necessary licenses and permits were in place; all props and players were in position. At long last, the curtain rose on a production two years in the making. City officials and civic promoters were all delighted to see such a fine troupe of players energetically engage in their diverse and apparently well-directed activities. Barely familiar with relocation plots or with this cast of characters, the producers at

Artspace were thrilled by merely seeing action on the set. The show was on!

Act I: Lengthy and with little action, the opening act merely set the stage for things to come, featuring nothing more than extensive procedures to prepare the play's protagonist, Shubert, for the powerful vibrations soon to be upon him. Complete removal of all interior non-bearing walls preceded fabrication of an extensive network of steel girders providing inside support for the motion-sensitive outer brick walls. Down in the basement, heavy shoring and cribbing were installed to support the sloping concrete floor that, before being left behind, would have to support a large formation of transport dollies and a multitude of steel beams, as well as the gazillions of bricks riding on them.

Act II: Another long and tedious affair, the second act did feature a hint of visible action while furthering the plot in preparation for future events. After the crews of Matyiko and Stubbs properly braced the walls and shored up the floor, the men and equipment of International Chimney went to work cutting beam-insertion slots through the base of all four exterior walls. When completed, this task left one hundred various-sized openings through which fifty various-sized steel beams were inserted above the remnant foundation.

The first beams in were the four main load beams, each one a welded pair of twenty-four-inch-deep wide-flanged steel beams weighing 162 pounds per linear foot (2X24WF162). Inserted front-to-back under the terra-cotta facade and extending through the stageless rear wall, these four mains were arranged in balance across the building's eighty-foot width with the two outer beams almost directly beneath the side walls. Above and horizontally perpendicular came twenty cross-steel beams on four-foot centers. While most of the cross-steel pieces were fourteen-inch beams weighing 145 pounds per linear foot (14WF145), two thirty-six-inch-deep cross-steel beams weighing 250 pounds per foot (36WF250) were placed under the forward balcony ends near the center of the load. Respecting the weight of the front and rear walls, two additional thirty-six-inch beams were placed slightly beyond the building footprint, one at each end, as the outermost pieces of cross-steel. For optimum load distribution, dozens of short needle beams were then inserted horizontally perpendicular and above, spanning the two endmost pieces of cross-steel under the heaviest two walls at front and rear.

The plan for jacking the Shubert Theater was very similar to that used for the Gem Theatre: Matyiko's long-stroke, nineteen-circuit jacking machine and a simple two-way splitter would supply thirty-eight fifty-ton jacks arranged in three distinct loading zones. For the Shubert, Zone One supported the lighter area near the stageless rear wall while Zone Two and Zone Three shared the heavier front section. Also similar to the Gem experience, Pete augmented his lifting capacity with helper jacks powered by three separate, self-contained hydraulic systems—one for each zone. With high-pressure hydraulic pumps and the latest in pressure control valves, these three common pressure systems would work in perfect harmony with the unified pressure of the jacking unit during all phases of operation. With thirty-four helper jacks apportioned among the zones according to weight demands, a total of seventy-two fifty-ton jacks could raise the 2,908-ton Shubert with a healthy margin of safety.

Although splitting the output of Jerry's trusty "nineteen-holer" into thirty-eight circuits reduced the amount of jack ram extension, thus adding time and hassle to the lifting procedure, Pete preferred to have as many jacks as possible under positive control of the jacking machine for a greater margin of safety. However, any further splitting of jacking-unit circuits would render ram extensions too short to be practical. Although a second nineteen-circuit jacking machine could eliminate the need for helper jacks, Pete's idea of three independent systems supplying helper jacks in separate zones was the simplest and safest way to go. Unfortunately, when the time came to begin jacking, the Shubert performance replayed the Gem experience: due to another dolly delivery delay, there were insufficient fifty-ton jacks available. In order to similarly expedite the operation, smaller jacks were grouped together to provide each jacking point with a ram pressure equivalent to the larger jacks. In some cases, it took four fifteen-ton crib jacks to do the job of one big one. Alas, directors of really big shows can never stop *thinking it through*.

Act III: Finally, five months after the curtain went up, real action was seen on stage. On January 16, 1999, Matyiko depressed the control lever of his beloved jacking machine, and hydraulic fluid at 5,000 psi pushed through nineteen slave circuits toward thirty-eight jacking stations. Simultaneously, more hydraulic fluid of similar pressure from the three independent power sources pushed toward sixty-two substitute helper jacks. A jungle of black rubber hose, snaking endlessly through a forest of crib piles, suddenly surged to life. One hundred jack rams of every conceivable size squeezed out of their containers and pushed relentlessly against four massive steel beams. Very slowly but very surely, a horizontal crack in the foundation wall grew ever wider, and the Shubert Theater gained altitude. "It's levitating!" someone yelled.

Enthusiastic audience response and intense media attention would later identify this moment as an early high point in the production. Meantime, the program's director was seen smiling down at his far-from-muddy boots, pawing lightly at small bits of well-frozen terrain. Thinking back forty-five years, seventy-seven-year-old Pete Friesen was reviewing the excitement in the eyes of Vic Janzen and John Loewen at the maiden flight of his UHJS. "It's levitating all right," Pete chuckled to himself.

While television crews and photojournalists soon wandered off in search of other exciting moments, and spectators eventually drifted into boredom-induced reverie, the professional players on stage remained committed to their roles. Once the half-million pounds of steel beams and the 5.316 million pounds of bricks had been elevated one full lift, it was time to build up the crib piles and block the load before depressurizing and resetting the jacks for yet another lift. It would take several days of repetitive jacking cycles before Shubert was high enough to accept transport dollies underneath.

Although less than two city blocks, the route from 22 Seventh Street to the Shubert's new home at 516 Hennepin Avenue near Fifth Street was tightly confined by other city structures. With little maneuvering room for tow vehicles and facing the prospect of multiple rotations of their cumbersome load, Friesen and Matyiko agreed to experiment with self-powered dollies for this move. Interested in the concept for many years, Pete had purchased a pair of hydraulically driven axles just before selling AMC in the mid-1980s. Donated to Matyiko, these two axles had been incorporated into one of six direct-drive dolly units recently manufactured for Expert Movers. Anticipating the need to have one powered dolly for every two non-powered units, the bold experimenters rented twenty additional self-powered units. As such, the "Pete and Jerry

Show" would feature twenty-six powered and forty-six non-powered units for a total of seventy-two dollies under the Shubert load.

Although similar in appearance, there were significant differences between powered and non-powered transport dollies. While the average non-powered dolly weighed in at about 3,200 pounds, the addition of hydraulic motors and associated hardware pushed the weight of powered units up to 5,500 pounds. Moreover, all powered dollies were not created equal. Although both were propelled by one hydraulic motor mounted on the unit, Expert's dollies and the rented units had different means of power transmission: on Expert's "direct-drive" dollies, power was transmitted from the hydraulic motor directly to the axle, whereas on the "chain-drive" rental units, power was transferred to the axle through a short chain-and-sprocket assembly, like a bicycle. Another difference existed within Expert's fleet: the one dolly containing Pete's original pair of axles had a larger motor than the other six units, and thus raised the specter of inharmonious performance. One thing was certain: many pairs of eyes would be intently focused on the first operation of these self-propelled dollies.

Three days and fourteen jack-and-block cycles after Shubert's initial lift-off, there was finally enough room under the main beams for insertion of the transport dollies. The famous old playhouse now sat level, eight feet above its remnant foundation, lounging on three layers of steel beams resting on one hundred hydraulic jacks sitting on a network of sturdy crib piles rising from a sloping concrete floor supported by more crib piles underneath.

Having completed a repetitious multi-day jacking task, the hardworking crew now began the multi-day ordeal of herding forty-six 3,200-pound dollies and twenty-six 5,500-pound dollies into place. Immediately, the two types of powered dollies displayed variations in personality. "The older design of the chain-drive dollies seemed to give them minds of their own," Matyiko recalls. "We had a real tough time getting them to go where we wanted, and although it was time consuming, we had to take the chains off the sprockets to get many of them into position. On the other hand, by simply removing hydraulic pressure, the direct-drive units freewheeled more easily into place. Obviously, we [at Expert] were on the right track. Later, we started using bigger motors, but we decided all our own self-powered dollies would be direct-drive models."

Eventually all seventy-two dollies were gradually shuffled into place. Eight rocker beams were installed across eight rows of dollies, immediately below and horizontally perpendicular to the main load beams. Each ninety-foot rocker beam was a welded pair of 14WF145s, and each pair added thirteen tons to the total load. With the installation of this fourth layer of steel, the Shubert was now resting on a network of fifty beams adding 250 tons to the overall weight. In due course, the entire load was transferred to these eight rocker beams resting on seventy-two fifty-ton dolly jacks, all now present and accounted for.

In compliance with Pete's three-zone loading method, the dollies were arranged under the rocker beams to provide maximum support for the building's walls and other heavy sections; as such, a high proportion of dollies were positioned under the balcony area at the building's heavy front end. Here, Zone Two and Zone Three shared forty dollies while Zone One utilized the other thirty-two in the lighter rear section. In compliance with tried and true tradition, the Shubert Theater would float home on three zones of common pressure. For purposes of accessibility and control, the twenty-six powered dollies were assigned stations on or near the perimeter of the seventy-two-dolly formation, and each powered type would be supplied by an independent hydraulic system. These two additional hydraulic pumps were attached to overhead support beams, along with the three helper-jack systems and the unified jacking unit also onboard for the ride. Prepared for transit, the jungle of black rubber hose was secured neatly along convenient beams before dropping straight down to assigned connections on dolly jacks and drive motors.

Meanwhile, down in the basement, thousands of timbers and crib blocks propped up that sloping concrete floor. With its upper surface made level with more blocks and lumber, the floor now supported 576 large rubber tires on seventy-two transport dollies with fifty-ton jack rams lifting the weight of eight duplex rocker beams, four duplex main beams, twenty-two cross-steel beams, and thirty-two needle beams carrying a seven-story pile of clay-fired brick known as the Minneapolis Shubert Theater. *Visualize.*

Act IV: Of shorter duration than the previous two, this fourth act presented the most dramatic action of the entire production, bringing thousands of spectators and hundreds of media personnel to their feet in awed appreciation. Although it was a mild winter by Minnesota standards, temperatures had recently dropped to -10°F (-23°C), where they would remain for duration of the performance. Despite these relatively chilly conditions, the theater-watching public of Minneapolis warmed to the occasion by stamping their feet and shouting encouragement to the parka-clad players onstage. On February 9, 1999, six hydraulic pumps whined to life amidst the general morning hubbub surrounding Block E. Only those nearby could hear the crack of a champagne bottle against the Shubert's rear wall, and only well-trained eyes on stage could detect the initial rotation of certain thirty-one-inch wheels. Jarred back from boredom-induced reverie, media critics and spectators alike dropped their jaws and raised their heads in disbelief as seven stories of granite and terra-cotta backed slowly away from the Seventh Street sidewalk.

Almost ninety years of age, old Shubert was finally leaving home and moving to a new pad; although the new home was not far away, there would be plenty of adventures along the way. Barely outside his abandoned back door, Shubert found he needed a new perspective on things. Having spent a lifetime with a generally southern point of view, the old guy needed a definitively eastern outlook if he wanted a life in his new neighborhood ... and it would be too late to change if he got there looking the way he did. It was now or never.

Given the lack of maneuvering room at the destination end, a required ninety-degree rotation of the dolly-borne load was carried out on the now-expansive parking lot surface of Block E, immediately adjacent to the now-abandoned theater site. Once the cumbersome load completely cleared its former foundation, the director called a halt to the action and began issuing instructions to the dolly wranglers. The compulsory quarter-turn rotation about the structure's vertical axis required the angle of each dolly frame and its articulating axle to be precisely readjusted according to careful calculations. By necessity, the new frame and axle angles all varied according to their particular positions in the overall formation. While undergoing individual realignment, each dolly was unweighted and held aloft by retraction of its own dual-action jack, while its share of the load was transferred to two temporary jacks powered by a separate hydraulic pump.

On the razed remains of Block E, old Shubert completed his programmed counterclockwise quarter-turn without a hitch. After setting the brakes and blocking the load, the director issued new instructions to the dolly wranglers: in the same manner as before, all 576 wheels needed another realignment, parallel to the rocker beams, for the first leg of the northbound journey. As well as physical and verbal encouragement, the dollies required constant attention for control of their fluid supplies. During every day's events, hydraulic pressures were continuously applied and released to various components, and every night, scores of valves were verified closed in order to block the pressure in place and secure the load. Riding herd on seventy-two dollies was more than a full-time job. On the Pete and Jerry Show, the crucial task of hydraulic valve control was assigned to responsible cast members. In the further interest of safety, all round-knobbed needle valves had already been replaced with red-handled ball valves that gave instant and obvious indication of their status.

*After backing away from Seventh Street and rotating ninety degrees on the infamous Block E, the 2,908-ton Shubert Theater load is heading north toward Sixth Street while riding on 72 dollies.*

After one change of attitude and two wheel alignments, our hero Shubert found his way across Block E and soon waited for a chance to cross Sixth Street. Early the next morning, rush-hour traffic was diverted while truckloads of crushed concrete and gravel were dumped, compacted, and graded across the full width of the street. As well as providing a firm rolling surface for dolly tires, this temporary fill also leveled out the route ahead where the side-slope of Sixth Street and rising ground to the north created a variation in terrain beyond the adjustment potential of the dolly-jack rams. It was hardly time to risk the hydraulic loading of a building that was floating along so well; a road full of gravel and concrete was a small price to pay for protection against the sudden risk of scattered granite and terra-cotta showers.

With their pedals to the metal, twenty-six hydraulic-driven dollies powered forward at many yards per hour, trucking the 6,400-square-foot behemoth out onto the street. Here, an ever-changing throng of admirers watched at least some part of old Shubert's daylong dash across Sixth Street. Slipping between cars so to speak, he was across and well clear before the street was returned to normal in time for afternoon rush hour. Undaunted by the unknown and unruffled by all the hoopla surrounding him, Shubert trundled resolutely northward, encouraged by occasional tugs from the director's trusty array of come-along winches.

A week after leaving home, Shubert was within sight of his new pad. Unfortunately, the basement extension of a nearby dining establishment undermined the direct route to his back door, and he was prevented from moving straight in. On the northern and western perimeters, several obstacles restricted any route for sidestepping around the unsupportive ground. Although perhaps technically possible, the sidestep option was declined because of limited space and the number of wheel alignments and additional duty days it would demand. Instead, to keep the show moving at a reasonable pace, the director suggested new choreography.

With the monstrous load parked abeam the restaurant's subterranean cavern, dolly wranglers realigned all 576 wheels to critical new angles prescribed by the project consultant. When everything was good to go, hydraulic power was reapplied to the self-propelled dollies, and the towering ensemble rolled slowly northeast, arcing around the unsupportive ground in a gentle right turn. At the project consultant's predetermined mark, the moving theater was brought to a halt, and all 576 wheels were once again realigned according to his calculations. With reactivation of the powered dollies, the hulking ensemble began rolling southeast, front wall leading, arcing in a gentle left turn toward its two-story concrete basement. On February 21, 1999, when the director crossed his arms above his head to signal completion of this gentle counterclockwise arc, old Shubert's memorable twelve-day odyssey came to an end. Arriving with style and grace befitting its legacy, the Shubert Theater was home. Perfectly positioned above its new foundation, the Shubert showed nary a brick or piece of terra-cotta out of place. The cameras clicked and rolled. The audience stood and cheered.

*Hard-hatted workers lend perspective to the theater's*
*terra-cotta façade as it rolls precisely into position.*

The director was happy. As production designer and operational consultant, Pete Friesen had guided another impossible mission to a successful resolution. Long recognized within his industry for invention and innovative thought, he had once again introduced original and effective choreography to get the job done in a safe and timely manner. Having long ago turned the world of jacking upside down and known for occasionally bending the rails, Pete had recently orchestrated a stylish pirouette to bring the Gem Theatre home, and now he would be remembered for two opposite-direction counterbalancing arcs that "sashayed" the Shubert Theater home. *Derch denche.*

Act V: All but devoid of visual action, the fifth and concluding act of this monumental production featured an early exit of its director and all principal players, followed by a protracted denouement during which the hero was tucked peacefully into his new bed in eager anticipation of a new life in the new neighborhood.

As soon as Shubert was poised above his new bed, the director exited stage left and returned to Lynden, Washington, where he took up the script for another large drama soon to be in production. As soon as old Shubert was tucked in, Matyiko and his merry band of movers headed for the east coast, followed shortly thereafter by the men and equipment of ICC. While Larry Stubbs and local contractors completed final touches to the scene, scores of dollies and beams, hundreds of jacks, and thousands of crib blocks were organized and summarily dispatched to destinations far and wide. As soon as the set was cleared of props and people, George Kissinger of the municipal development agency gave a green light to the Block E shopping-mall developers and transferred Shubert Theater responsibility to the Artspace organization.

As far as Kelley Lindquist and Artspace colleagues were concerned, the production had just made it onto the stage, and the real work of bringing their production home was still before them. Having been encouraged by the state's Historic Preservation Office and by the city's Heritage Preservation Commission, they had saved the historic building from the wrecking ball. Now, armed with almost a dozen studies outlining its feasibility, they enthusiastically undertook the task of enlisting broad private and public support to transform the old theater into a functioning element of a truly remarkable artistic vision. A large work in progress, the Artspace proposal brings federal, state, and municipal funds together with a majority of private investment into a total budget of $40 million

(2007) to finance complete restoration of Minneapolis's longest standing performance theater and to include it in their envisioned arts and education complex.

Now situated at 516 Hennepin Avenue, the Shubert Theater is in good company, one lot removed from another vintage building rededicated to the city's vibrant arts scene. The Hennepin Center for the Arts, housing a 250-seat theater as well as administration and rehearsal space for seventeen arts organizations, was originally constructed as a Masonic temple in 1888, and is also now listed on the National Register of Historic Places. This eight-story Richardson Romanesque structure is an attractive and most suitable neighbor for the relocated Shubert. Connecting these two heritage buildings, the Artspace design includes a graceful, modern two-story atrium serving them both as box office and community gathering place.

As an integral part of the larger vision known as the Minnesota Shubert Performing Arts and Education Center, the thousand-seat Shubert Theater will host a chamber orchestra while providing performance space for approximately twenty arts groups. With construction expected to be well underway by time of this publication, a grand opening is planned to coincide with the hundred-year anniversary of the Shubert's inaugural performance. The current Act V is scheduled to conclude in 2010.

Meanwhile, the producers are happy. The people of Artspace have successfully brought together two historic buildings into a unique and functional center for the performing arts and in so doing have made a significant contribution toward the revitalization of their city's downtown core. While considered by many as the organization's biggest success, the Minnesota Shubert Center was only one of many Artspace success stories. Since formation in 1979 as an advocacy group and then becoming a proactive developer, the organization has expanded well beyond its hometown. In its first thirty years of existence, Artspace has already developed twenty-two "Live/Work" projects for artists in thirteen states and been recognized as America's leading non-profit real estate developer for the arts.

*Computer-graphic image of the Shubert Theater in place on Hennepin Avenue beside the former Masonic Temple building of 1888—Minnesota Shubert Center.*

The executive producers are also very happy. City officials and municipal agencies have successfully orchestrated rejuvenation of a downtown sector that seemed to be sliding out of control. Indeed, the city's initial $4 million investment that rolled the Shubert into line with three other fully restored vintage playhouses on Hennepin Avenue is part of a larger plan. Even before restoration, the relocated Shubert is bringing the city's old theater district back to life. With improvements to rapid transit and pedestrian amenities, there is new life in the neighborhood and a renewed sense of connection within the inner-city landscape.

When the Minnesota Shubert Center for Performing Arts and Education opens its doors in 2010, Minneapolis will celebrate the end of a lengthy rehabilitation and the launch of a new era in the community's long tradition of live theater. While there may never again be forty "legitimate" theaters in town, the restored Shubert, State, Orpheum, and Pantages theaters will long remain reminders of that bygone era. Including the renowned Guthrie Theater nearby with its three performance stages and 32,000 subscribers, it is safe to say the city's theater district is alive and well. Including its wealth of smaller playhouses, the Minneapolis-St. Paul Region is second only to New York City in the number of live theater seats per capita and, after Chicago, is the third-largest theater market in the nation. The relocated Shubert Theater can be seen as yet another "outward and visible sign of inward and probable culture."

A 1999 entry in the *Guinness Book of World Records* cites the 5.816-million-pound Shubert Theater in Minneapolis as the heaviest building ever moved on pneumatic tires.

# 17

# Hatteras

On his return to Spain in 1524, the Italian navigator Giovanni da Verrazzano reported having seen "what must certainly be the Oriental sea … the one which goes about the extremity of India, China, and Cathay." Coasting north with the Gulf Stream, far to the south of where Block Island was first placed on his chart, Verrazzano gazed across a narrow strand of sand beyond which appeared another vast ocean extending to the western horizon. However, all notions of such easy passage to the Orient soon evaporated. By the end of that same century, dozens of ships had explored this narrow strand of sand, proving it to be a two-hundred-mile-long chain of barrier islands separating Atlantic waters from a thirty-mile-wide inland sea. The Northwest Passage, the Holy Grail of maritime trade, would require three more centuries of exploration. Meanwhile, a large new landmass named North America had become available for exploitation and habitation.

After two failed attempts at colonizing islands in that inland sea, the first permanent English settlement in the New World was established during 1607 at nearby Jamestown in what would become the colony of Virginia. Fifty-six years and three English kings later, a royal charter of 1663 authorized creation of another colony immediately to the south. This new Carolina colony was then divided into separate north and south jurisdictions in 1729. Sixty years and one revolutionary war later, the vast inland sea and the long chain of barrier islands were part of the new state of North Carolina.

By then, disease, famine, and warfare had all but eliminated the

Algonkian-speaking Native Americans who had inhabited the region since time immemorial. Immediately prior to European contact, approximately five thousand Croatan people lived on one of these barrier islands they called *Hatteras*. Thought to derive from the Croatan term for "an area of sparse vegetation," Hatteras refers to a windswept homeland of ever-shifting sand dunes and very few trees. Today, seven small communities exist on Hatteras Island, the largest of the barrier island chain that eventually became known as the Outer Banks. The most easterly projection on this island's fifty-mile arc is called Cape Hatteras.

Offshore from Cape Hatteras, an ever-changing pattern of underwater sand bars extends ten miles into the Atlantic Ocean where the Virginia Coastal Drift, an extension of the southerly flowing Labrador Current, is pinched landward by the strong northbound flow of the Gulf Stream. Here, on Diamond Shoals, hundreds of ships from many nations have run aground along an almost featureless shoreline. Like Sable Island off Nova Scotia and Cape Cod in Massachusetts, this patch of unruly water off Cape Hatteras became known as a "graveyard of the Atlantic." Recognizing Diamond Shoals as serious hindrance to coastal shipping and commerce, the U.S. Congress allocated funds in 1797 for construction of a lighthouse at Cape Hatteras. Completed in 1803, this light was immediately seen as inadequate: a ninety-foot-high sandstone tower supported eighteen small whale-oil lanterns whose illumination barely reached beyond the shoals in clear weather conditions. The light was also vulnerable: winter storms were known to shatter the windows and snuff out its lights for days and nights at a time.

In 1852, Congress established the Lighthouse Board—including scientists, Army engineers, and Navy officers—to create a unified and continuous system of navigational aides along the nation's coasts. The board addressed concerns at Cape Hatteras by extending the tower to a height of 150 feet and installing a recently invented first-order Fresnel lens with its much stronger, flashing-white light. It was one of the most dependable lights on the Atlantic coast until Confederate forces absconded with the lens in 1861. At the conclusion of the Civil War, studies suggested that replacement of the Hatteras light tower would be more economically viable than repairing the damage sustained during recent military action and severe weather. Acting on recommendation of the Lighthouse Board, Congress allocated $155,000 for construction of a new Cape Hatteras Lighthouse. Motivated by growing awareness of coastal erosion, the decision makers situated the new lighthouse six hundred feet inland of the old tower and 1,500 feet back from the high-tide line.

In November 1868, a Yankee contractor disembarked from a Lighthouse Board service vessel at the Hatteras Island village of Buxton; his name was Dexter Stetson, and he had come to build the new lighthouse. Contrary to some fears, fifty-three-year-old Stetson fit in well with the local folks, and almost one hundred of them found steady work on the project for about $1.50 per day. Despite dreadful weather, much was accomplished during that first winter. Stetson and crew dug a large hole in the sand, about seven feet deep and sixty feet across, where they would install the lighthouse's planned forty-five-foot-diameter foundation. Finding the floor of this excavation to be highly compacted sand lying several feet below the freshwater table, Stetson immediately revised the original blueprint. Facing the difficult prospect of driving wooden pilings into dense sand as hard as concrete, he chose to float the towering structure's masonry base on two horizontally perpendicular courses of wooden timbers, all hewn from local yellow pine. As such, reasoned the lighthouse builder, the timber matting would easily support the weight of the structure while being preserved by immersion in fresh water. It remains unknown if Dexter Stetson required or received any authorization for such a drastic change to the Lighthouse Board's approved design.

Erecting a cofferdam and utilizing steam-driven pumps to keep his excavation dry, Stetson's crew installed multiple layers of rough-hewn granite block to a height of five-and-a-half feet on top of the timber mat. Above this, they mortared together five octagonal courses of granite blocks with the four uppermost courses above grade and stepped back eleven inches from the one below. Above this forty-five-foot-diameter plinth came a twenty-five-foot-high, gently tapered, octagonal base, composed of red brick with stylish white granite accents at the corners and a fine granite staircase leading to a handsomely decorated entrance. Above this attractive and solid base-section came the tricky part—a circular double-walled tower of mortared brick tapering skyward for another 150 vertical feet.

Think of the tower as a brick-walled cylinder inside a brick-walled cone. The inner cylinder, containing the spiral staircase, has a consistent inside diameter of eleven-and-a-half feet from bottom to top; the thickness of its brick wall, however, decreases with height, from twenty inches at the bottom to eight inches at the top of the shaft. By contrast, the inside diameter of the outer cone decreases with height, from thirty-seven-and-a-half feet at the bottom to twelve-and-a-half feet at the top; the thickness of this brick wall also gradually decreases with height, from forty-six inches at the bottom to a point, 135 feet above ground level, where it merges with the cylinder wall within. In the space between the cylinder and cone, twelve vertical ribs or cross-walls, each four bricks wide, contribute to the tower's overall strength and rigidity.

Something must also be said for the strength and endurance of Dexter Stetson and his workers, who labored almost incessantly for nearly two years to complete their task. They had neither hydraulic jacks nor electric winches, and they were without any form of motorized ground transport. What rudimentary tools they did possess—for cutting, hauling, and leverage—were all powered by human effort with occasional assistance from draft animals. Before being maneuvered into place in the construction, hundreds of heavy granite blocks and 1.25 million clay-fired bricks were offloaded from barges onto lighters and then hoisted onto tramcars before being pushed and pulled to the jobsite. A similar amount of respect must also be given to Stetson and crew for their attention to detail. Without laser-levels or other sophisticated measuring devices, they made marvelous use of a plumb bob and the good old human eyeball in building a structure measuring 208 feet from the base of its broad foundation to the top of its tiny roof. History speaks long and well about the quality of their workmanship.

In the autumn of 1870, a first-order Fresnel lens arrived from Paris and was hoisted into position atop the completed brick tower, now capped by a narrow steel gantry around the glass-paneled lantern room. Appropriately, the same lens "liberated" from the old sandstone tower nine years prior had found its way to France for reconditioning. Beneath the new whale oil lamp and lens, an iron staircase of 247 steps spiraled down to a ground-level storage room opening to a granite staircase and eleven more steps to the sandy soil. The keepers of Cape Hatteras Light would be very fit people. After erecting additional living quarters to house the necessary three families of keepers, Dexter Stetson packed up his tools and went thirty-five miles north to build another lighthouse at Bodie Island.

At sunset on December 16, 1870, the new Cape Hatteras Lighthouse flashed into service with a bright, white light shining across Diamond Shoals and far beyond every seven and a half seconds. At 208 feet in height, it was the highest maritime beacon in the United States and the tallest brick lighthouse in the world. With the subsequent addition of a distinctive black-and-white barber-pole paint scheme to enhance daytime recognition, the light soon became a coastal icon, admired and appreciated from both land and sea. However, despite a functioning array of handsome light stations on the barrier islands, something was not quite right in the state of North Carolina. Scientific analysis would eventually confirm what many long-term beachcombers had been suggesting: the Atlantic was devouring the state's eastern edge at an alarming rate. Barrier islands are some of the least stable landmasses on earth. Those like the Outer Banks, which are not anchored on a coral reef foundation, are especially susceptible to transformation. By 1919, the ocean had advanced to within three hundred feet of the Cape Hatteras tower, originally constructed 1,500 feet back from the shoreline. By 1930, interlocking steel groins were installed along the beach as a preventative measure. These were but the first of many steel and concrete barriers installed in front of the lighthouse during the next seventy years.

In 1936, two years after an electric bulb replaced the oil lamp, ocean waves began lapping at the base of the tower. Having recently acquired control of the lighthouse from the Bureau of Lighthouses (formerly the Lighthouse Board), the U.S. Coast Guard was forced to turn off the light and lock the door. While an electric light on a 150-foot steel tower farther inland satisfied navigational requirements, the Coast Guard transferred ownership of the masonry structure to the U.S. National Park Service that had already expressed interest in the site. However, with the outbreak of World War II, all park planning was put on hold. The Coast Guard used the tower as a lookout point across Diamond

Shoals, where crowded sea-lanes provided easy pickings for marauding German submarines. Before the U-Boat threat was eliminated, one offshore lightship and nearly sixty commercial vessels were destroyed. For several years, this Graveyard of the Atlantic was better known as Torpedo Junction.

As peace returned to the Outer Banks, so too did the sand. In little more than a decade, the width of the beach in front of Cape Hatteras Lighthouse had increased from zero to one thousand feet, for which a combination of natural process and human enhancement can be credited. Encouraged by this trend, the Coast Guard leased back the tower-top navigation lantern from the Park Service and returned Cape Hatteras Lighthouse to service in 1950. Maintaining ownership of the lighthouse structure, the Park Service began acquiring land in its vicinity while struggling to define a balanced vision for some form of coastal protected area that might enhance human enjoyment while respecting the area's unique ecology. It was a long and difficult process. Finally, 28,500 acres of land and seventy miles of shoreline from both sides of the barrier islands were designated as the country's first coastal recreation area and transferred to the federal government.

Formally dedicated in 1958, Cape Hatteras National Seashore was the subject of considerable rancor and legal debate until the end of the following decade, when all former landholders were finally satisfied with their compensation. By this time, a new bridge and highway had brought a new wave of tourism to the Outer Banks. Unfortunately, while tourists migrated toward the light in ever-increasing numbers, the sands were once again drifting away from its base at an alarming rate. Two recent decades of relative shoreline stability had proven to be only a lull in nature's progress. Shoreline enhancement projects were again undertaken in earnest. Between 1966 and 1973, almost 2 million cubic-yards of sand were deposited in front of the light tower with almost no effect on the erosion rate. Several strong "nor'easters" in the winter of 1980 completely inundated the remains of the original 1803 tower and pushed high tides within fifty feet of the existing light. For the first time in seventy years of active beach management, emergency protective measures were initiated. By the end of the following year, the third such emergency measure saw the innermost barrier groin extended inland by an additional three hundred feet, while many tons of rock and concrete rubble were placed around the tower's base. By then, Senator Jesse Helms and Governor Jim Hunt had united to sponsor a statewide Save Cape Hatteras Lighthouse Committee.

Public workshops and an environmental assessment in 1982 suggested that a seawall, or revetment, encircling the lighthouse was the best option for its long-term protection; the U.S. Army Corps of Engineers' wave-tank modeling of the concept was completed in 1985. By the time funding was secured for construction of the seawall in 1987, a recently created private organization, the Move the Lighthouse Committee, had presented documentation about advances in relocation technology unavailable during the earlier planning process. Motivated by this new information, the National Park Service contracted with the National Academy of Sciences for an independent review to determine the very best long-term protection for the lighthouse while considering structural risks, environmental issues, visitor factors, and total cost.

Presented in 1988, the final report from the National Academy of Sciences recommended relocation as the best option for saving Cape Hatteras Lighthouse from the sea. After soil testing and another environmental assessment, the Park Service announced a preference for the relocation option, and in 1990, contracted with ICC to perform structural-integrity work to ensure the lighthouse could withstand the rigors of travel. When this restoration work was completed with satisfactory results in 1992, the Park Service started the big wheel rolling toward relocation while promoting interim measures to keep the tower "afloat." While scientists and consultants assessed site locations and erosion rates, 1993's Hurricane Emily damaged the lantern deck handrails and windows. The next year, Hurricane Gordon passed close enough to breach the sand dunes north and south of the lighthouse, promoting extensive erosion. By 1996, the landward end of the south barrier groin had been extended inland by another two hundred feet while 1,500 large sandbags attempted reinforcement of the eroding escarpment at the base of the tower.

In 1997, a faculty committee at North Carolina State University issued a report endorsing the 1988 findings of the Academy of Sciences while warning that "if Cape Hatteras Lighthouse is to be preserved for enjoyment by future generations, it must be moved and it must be moved *now*." In 1999, eleven years after the original recommendation, with a federal appropriation of $11.8 million, the Park Service awarded a design-build contract to ICC for the relocation. After more than ten years of hard work, the Move the Lighthouse Committee had finally got its point across. This group of engineering-minded lighthouse lovers had brought the idea of relocation to the attention of the Park Service back in 1987. Armed with their own book, *Move it or Lose it!*, this spirited group of relocation advocates was already lobbying the structural-moving industry as well as politicians at every level when the final report from the National Academy of Sciences was released in 1988.

Coincidentally, the front cover of *The Structural Mover* magazine's April 1988 edition presented a striking photograph of Cape Hatteras Lighthouse surrounded by dilapidated snow fence and storm-thrashed polypropylene sandbags. The IASM enticed readers to this cover story with a related caption: "A Light Move?" Inside, the magazine's featured article offered a brief summary of the interim report on "Options for Preserving the Cape Hatteras Lighthouse" from the National Research Council and the National Academy of Sciences. Together with historical background, the article clearly identified relocation as the preferred option for long-term preservation of the lighthouse. As noted by the magazine's publishers, "A technological report backing this type of recycling project should have an invaluable impact on future decisions involving our industry."

Coincidentally, another article in this same magazine issue was entitled "Mr. Mover" and featured a photograph of Pete Friesen in convention mode. Acknowledging this "Mr. Mover" as one of the IASM's founders, this brief article announced Pete's plan to retire from active structural moving while moving himself back out west whence he came. "The Association wishes Mr. Mover well. Pete, may the fairways be smooth and always be centered underneath when you drive the little white ball."

Pete Friesen played far less golf than he thought he would. Although AMC ended up in capable hands, Pete's consulting agenda showed far more on-duty hours than tee-off times. After the action-packed five-year run with Dell Davis in Chicago, there had been the three lighthouses and a gymnasium to move in New England, followed by the smokestacks in Pennsylvania. It had all been fun. Pete met all sorts of interesting people, and he came to know many an interesting old building. He was now hooked on the historical preservation of architectural treasures, while still enjoying opportunities for pushing the industry envelope. Over the course of recent moves, George Gardner, Jerry Matyiko, and Pete had engaged in many a conversation about a particular black-and-white-striped lighthouse that had been on most structural-moving minds since 1988.

While orchestrating their 1997 theatre performance in Detroit, the trio was invited to submit a bid for the proposed relocation of Cape Hatteras Lighthouse. As soon as the Gem was successfully pirouetted into place, Pete Friesen headed home to his Lynden office, where he designed a workable method for moving the lighthouse structure while helping George and Jerry complete a comprehensive bid submission. By the time of their encore theater move in Minneapolis, the Three Houseketeers had been awarded a contract for the 2,900-foot relocation of Cape Hatteras Lighthouse. As soon as the Shubert was successfully sashayed into place in February 1999, Pete headed to Lynden and applied himself to refining the plan for relocating the 208-foot-high lighthouse. Pete Friesen was again busy *thinking it through*.

Although major questions about moving this lighthouse had been addressed by feasibility studies, fine-tuning was required. While happy with his overall plan, Pete remained highly disturbed by an important factor—the hydraulic jacks. A pioneer in the field, Pete Friesen knew a thing or two about hydraulics, and especially, he knew something about hydraulic jacks. As much as anyone in the business, Pete knew all jacks were not created equal. While some of the latest large-bore hydraulic jacks had capacity ratings anywhere between thirty-five and one hundred tons, depending mostly on the amount of applied hydraulic pressure, all of them were only as good as their inside seals and the finish of their cylinder's inner wall. Without a smooth finish and very close tolerances, the semi-flexible seals around the piston rings are unable to fully block passage of hydraulic fluid between the piston and inner cylinder walls. As a result, these jacks will not hold sufficient pressure to maintain their advertised weight capacity.

The first hydraulic crib jacks designed by Pete and manufactured by Peters Brothers of Vancouver in 1955 had extremely fine inner tolerances—three-one-thousandths of an inch. Although only fifteen-ton jacks, they consistently operated to rated capacity. They were reliable. During four subsequent decades in the structural-moving business, Mr. Friesen struggled with several models of hydraulic jack, as well as with some of their builders and representatives. Of course, the quality of materials and tolerances in assembly often vary significantly among manufacturers. Performance can also vary noticeably among individual units of any one type. Being away from the action and its inherent danger, some jack providers were blasé about the situation, shrugging the problem off onto part suppliers or assembly workers. Only with concerted effort could people close to the action, like Pete Friesen, be relatively certain about their jacks' lifting capacity and reliability. The only way to know any jack's lifting power is to test it under load within its rated capacity. A long time ago, Pete had learned a valuable lesson: the time it takes to pre-test jacks and hydraulic hose is time well invested.

Before having accepted the role of consultant for the 1993 relocation of Southeast Light on Block Island, Pete had insisted Expert House Movers recondition all its jacks, installing adequate seals and ensuring their inside tolerances would not exceed three-one-thousandths of an inch. Encouraged by only one jack failure on that job, Pete made the same request for subsequent major projects. Now, Pete insisted that Expert similarly recondition all hydraulic jacks before he would consult on the Cape Hatteras Lighthouse project. Also on his recommendation, all of these reconditioned jacks were pre-tested on-site before being subjected to the weight of the actual load. Seeking a margin of safety well above the bare minimum, Pete had the jacks tested at significantly higher pressures and was seriously disappointed when few of these latest heavy-duty jacks could sustain more than 7,000 psi—a capacity of seventy tons. Pete was in anguish: the numbers were not good enough. At best, he could only fit one hundred jacks into the available surface area beneath the lighthouse, and only by pushing his jacks to the extreme could he have 7,000 tons of potential lift for a load estimated at 5,000 tons. At best, his safety margin was only 40 percent—not good enough. Ideally, Pete preferred to operate his jacks well below their maximum capacity while maintaining a lifting capacity 50 percent greater than his total load. Too many things can go wrong:

failure of one small component can quickly lead to multiple jack failures, precipitating disaster. Considering the magnitude of this lighthouse project, even a safety factor of 50 percent was barely acceptable insurance against unforeseen circumstance. For an iconic structure of this magnitude, there is really no such thing as too much insurance. With people's lives at stake, there is really no such thing as too much safety. Pete didn't like the numbers, and he looked for ways to improve the odds.

Still at home in Lynden, Pete paced and pondered for several days, all too aware of the work well underway at Cape Hatteras. By this time, ICC crews had cut into the tower foundation and cleared vegetation from the move corridor; Expert House Movers had already successfully repositioned the principal keeper's house, the assistant keepers' duplex, the oil house, and three cisterns. There was only one more thing to go—the lighthouse. As always, Pete looked for his subconscious intuition to augment his warehouse of hard-won knowledge in coming up with a solution. Along with years of experience, Pete also carried healthy respect for his gut instincts. At the moment, these instincts were in total harmony with his mind. Both were adamantly opposed to his heart's desire. "I was at wits' end," Pete recalled. "As much as I wanted to do the job, I could not find a way to do it safely … the more I tried to find a way, the more I knew it was impossible. Finally, one day, I gave up and I went to bed very frustrated … I was really down. I knew that in the morning, I had to make a telephone call that would shut the whole job down while we reworked the jacks.

"I don't know how the good Lord works," Pete continued, "but God somehow finds a way of looking out for us. I woke up in the morning with this idea of further isolating the jacks into separate cells within the three zones underneath the lighthouse. That way we would have duplicate hydraulic circuits in each zone and have much greater protection in case of jack failure. I sure wasn't conscious of thinking this up, but it must have come through me somehow, because there it was in the morning, bright and clear as the day. All of my safety problems were solved … I was very relieved about not having to make that telephone call … I felt blessed."

*Cape Hatteras Lighthouse keepers' quarters being moved*
*3,000 feet from their original site.*

One can only imagine the amount of apprehension experienced by the specialists at the National Park Service who, after two decades of consideration, had finally committed to relocation of the Cape Hatteras Lighthouse. Although their agency had witnessed two successful relocations of lighthouses under its jurisdiction in New England, neither move was anywhere near as challenging as this one. The move of Southeast Light on Block Island did not carry the same amount of public scrutiny and political pressure as this one. Although the men and the machinery given the task of moving Hatteras Light were all well-proven, one never knew when a bit of bad luck might waylay the best-made plans. Fortunately, this project's $11.8 million budget was suitable to the enormity of the task. Alongside the work of the Three Houseketeers, surveyors and soil testers had completed the necessary groundwork leading up to the move, and several masonry contractors were already assigned to finishing touches required once the lighthouse was in place. Meanwhile, the site was crawling with engineers of all stripes: structural engineers, civil engineers, chemical engineers, geotechnical engineers, environmental engineers, hydraulic engineers, and even electrical engineers.

David Fischetti of Cary, North Carolina, was among the engineers. Long-opposed to the seawall/revetment plan that would have made the lighthouse an island off a receding shoreline, Fischetti was the founding president of the Move the Lighthouse Committee. As part of an original relocation design team, Fischetti had suggested the participation of those same contractors who had recently moved Southeast Light on Block Island and who were then relocating the Gem Theatre in Detroit. His company, DCF Engineering, subsequently became part of the Hatteras relocation team, producing structural drawings for ICC and designing the new foundation.

Jerry Stockbridge was another of those engineers who literally crawled about the lighthouse. Representing the firm of Wiss, Janney, Elstner and Associates from Northbrook, Illinois, Stockbridge conducted extensive testing of lighthouse materials prior to the move and installed a complex monitoring system for the transit phase. His analysis showed the 130-year-old mortar as equivalent to a modern-day Portland cement-lime-sand mixture, and his core samples established an estimate for acceptable levels of stress to the brick and granite components. Having determined the lighthouse could be as much as five degrees off vertical before being over-stressed, he established a safety limit of one-half of one degree from vertical. Stockbridge engineered a network of fifty-six sensors feeding real-time data to his sophisticated computer program, monitoring verticality, vibration, deformation, and other potentially stressing conditions. Upon sensing any abnormality, the computer would sound a klaxon and make telephone calls until appropriate corrective action was taken.

Bill Jahns is not a professional engineer, and he spent very little time at the Cape Hatteras jobsite. However, he would still make a vital contribution to the relocation. A former employee of Modern Hydraulics and self-described jack-of-all-trades, Jahns is best regarded as a "pressure engineer" who has been successfully designing and manufacturing his own line of hydraulic equipment since 1985. Based in Elburn, Illinois, Jahns Structure Jacking Systems (JSJS) provided Expert House Movers with its modified double-stroke-length, nineteen-circuit jacking machine used for Southeast Light and subsequent heavy moves. In summer 1998,

Jahns was informed about the Cape Hatteras project, and he immediately went to work building the brand-new sixty-circuit jacking machine he had been discussing for some time with Matyiko and Pete.

Mike Booher is a professional photographer and sometime-resident of Hatteras Island who was familiar with the lighthouse and the campaign to save it. Signing on as official photographer, Booher volunteered to provide the Park Service with quality visual records of the project in exchange for near-exclusive access to the jobsite. Booher and author Lin Ezell later collaborated on a book about Cape Hatteras Lighthouse and its 1999 relocation. Readers interested in a more comprehensive description are encouraged to consult their fine work—*Out of Harm's Way: Moving America's Lighthouse.*

Motivated by growing public curiosity about the project, the Park Service supplied live video coverage and near-continuous updates on a dedicated Cape Hatteras Lighthouse Web site. Recognizing an engineering feat of historic proportion, local, national, and international media were soon attracted to Cape Hatteras. This gathering throng of "news engineers" soon proclaimed the relocation of Cape Hatteras Lighthouse as the "Move of the Century."

ICC began physical work at the site in December 1998. Company president Rick Lohr and project manager Joe Jakubik organized their men into two crews working simultaneously on different chores: while one crew prepared the move corridor, the other prepared the lighthouse. After dismantling, cataloguing, and storing all components of the external granite staircase and bricked pathway from the oil house, the lighthouse crew excavated around the base of the tower, down to the level of Stetson's yellow pine timbers. In the process, they uncovered masonry footings and sections of an ornamental wrought-iron fence that originally encircled the structure before becoming lost in the shifting sands of time.

Beginning in February 1999, the ICC crew used a diamond-studded cable saw to sever the lighthouse from its base. Below the plane of separation, heavy-duty concrete drills and splitters were used to remove the lowest course of granite plinth plus six vertical feet of granite foundation from below the tower. While chunks of granite were laboriously chiseled out several feet at a time, long sections of ten-inch-deep beams were stitch-welded together and placed into position as steel matting on top of the original wooden timbers. As the granite was removed, the weight of the lighthouse was gradually transferred onto steel shoring towers set on the steel matting. Each one of many four-foot-high shoring towers was composed of four steel posts cross-braced together. Inserted in the base of each post, fifty-ton jacks shimmed every shoring tower tight and level to base of the big tower.

On February 28, 1999, Cape Hatteras Light was switched off, never again to shine from this long-familiar location. By this time, ICC had already brought in even heavier heavy-duty equipment and instituted a night shift to hammer away at a granite foundation proving tougher than anticipated. Nearing midnight on April 1, ICC's hard-rock miners finally reached the center point of the foundation; they found a lead-encased grounding rod and a wooden surveyor's stake left by Stetson's men 130 years before. By the end of April, after eleven weeks of intense labor, all 334 cubic-yards of granite foundation had been removed. Without its eight-hundred-ton base, the Cape Hatteras Lighthouse rested on 134 steel shoring towers and 536 fifty-ton jacks sitting on heavy steel matting atop two layers of wooden timbers lying in the wet sand. Stetson would have been pleased.

*With excavations underway beneath it, the light tower is temporarily supported by two main beams, several cross-steel beams, many shoring towers, and one remnant of its original foundation.*

Although symmetrical with a relatively low center of gravity—sixty-six feet above ground—the circular structure of Cape Hatteras Lighthouse presented more than one challenge to the modern-age engineers who were preparing to move it. Of major concern was the need to arrange sufficient heavy-duty jacks into straight lines under a circular base while still adhering to the principles of three-zone loading. Pete had given much thought to the problem and discussed various options with his "mission impossible" cohorts. They soon came up with a plan that George Gardner put onto paper and Matyiko now put into action.

The crew from Expert House Movers began inserting their steel load beams into the carefully aligned array of shoring towers. First to be installed were seven eleven-ton main load beams, each one being a welded pair of seventy-two-foot wide-flange steel beams, twenty-four inches deep and weighing 162 pounds per linear foot (2X24WF162). While modified over the years, most of these main beams had seen service on Block Island and subsequent heavy moves. All of the duplex main beams on this job were similarly welded to allow for insertion of hydraulic jacks into a six-inch space between the pairs. Before installation beneath the tower, each main load beam was outfitted with its share of heavy-duty hydraulic jacks, bolted between the beam pairs with their rams extending downward toward the crib piles.

According to the consultant's design, all one hundred jacks were systematically arranged within the forty-five-foot-diameter base area and positioned to provide the five innermost beams with 90 percent of the lighthouse load. Also, the one hundred pre-positioned jacks were arranged into the required three zones for anticipated horizontal movement. Zone One, toward the leading edge of the circular base, contained thirty-six jacks; Zone Two and Zone Three shared the remaining area with thirty-two jacks in each. To guard against the possibility of multiple jack failures, each zone was further divided so as to supply every second jack from a different hydraulic circuit. According to Pete's cell-creation idea, Zone One contained six separate hydraulic circuits, all supplying non-adjacent jacks; Zone Two and Zone Three each contained five circuits supplying non-adjacent jacks. Thus, while somewhat lacking in jack power, Pete now had the redundancy he needed for safety. One hundred jacks supplied with a moderate pressure of 6,000 psi would provide approximately 6,000 tons of lifting capacity beneath 5,000 tons of load. If all went well, they could utilize lower pressures; if necessary, they could compensate for jack failures by increasing pressure to other circuits.

Above and horizontally perpendicular to the main beams came fifteen pieces of cross-steel on four-foot centers, each piece a 14WF145 steel beam with experience on previous heavy moves. Together, the cross-steel and mains formed a 72' by 60' grid supporting the lighthouse. For added rigidity, four thirty-six-inch-deep strong-back beams were welded at their corners to form a stabilizing box around the grid. By late May, more than five hundred tons of supporting steel were in place beneath the four remaining courses of granite plinth. According to Pete's calculations, a total load of 4,800 tons had to be raised seven feet to allow for insertion of roll-track beams and creeper-dollies to carry Cape Hatteras Light safely home. *Derch denche.*

After settling into accommodations near Cape Hatteras in the spring of 1999, Pete donned his consultant's hardhat and re-introduced himself to the jobsite and his fellow workers. After meeting with Park Service facility manager Dan McClarren and ICC's site supervisor Skellie Hunt, Pete happily reconnected with his fellow Houseketeers. George Gardner had been on site since day one and now offered Pete an armload of his latest drawings and blueprints for their mutual review. Once reacquainted with the paperwork, Pete helped Jerry Matyiko and his Experts assemble a truckload of new toys recently arrived from Bill Jahns. Along with a huge shiny-red UHJU came six large hydraulic manifolds, three small hydraulic manifolds, two five-horsepower hydraulic power packs, and five six-foot-long push-rams rated at thirty tons each. Batteries were not included.

Eventually mounted on a gantry constructed atop the main beam extensions at the rear of the load, the shiny new jacking unit was a monstrous sight to behold. Containing all the latest bells and whistles, it featured an expansive control panel for operation of a very large master piston and sixty slave circuits. The master cylinder measured five feet in length and eighteen inches in diameter; the slave cylinders were five feet in length and slightly more than two inches in diameter. Built especially for the Cape Hatteras project, this big red machine was designed to do far more than just push hydraulic fluid. Weighing in at 36,000 pounds and costing $250,000, "Big Red" remains a one-of-a-kind specialty item. Hoses are not included.

*The 78-year-old project consultant and Big Red, the latest version of his 45-year-old invention.*

Using fifty of the sixty available slave circuits, all one hundred jacks were connected to Big Red through simple line-splitters. To safeguard against possible failures, individual jacks of each pairing were located some distance apart within the overall jack arrangement. Also, for safety and ease of operation, numerical identification and color-coding were applied to all components within the hydraulic circuitry. Supplying sufficient quantities of hydraulic fluid was Expert House Movers' custom-made provider "The Blue Monster"—a fifty-gallon tank and a large diesel engine driving six hydraulic pumps. By early June, everything was in place. It was time to jack the lighthouse high enough to insert creeper-dollies and roll-tracks.

This phase of the project did not begin well. Very soon after Matyiko first engaged hydraulic pressure, a significant fluid leak developed behind the jacking-unit control panel. When all attempts failed to rectify the fault, the call went out to Elburn, Illinois. Within hours, Bill Jahns and sons were on the job in Cape Hatteras, replacing a multitude of small swivel connections in their new jacking machine system. About half of these small components, from one particular supplier, proved to be defective. Thirty-six hours later, the repair was complete, and the repairmen headed back home. This would be the only problem with the new jacking machine on this job, and it was the only time Bill Jahns got to visit the jobsite. "I regret it now," Bill recalls. "I wish we had stayed around for more of the spectacle, but we were a small family business, and we had fallen behind with our other customers while we were building the new machine over the previous six months ... we had to get back."

After proper parts were installed, the jacking-unit control lever was again selected downward, and high-pressure hydraulic fluid was directed to a master piston that mechanically extended the slave pistons. With control panel valves set accordingly, the jacking unit supplied unified pressure through splitter manifolds to each of the one hundred jack rams that extended downward against their crib piles and raised the load. After several short jack extensions to properly shim all beams tight and level against bottom of the lighthouse, the load was then raised in increments of twelve inches over a four-day period. Between twelve-inch lift cycles, independent safety cribs supported the load while jack rams were reset. Jacking-unit pressure gauges now confirmed the total load at 4,830 tons, of which 430 tons were steel load beams.

When the necessary elevation had been attained, the lighthouse movers inserted roll-track beams directly beneath and parallel to the main load beams. Each of the seven roll-track sections was a welded pair of 14WF145 beams topped with a plate of hardened T-1 steel. Placed on top of this crib-supported roll-track, one hundred Hilman creeper-dollies, each capable of carrying seventy-five tons, were attached to the one hundred downward-projecting jack rams. With hydraulic pressure re-applied, the jack rams accepted the load from shoring towers, and safety cribs were soon removed. At this point, the 1.25 million bricks and thirty-six remaining granite plinth blocks of Cape Hatteras Light were perched atop fifteen cross-steel beams sitting across seven main load beams containing one hundred hydraulic jacks riding on one hundred creeper-dollies about to roll along seven roll-tracks being supported by nine thousand crib blocks standing on ten inches of steel matting resting on two layers of yellow pine timbers in the wet sand of Hatteras Island. *Visualize.*

Before moving forward, several outstanding factors required attention. First and foremost, the road ahead needed work: having been expertly graded and well compacted across its hundred-foot width, the 2,900-foot corridor needed additional help to properly support the roll-tracks. For this purpose, ten-inch beams were spot-welded together in groups of five in lengths of thirty and forty feet. Placed end-to-end across the move corridor, these grouped beams distributed the 4,830-ton load as evenly as possible. Spacer bars, welded horizontally perpendicular between these five-beam sections stabilized the steel matting and served as guides for accurate placement of the roll-tracks above them. Once the lighthouse was moved far enough forward, the seventy-foot lengths of similar grouped-beam matting would be lifted from the bottom of the excavation and added to the collection of cross matting to be leapfrogged ahead of the traveling lighthouse.

Preparations were also in progress behind the lighthouse, where the five large push-rams were mounted onto the five innermost roll-track extensions. As usual, the push-ram cylinders were attached to the load, while their ram ends were affixed to the roll-tracks. In this case, each cylinder base was bolted to the aft end of its main load beam while its ram tip, instead of being pinned to a bracket assembly, was contained by the Houseketeers' most recent invention. Their new "Jack-in-the-Box" was exactly that—a 150-ton hydraulic jack within a square steel housing. Clamped firmly to the roll-track, the box would anchor the ram piston that pushed the load forward under pressure. Applying and releasing hydraulic pressure at the five boxes would be far more time-effective than the customary chore of undoing and re-tightening scores of bolts each time push-rams were reset. For identification purposes, the five push-rams were given names: the centermost push-ram was named *Mr. Pete* in honor of the project's consultant, and those either side were named *Johnny, Joe, Jim,* and *Jerry,* honoring, in order of seniority, the four Matyiko brothers on the jobsite. Sons of company founder "Big John," they were the eldest of nineteen Matyiko family members on Expert's fifty-five-person Cape Hatteras crew.

*A hydraulic-actuated "jack-in-the-box" push-ram anchor on a roll-track.*

Before pushing off, however, the lighthouse movers needed to change their hydraulic configuration from the unified pressure of jacking mode to the three zones of independent common pressure required for horizontal travel. In the early years, conversion from unified lifting mode to three-zone travel mode required a lot of mucking around underneath the load with jacks and hoses, and sometimes with cribs and dollies. Pete's second-edition jacking machine of the late 1950s was quick to offer an additional circuit to facilitate the unifying procedure; however, transition to three-zone loading remained pretty much a manual affair. While later editions of his machine, such as Expert's well-traveled nineteen-circuit "Old Faithful," could accomplish the pre-loading procedure at the control panel, transition to three-zone travel mode usually entailed considerable equipment adjustment beneath the load. Here at Cape Hatteras was the latest and greatest in jacking machines. Big Red could do it all! By manipulating 120 circuit valves and twenty-nine zoning valves—and other magical things—a trained operator could quickly transform all hydraulic circuitry from the unified lifting mode to the three-zone travel mode. Presto! It was soon done without any mucking around down below.

In final preparation for impending horizontal movement, two portable

power packs—each a five-horsepower engine and a five-gallon tank—
supplied hydraulic pressure to clamp each Jack-in-the-Box to its roll-track
extension behind the load. To power the push-rams, sixteen outlets from
Expert's faithful nineteen-circuit jacking machine were routed in groups of
four through a collector manifold to each of the four primary ram cylinders.
*Johnny, Joe, Jim*, and *Jerry* would push the load forward with unified pressure,
while *Mr. Pete* went along as a standby. While the two power packs were
hand-carried, Old Faithful would follow along on a truckbed, and Big Red
would travel on its gantry affixed to the main load.

At 3:05 PM on June 17, 1999, Jerry Matyiko pushed gently downward
on the control lever of Old Faithful, and the Cape Hatteras Lighthouse
moved four inches in a southwesterly direction. After a satisfactory
equipment check, two five-foot push cycles were completed on that first
day. Seventy feet of progress on the second day saw the lighthouse clear
of its old foundation and onto solid ground, where progress proved
better than expected. Thanks primarily to efficiency of the Jack-in-the-
Box invention, the lighthouse rolled along at an average speed of one
foot per minute, as opposed to the anticipated rate of one inch per
minute. Further, the ride was extremely smooth; personnel riding inside
the light tower reported no sense of movement whatsoever.

*Behind the lighthouse load, used roll-track sections are unbolted and leapfrogged ahead while*
*push-rams are adjusted forward. The Blue Monster hydraulic provider sits at the left end of*
*the gantry while Big Red the jacking machine sits to the right under protective tarpaulins.*

While the road crew ensured a continuous supply of steel matting and roll-track out front, the back-end crew settled into rhythm with their 120 tons of unified hydraulic pressure: releasing and resetting track clamps; pressurizing and depressurizing push rams; pushing and rolling their heavy load forward ... five feet at a time. Suddenly, the klaxon wailed, and telephones started ringing all the way to Northbrook, Illinois. The monitoring system had detected a gross variance in verticality—the lighthouse was tilting beyond acceptable limits! With the operation at a standstill, Matyiko and Pete immediately consulted a plumb bob hanging from base of the lantern deck down through the spiral staircase within the tower. When it pointed directly to the center point of the concrete floor below, the lighthouse movers knew they were still in business. Further investigation revealed a small electric wire from one of the fifty-six electronic sensors had been severed by seventy-five tons of creeper-dolly. The show was soon back on the road, aided by a 180-foot plumb bob hanging calmly in place.

*The "Move of the Century" in progress:*
*steel matting and roll-tracks being laid out*
*before the 208-foot tower of 1.25 million bricks.*

At 1:23 PM on July 9, 1999, the Cape Hatteras Lighthouse arrived over top of its new concrete footing, 2,900 feet from its original site.

For the first time in 130 years, it was again 1,500 feet away from the voracious waves of the Atlantic. With daily progress ranging between zero and 355 feet, the lighthouse had traveled an average of 130 feet per day. Once again, the Three Houseketeers had successfully completed a mission many professional engineers had proclaimed impossible. Unbeknownst to twenty thousand cheering spectators and scores of media personnel, the twenty-three-day odyssey had not been without incident. Nine of the one hundred hydraulic jacks beneath the lighthouse had failed along the way. Fortunately, because of the crew's experienced professionalism and because of the project consultant's commitment to safety, there were no adverse effects.

"Well, Pete, I heard you were good, but I had no idea you were this good," commented Jerry Stockbridge, the sensor guy, with an outstretched hand. "There is not one new crack in the brickwork anywhere … and the old cracks haven't grown a hair."

"Thanks, Jerry," responded Pete. "I'm happy about what I could do here, but it takes more than one person … we had many of the best people on this job."

During the next several weeks, while the lighthouse was being jacked down to its proper elevation, numerous media reports toasted success of the engineering feat in newspapers and on television. Among these many reports and special features, a heartfelt letter from a Susanna Rodell to the editor of the *Raleigh News and Observer* found its way onto the National Park Service Web site. It aptly summarizes public perspective on the Cape Hatteras Lighthouse relocation:

> I was watching a mammoth act of human will, a huge, unusual effort being made to save something solely because of its place in our emotions, in our collective history. It was, and is, an enormous act of love. All these humans—from the guys in hardhats driving the forklifts to the members of all the historical societies to the engineers to the Park Service folks—are working their hearts out … Watching the operation, you can't help thinking about the pyramids. It does the heart good to know that here in the late twentieth century people are still willing to put all this collective wisdom and energy—not to mention millions of bucks—working to save something that's really just

a symbol, not religious, not political, just something tall and grand and old that has stood there all those years delivering the purest gift imaginable—Light!

Understandably, everyone involved in the project wanted the relocated lighthouse to be at least as durable as the original. Accordingly, a 60' by 60' concrete footing, four feet thick and heavily reinforced with epoxy-coated rebar, was the substitute for Stetson's original yellow-pine anchor. On top of this footing, gazillions of paver-type masonry blocks would be mortared together into a solid foundation, duplicating the original foundation of layered granite block. However, several weeks into this phase of construction, the twelve masons and six laborers so employed were suddenly called off the job.

Hurricane Dennis hit the Outer Banks on August 29, 1999 ... and it hit hard! The original site of the Cape Hatteras Lighthouse was soon totally overwhelmed by the ocean. At its new location, awash in more than a foot of seawater, the refugee lighthouse survived the five-day storm with only a few broken windows. Returning to the ravaged jobsite in hip-waders, Stockbridge found fifty-six electronic sensors in complete ruin, and at the miniature weather station atop the lantern casement, he found his anemometer snapped in half—the last recorded wind reading was 128 miles per hour.

The partially completed lighthouse base was already as wind-resistant as the original. Between subsequent seasonal storms, masonry workers finished bricking in the new foundation and removed the last of the shoring towers and cross-steel beams. Once the lowest course of original granite plinth was placed atop the completed foundation, everything below was covered by a back-fill of very sandy soil. Looking as good as new and as good as ever, the Cape Hatteras Lighthouse went back into service with a ceremonial relighting on the evening of November 13, 1999. Two thousand-watt rotating lamps once again flash a white light—every seven-and-a-half seconds—across Diamond Shoals and far beyond. While the Coast Guard continues to operate Cape Hatteras Light as a maritime navigation aid, the National Park Service manages the lighthouse structure as a National Historic Site within a coastal recreation area now attracting more than 2 million visitors annually.

First envisioned in the 1930s and dedicated twenty years later,

Cape Hatteras National Seashore was a learning experience for all concerned. While simultaneously redefining its own mandate, the Park Service invented and introduced a new protected-area designation that became successfully integrated into the national conscience as well as the national parks system. Along the way, politicians and government agencies at all levels were compelled to reevaluate priorities and confront changing values. In the process of battling the Atlantic Ocean for control of barrier-island real estate, the government, the Park Service, and their engineers gradually came to understand the true power of their adversary. Defending one section of beach invariably contributed to heavier losses at another. As finally became apparent, they were not being overwhelmed by erosion; they were being exhausted by an endless supply of sand being transferred laterally along the coast by wind and current—deposition. While constantly changing shape, the barrier islands of North Carolina also move incrementally landward, as high winds and over-wash inexorably transfer coastal detritus across the low-lying land onto its leeward side. Regardless of North Carolina's desires and America's intent, Mother Nature will continue pushing the Outer Banks westward at a rate of approximately five feet per calendar year.

The 200-mile arc of these barrier islands has been a learning curve for everyone. Gradually, residents of the eastern seaboard have come to accept the ocean they live beside. Finally, most people see the Atlantic as not their enemy. It is just doing what the ocean does. Here as elsewhere, people are becoming concerned about the ocean and its health; after all, it is a major component of the natural system supporting ourselves and everything we cherish. Throughout Cape Hatteras National Seashore, park rangers, signboards, and interpretive centers freely share ocean-awareness information while celebrating the nation's maritime heritage.

When Cape Hatteras Lighthouse reopened to the public in early 2000, the senior class from Cape Hatteras High School was the first organized group to climb its 258 steps. According to current rates of beach transference, at least one hundred more graduating classes and many more millions of park-goers will have a similar opportunity before the iconic black-and-white tower again becomes a candidate for relocation. While unable to accurately predict the presence of people or the state of the public will in 2099, we already know appropriate technology exists to save this and any other cherished lighthouse from the sea. In the meantime, the 1999 relocation of Cape Hatteras Lighthouse has attracted worldwide recognition and a number of very significant engineering awards as the "Move of the Century."

The *Guinness Book of World Records* recognized Cape Hatteras Light as the Tallest and Farthest lighthouse move of all time. The American Consulting Engineers Council honored the Cape Hatteras relocation project with its Grand Award for excellence in engineering design. The IASM honored the Three Houseketeers—ICC, Expert House Movers, and Friesen Consulting—by presenting them with its IASM Millennium Award. Having designated Cape Hatteras Lighthouse a National Historic Civil Engineering Landmark, the American Society of Civil Engineers (ASCE) also honored the lighthouse relocation team with the nation's most prestigious engineering award, the Opal.

Inviting the Cape Hatteras relocation team to the Opal 2000 awards ceremony, ASCE President Delon Hampton wrote, "No gathering of Engineering's brightest and best would be complete without you, Pete Friesen."

*The Opal: annual award for engineering excellence presented by ASCE to the team of professionals who successfully relocated Cape Hatteras Lighthouse.*

# 18

# Newark

For generations unknown, the Lenni Lenape people comfortably inhabited a verdant plain on the east coast of America where they found rich nourishment in several large tidal estuaries and in the forest beyond. Augmenting seasonal rounds of subsistence-gathering with agriculture in the form of maize, beans, and squash, the Algonkian-speaking Lenape nation was once comprised of fifteen thousand people living in eighty semi-permanent sites. Known to be easygoing folks who often mediated disputes among their Algonkian neighbors, the Lenape were also known for their willingness to engage in trade, even with the pale-faced beings arriving from across the eastern sea. Descendants of the Lenape who had paddled out to meet Giovanni da Verrazzano in 1524 traded with the Dutch settlers who followed Henry Hudson into their tidal domain three generations later. Unfamiliar with the European concept of land ownership, one Lenape tribe traded away agricultural rights on their rocky Manhattan Island territory to colonists of New Netherland. Three generations later, having become known as Delaware Indians, the Lenape People all but disappeared, consumed by disease and warfare.

Established in 1613 and fortified twelve years later, the Dutch fur-trading post on Manhattan was incorporated as the city of New Amsterdam in 1653. Twenty years later, as a result of wars mostly fought elsewhere, the New Netherland colony defaulted to control of the British Crown, and the city of New Amsterdam was promptly renamed New York. After eliminating Dutch influence in North America, England reorganized its New World holdings: during the closing decades of the seventeenth century, colonial boundaries were drawn and redrawn, governors were moved and removed, and colonial assemblies were disbanded and reactivated. From the city of New York, an appointed governor and his appointed council administered the province of New York. Eventually, a small colonial assembly elected from and by the colonists satisfied, at least in appearance, a constitutional clause regarding "no taxation without representation." By 1700, there were five thousand souls—mostly Dutch, English, and natives—inhabiting the islands at the mouth of Hudson's River, where a fine natural harbor hosted the colonies' largest destination for African slaves as well as a haven for English privateers who raided enemy shipping in western Atlantic sea lanes.

In 1754, Great Britain (England and Scotland united in 1707) launched an all-out offensive against France for control of the North American colonies. Known elsewhere as the Seven Years' War, this conflict was known in the British-American colonies as the French and Indian War. The British forces proved victorious, and under terms of the 1763 Treaty of Paris, France ceded Canada and all French territory east of the Mississippi River to Great Britain. Hoping to maintain peace with native peoples and preserve control of the fur trade, British authorities issued a proclamation by which the original thirteen colonies could not expand westward beyond the Appalachian divide. Angered by the loss of their western dreams and no longer in need of British protection against the threat of French Canada, the thirteen colonies grew increasingly disturbed about ever-increasing levels of taxation that funded European military campaigns. Spurred on by proto-patriotic organizations, the colonies each developed their own provincial congress in parallel with, and gradually replacing, official British administrative councils. Soon thereafter, a long-simmering fire erupted into a full-blown inferno. After the 1783 Treaty of Paris officially ended the War of Independence, the city of New York became the first capital of the United States.

Bolstered by post-war immigration of "Yankees" from New England, the city's population doubled by the turn of the nineteenth century. Having successfully rebelled against all territorial restraint, the United States expanded westward with unbridled fervor. Opening in 1825, the Erie Canal provided a vital transportation route to western lands of new opportunity. Funneling through New York, many newcomers to America found their land of opportunity right in New York City, where they discovered ready employment in scores of factories manufacturing all the necessities for life on the frontier.

By 1830, this city of two hundred thousand people had become North America's trade center. As a result of the Irish potato-famine diaspora, the city's population tripled in less than two decades. By 1880, widespread immigration from virtually everywhere had pushed the city population beyond 1 million. With the 1898 incorporation of neighboring boroughs—Brooklyn, Queens, the Bronx, and Staten Island—New York entered the twentieth century as a megacity of 3.5 million residents. In 1925, with almost 6 million inhabitants, New York would surpass London as the largest city in the world. While Manhattan grew skyward as a global financial center, all regions of the city were connected by improvements to transportation infrastructure: as inter-urban travel was facilitated through two major railroad stations, inter-borough rapid transit was introduced by beginnings of the city's vast subway system in 1904. While a network of tunnels and bridges catered to Henry Ford's latest creations out of Detroit, something was also needed to accommodate the Wright Brothers' recent accomplishments at Kitty Hawk. Tested above the trenches of WWI in Europe and proven by the new U.S. Air Mail service, the airplane had become an established fact of life by the early twentieth century. Aviation had arrived, and New York City needed an airport.

In 1928, construction of the city's first public airport began on sixty-eight acres of level swampland west of the Hudson River in the adjoining state of New Jersey. Officially opened later that year, the new airport would continue growing across the boundaries of two adjacent cities, Elizabeth and Newark. The latter city, having been incorporated in 1836, was the economic center and largest municipality in New Jersey. Located only nine miles from Manhattan's Central Post Office, Newark Airport became the eastern terminus for the U.S. Postal Service as well as the nation's first commercial airport. With completion of construction in 1931, Newark Airport celebrated the first paved runway, the first control tower, and the first airport weather station in the country, while also launching dedicated passenger service to the west coast—a thirty-six hour flight. The busiest airport in the United States, Newark was soon regarded as the busiest anywhere—handling approximately one-third of the world's passenger traffic. Commercial air travel was growing, and Newark Airport needed a passenger terminal.

When it opened for business in 1935, the passenger terminal at Newark Airport was considered the most modern of its time. Constructed with a $700,000 budget, it offered thirty-three thousand square feet of usable space on two floors, topped by an air traffic control tower. Referred to as International Modern design, its graceful Art Deco style featured extensive use of glass, steel, and concrete in a structure of simple geometry and minimal ornamentation. Appropriately, the main body of the building was appended on each side by angular wing-like annexes. Designated as Airport Building 51, it was the first air passenger terminal in the United States and second in the world, after one at London's Croydon Aerodrome built seven years prior. Dedicated by aviation pioneer Amelia Earhart, Building 51 became the centerpiece of America's busiest airport. Then, with the opening of LaGuardia Airport in 1939, New York's air traffic became split between two airports, and the distinction of busiest airport defaulted to Chicago's Midway International. Immediately thereafter, all passenger operations ceased at Newark while the U.S. Army used the airport as a logistical staging point during WWII.

At the conclusion of hostilities, responsibility for Newark Airport was transferred to the Port of New York Authority. Created in 1921 to resolve decades of intense inter-state conflict over use of the lower Hudson River and its harbors, this agency had overseen development of vehicle bridges and tunnels within its fifteen hundred square mile jurisdiction. Later renamed the Port Authority of New York and New Jersey, the agency would ultimately be responsible for most transportation facilities within the New York metropolitan area, including the three major airports—Newark, LaGuardia, and John F. Kennedy.

Facing dramatic growth in air travel during the early 1950s, the Port Authority began the first of many multi-million-dollar upgrades to their airports. With installation of runway lighting, Newark (call letters EWR) became the nation's first commercial airport fully certified for nighttime operation. Also necessary was a new $8.5 million terminal to replace the original Art Deco building, which was already proving inadequate. Early in the 1960s, the airport was expanded by an additional 325 acres. In the 1970s, two triple-tiered terminal buildings were constructed, and in the 1980s, a third terminal was added. In the 1990s, an airport monorail went into operation between terminals.

By1998, regional governments had invested more than $20 million and the Port Authority almost $2 billion in Newark Airport; this same year saw commencement of a $3.8 billion modernization plan for an airport now accommodating thirty air carriers and 30 million passengers per year. The seventy-year-old airfield was expanding yet again, and it would soon occupy two thousand acres of swampland, now politely known as New Jersey "meadowlands." By this time, the airport had been renamed Newark International Airport, and its original Art Deco terminal had been placed on the National Register of Historic Places. Housing airport administrative offices, Building 51 now sat directly in the path of necessary runway extension.

After determining the heritage building was sturdy enough for travel, the New Jersey State Preservation Office approved a three-quarter-mile relocation to another airport site, well clear of the runway extension. Coincidentally, the budget for relocating Building 51, arranged through the Federal Aviation Administration, equaled the $6 million figure required for construction of the original airport seventy years before. After receiving the green light, the Port Authority enlisted Prismatic Development Corporation of Fairfield, New Jersey, as general contractor for repositioning and incorporating the former terminal building into a new administrative complex. Prismatic soon contacted ICC, who soon contacted Expert House Movers, who were soon on the telephone to Friesen Consulting in Lynden, Washington.

$$* \quad * \quad * \quad *$$

"I dunno, Pete ... it just looks too big," said Jerry.

"Well, Jerry," Pete responded, "just think of it as a small job requiring more men and equipment."

Jerry Matyiko and Pete Friesen were standing on the roof of Building 51, surveying its 24,000 square-foot expanse and assessing its overall weight while attempting to visualize how it might reasonably be moved. It was the summer of 2000, one full year after these two structural movers had seen Cape Hatteras Lighthouse relocated to its new site. Now, from their rooftop vantage point at Newark International Airport, they recognized a familiar figure crossing the parking lot below. Carrying a large roll of original construction drawings and sporting a large grin, George Gardner looked up and waved toward the rooftop. The Three Houseketeers had accepted another "mission impossible." As subcontractor to Prismatic, ICC would oversee the relocation phase while engineering the necessary technical paperwork and doing the heavy masonry work. As now customary, Jerry Matyiko and his merry band of Expert House Movers would provide most of the equipment and physical labor while the project consultant, Pete Friesen, would be responsible for the overall concept and design of the move.

Although the project consultant had originally defended the feasibility of moving the long and angled structure in one piece, the Three Houseketeers ultimately decided in favor of ease and simplicity: the two wing-like annexes would be severed from the main body, permitting the old passenger terminal to be moved in three "easy" pieces. With concrete floors and two full stories, each 60' by 40' annex was expected to weigh about 1,300 tons; the 240' by 60' main section, containing a large foyer under the control tower and proportionally less concrete floor, was estimated to weigh 5,300 tons. In terms of total weight, the Newark move amounted to moving one Cape Hatteras Lighthouse and two Fairmount Hotels as parts of the same project.

Although by size alone, this project would tax their collective wisdom and ingenuity, the movers were upbeat and confident about safely moving Building 51. For one thing, they had seen the original drawings, and they were confident that man had built this building. More importantly, while working together during the past decade, they had seen their own design concepts and operational techniques prove successful on other large and complex relocation projects. They were a smooth-running team of experienced professionals using the best equipment available. Joined by scores of the most capable and hard-working practitioners in the business, they would get this job done ... somehow.

"So many good golf-weather days and so little time," mused seventy-eight-year-old Pete Friesen through his office window. Pete returned home and refined the master plan while Expert House Movers and ICC began positioning men and equipment at Newark International Airport in July 2000. As soon as the building had been vacated and stripped of interior furnishings, ICC and Expert went to work, and as usual, the object of their attention soon offered up a few surprises to challenge their best-laid plans. Off the top, when its waterproof membrane was removed, the building's concrete roof was discovered to be far thicker in places than imagined: its drainage slope had been incorporated into concrete castings that were four inches thick at the eaves and sixteen inches thick near the peak; it weighed almost two hundred pounds per square-foot in places. This discovery prompted hasty revisions to the load plan in order to accommodate an increase in overall weight and to provide additional support beneath central portions of each roof section.

Another surprise came when the ICC crew put their diamond-studded cable saw to work: unlike many older heritage buildings they had moved, this more modern structure had a frame of concrete strengthened with rebar. Immersed within the concrete frame, many of these steel rods also extended into adjacent building sections for structural integrity; therefore, they would complicate the process of cutting vertical separation lines between the wings and center section. Yet another surprise was discovered underneath the building: an unconventional arrangement of supporting columns demanded unforeseen modifications to their plan for severing the structure from its concrete footings.

Of even greater concern was the water table that lay only a few feet below the footings: excavating in the porous meadowlands soil demanded constant use of diesel-driven pumps to keep the water level at a workable depth. The high water table inspired some creative thinking among the structural movers. Fortunately, the design of Building 51 was conducive to such thinking: it rested on concrete grade beams— two interior beams on the long axis plus the four under perimeter walls—all of sufficient depth to permit insertion of their twenty-four-inch-deep main load beams within the same vertical profile; that is, bottom edges of the main beams would be level with bottom surfaces of the grade beams. As such, twenty-four inches of main-beam space would be incorporated within the building's vertical profile rather than occupying a layer beneath it. By reversing their normal procedure and placing cross-steel *beneath* their main beams, the building movers could avoid digging several more feet below the water table. Surrounded by life-threatening challenges, these people were not interested in draining a swamp.

With a plan in place, excavations intensified around the building's east wing that was to be the first section moved. Because of its angle of attachment, this wing's longest outside wall measured almost eighty feet when severed from the center section. As soon as there was room to work, four one-hundred-foot main load beams were maneuvered into position, each one a pair of twenty-four-inch-deep wide-flanged steel beams weighing 162 pounds per linear foot welded together with a space between for inverted jacks (2X24WF162). Containing forty heavy-duty hydraulic jacks positioned in accordance with the consultant's determination of the wing's weight and center of gravity, the four main beams were shuffled into place: one was slightly outside the front wall, one was slightly outside the rear wall, and two were inserted through notches in the end-wall grade beam and parallel to the interior grade beams.

Beneath and horizontally perpendicular to the main beams came eight sixty-foot cross-steel beams, each being two 14WF145 beams stitch-welded side-by-side with a narrow space between. Because of the building's solid reinforced-concrete framework, the cross-steel beams could be placed on eight-foot centers, instead of the more usual four-foot spacing, while maintaining the necessary degree of load distribution. Anchored by short lengths of square steel tubing placed above the main beams and below these cross-steel beams, threaded steel rods were then inserted through the narrow space between and outside each cross-steel pair. Thus, with three at each main-beam intersection, forty-eight of these "Williams" rods held the eight cross-steel beams in place. With the cross-steel snugged tight against bottom of the main beams, a stable 100' by 60' lifting platform was in place beneath the 1,300-ton east wing.

Within the structure, measures were taken to deal with the weight of the concrete roof. Through a shoring and bracing network of steel posts, jacks, beams, and crib blocks, the roof's weight was distributed across both floors and transferred down to the load beams. With everything secure inside and below, the task of raising the east wing began. Forty heavy-duty hydraulic jacks, inverted and inserted in the duplex main beams, were connected to the Big Red jacking machine of Cape Hatteras fame. Utilizing forty of Big Red's sixty slave circuits, the forty jacks were arranged in three distinct lifting zones identified by the project consultant's design. A far cry from the fifteen-ton crib jacks Pete designed in the 1950s, the new generation of large-bore lifting devices can raise fifty tons when supplied hydraulic pressure at a nominal 5,000 psi; with 6,000 psi, they will lift sixty tons, and if pushed by necessity, they are capable of seventy tons and beyond ... albeit to the detriment of stressed seals and diminished life expectancy. Pressurized to 5,000 psi, the forty jacks under the east wing were essentially fifty-ton jacks with a total lifting capacity of two thousand tons, offering a healthy 50 percent safety factor for raising the 1,300-ton structure.

With Expert's custom-made hydraulic provider, the Blue Monster, ensuring an ample supply of fluid, the Big Red jacking machine provided forty circuits of unified pressure to forty strong jacks that would easily handle a mere 1,300 tons. Nevertheless, it still required several tedious days of hucking blocks and resetting jacks to raise the load, fourteen inches at a time, to the required height of eight feet above grade for inserting two more layers of steel and forty transport dollies.

Although the decision to place the cross-steel under the main beams had kept the operation out of deep water, it necessitated an extra layer of steel for proper alignment of the dollies; otherwise, the necessary dolly-top rocker beams would be parallel to the cross-steel beams instead of perpendicular. To compensate, four one-hundred-foot spacer beams were inserted beneath and perpendicular to the cross-steel beams; each spacer beam was three 10WF54 beams welded side-by-side. For maximum support, these flimsy spacer beams were positioned directly below and parallel to the main load beams. The amount of vertical space consumed by these ten-inch-thick spacer beams was far more acceptable than having the twenty-four-inch-thick main beams protrude below the grade beams, notwithstanding the substantial depth of additional excavation required to get them there.

Beneath and horizontally perpendicular to the four spacer beams, ten sixty-foot rocker beams, each a welded pair of 14WF145 beams, were placed atop ten rows of transport dollies. As such, each row of four dollies became a united and stabilized unit, and the ten rows of dollies were properly aligned perpendicular to the main load beams. Composed of twelve self-propelled units and twenty-eight non-powered units, the forty-dolly formation was then made road-worthy by connection of all steering tongues, via lengths of linked chain, to come-along winches for directional control. Ready to roll, the 80' by 40' two-story east wing of Building 51 was sitting on four duplex main beams and eight duplex cross-steel beams resting on four triplex spacer beams and ten duplex rocker beams riding on forty hydraulic jacks carried by forty transport dollies on 320 wheels. *Visualize.*

*Rear view of a self-propelled transport dolly with jack ram extended beneath rocker beams, spacer beams, and cross-steel beams secured by threaded steel rods to the main load beams above.*

Adjustments at the jacking machine control panel soon converted the hydraulic circuitry from the unified-pressure lifting phase to three zones of independent common pressure for the transport phase. With the weight of support beams and dollies added to the weight of the heavy shoring within, the total load was now about 1,400 tons; as such, it was twice the weight of Liebermann's Jewelers in Joliet, where Pete had initially applied his three-zone loading principle to dollies in 1976. One late-fall day in 2000, the east wing of Building 51 nonchalantly separated from its central core and motored serenely away to a semi-remote storage area where it would remain perched on crib piles. In due course, after weeks of intense labor, the west wing was similarly raised from its footings and moved to storage. Awaiting the relocation of their main body section and their subsequent reattachment, both wings were "waiting in the wings."

Meanwhile, the center section had become somewhat longer than first envisioned. When the angled wing sections were separated, twenty feet of their interiors had to remain attached to both ends of the center. Still sixty feet wide, the center section was now 280 feet long. While its footprint was almost identical to Chicago's Armitage Plaza mall that Pete had moved with Dell Davis ten years prior, this load was almost ten times heavier. With a glassed-in air traffic control tower sitting atop two-and-a-half stories of heritage building being moved almost three-quarters of a mile on rubber tires, this job would be far more demanding than sliding a one-story shopping center a distance of sixty-six feet. In fact, the steel beams used beneath this one building section weighed twice as much as that entire shopping mall. Forecast at almost 7,000 tons total load, this center section of Newark Airport's sixty-five-year-old passenger terminal would be the heaviest structural relocation ever attempted by Pete Friesen.

Although far grander in scope, the procedure for moving the main body of Building 51 was very similar to that used for removing its two wing-sections. After the control tower was braced and protected, an extraordinary amount of internal shoring was installed to distribute and transfer weight of the heavy concrete roof. After excavating around the structure and completing preparations beneath it, the Experts inserted their load beams. The four main beams were identical in design to those used for the wing sections, each one a welded pair of 24WF162 beams with space between for jacks. Fashioned by bolting various-length sections end to end and installed flush with the bottoms of the grade beams, these four main beams were similarly located: one 280-foot twin beam outside the front wall, one 280-foot twin beam outside the rear wall, and two 300-foot twin beams within the building footprint parallel to the grade beams. Outfitted with their share of inverted jacks and weighing about forty-six tons each, the four very long main beams were eventually wrestled into place. Beneath and horizontally perpendicular came thirty-six seventy-five-foot pieces of cross-steel on eight-foot centers, each piece being two 14WF145 beams stitch-welded with a narrow space between. Anchored by short lengths of square steel tubing placed above the mains and below the cross-steel, 432 lengths of threaded Williams rod snugged tight a 22,500-square-foot lifting platform beneath the center section of Newark's original passenger terminal.

Designed with two vertical expansion seams, this building's center section demanded more protection than its shorter wing components. In order to counter the inherent flexibility allowed by these rubberized expansion joints, four strong-back beams were positioned around base of the center section and tightened against the exterior of all four walls; each of these four strong-backs was a welded pair of thirty-six-inch beams, each single beam weighing 250 pounds per linear foot (36WF250). Welded together at the corners and secured to top surfaces of the main load beams, they provided a rigid, boxlike container to prevent undesirable movement within the structure during its journey. Not counting weight of the nuts and bolts and clamps and welds required to keep them in place, the four duplex strong-back beams alone added 160 tons to the overall load. Adding in 400 tons of cross-steel and 190 tons of main beam and jacks, there were now 750 tons of steel already affixed to the center section of Building 51. Incredible as it might seem, the weight of these steel support beams *alone* was one hundred tons more than the combined load of the Armitage Plaza shopping center and its supporting steel.

Here at Newark International Airport, with 750 tons of steel beams supporting the center section of old Building 51, it was jacking time again. According to his calculations for weight and center of gravity, the project consultant's plan called for 164 heavy-duty jacks now strategically located along the four main load beams. As one might expect, more jacks were assigned to the heavier wall and roof areas of their respective zones. For safety, each of the three "loading zones" received hydraulic pressure from several different circuits. The sixty slave circuits of Big Red would provide unified pressure through simple splitters to 120 of the 164 jacks that were all now in place.

As premiered at Detroit's Gem Theatre in 1997 and as performed several times since, the project consultant once again augmented his three zones of unified pressure with three separate circuits of regulated common pressure. While 120 jacks remained under control of the jacking unit, the other forty-four jacks were divided among three additional, self-contained hydraulic systems, each of which supplied common pressure to numerous jacks in one of three established lift-zones. Interspersed among the unified jacks, these forty-four common-pressure jacks were allocated according to lift requirements while being located apart from other similar helper jacks in the same zone or circuit. Automatic regulators in each helper system maintained its circuit pressure identical to that of its unified zone; therefore, all jacks in any one zone worked in unison, be they unified or common. The three separate helper circuits added safety to the overall jacking system while the ratio of three unified jacks for each common-pressure jack kept it manageable. Planning to utilize pressures of about 5,500 psi from their jacking machine and helper circuits, the movers would have 164 jacks pushing fifty-five tons for a total lifting capacity of 9,020 tons under a load that was now estimated at about 6,000 tons in total weight. The safety factor was 50 percent.

Jerry Matyiko selected the jacking-unit control lever downward: down went the jack rams and up went two-and-a-half stories of concrete-framed construction in a steady and balanced manner. According to jacking-machine pressure readings, the 750 tons of steel were supporting 5,400 tons of building and interior shoring towers. After the mandatory systems check, each dual-action jack ram was then retracted upwards, one at a time, while its crib pile was built higher against it. Once Big Red's master cylinder had been recharged with fluid, its control lever could initiate another lift. Thus, in a multitude of twelve-inch cycles over a period of several days, Building 51's center-section load was gradually elevated eight feet above the soggy ground. Bring on the dollies!

Between carefully positioned rows of crib piles, 116 non-powered dollies and 48 self-propelled dollies were wrangled into position beneath the center section of Building 51. According to the consultant's precise load calculations, 164 dollies were arranged in twenty-three rows containing six, seven, or eight dollies each. In anticipation of the long journey ahead, all powered dollies were positioned for ease of access and overall balance of driving power. Coincident with placement of the dollies came insertion of spacer beams to properly orient the dolly formation and also rocker beams to stabilize each row. Two 280-foot spacer beams were inserted beneath and perpendicular to the cross-steel and positioned directly below and parallel to the outside main load beams; two 300-foot spacer beams were aligned beneath the interior main beams. Similar to those used under the wing sections, these spacer beams consisted of three 10WF54 beams welded side by side. Being almost five times longer, these four spacer beams added more than sixty tons to the main-section load.

Beneath and horizontally perpendicular to the spacer beams, an eighty-five-foot rocker beam was placed across each row of dolly jacks. Similar to those used under the wing sections, each of these rocker beams was a welded pair of 14WF145 beams; being far more numerous, these twenty-three rocker beams added nearly 300 tons to the total main-section load. Once each rocker beam was in place, its share of the load was transferred to the dolly-borne jacks being pressurized beneath it. Gradually, row-by-row, the 5,400-ton structure plus about 1,100 tons of attendant steel were transferred to 164 jack rams riding on 164 eight-wheeled dollies.

Winter had arrived. Laboring with ice-cold steel and freezing equipment, workers were soon wearing thick mittens along with their felt-lined work boots and heavy parkas; under their hardhats, toques and ear-warmers were necessary items of daily dress. After weeks of cold and hard labor, 164 transport dollies and twenty-seven large pieces of supplementary steel were finally shimmed, shimmied, and secured under the center section of Building 51. It was time for horizontal movement. Tire pressures were checked, and all dolly axles were accurately aligned in the direction of first travel. From the self-propelled dollies, yards of hydraulic hose were strapped out of harm's way and connected to their independent power units already affixed to the load. Also onboard were the power units and hydraulic reservoirs of the three helper systems, their separate circuits now supplying common pressure to forty-four helper jacks now mounted on dollies.

Of course, Big Red was going along for the ride, providing unified pressure through slave circuits and splitters to 120 of the dolly-mounted jacks. When the time was right, Jerry Matyiko made the appropriate selections at the control panel: almost instantly and somewhat magically, Big Red's sixty slave circuits and their 120 hydraulic jacks were converted from the unified lifting mode to three separate zones of independent common pressure for transit. Equally quick and amazing, the automatic regulators in each of the three helper-systems adjusted to the common pressure in its particular zone, and wherever they were located, each of the forty-four helper jacks maintained the same pressure as the primary jacks in its zone. It was time for the pre-taxi checklist.

| | |
|---|---|
| Triple-Assist Three-Point Loading | ENGAGED |
| Jacking Control | NEUTRAL |
| Main Hydraulics | SELECTED ON |
| Jacking Unit Pressure | NORMAL |
| Hydraulic Quantity | FULL |
| Assist Pumps | THREE ON |
| Assist Pressures | ALL NORMAL |
| Dolly Drive Pumps | ALL ON |
| Dolly Angle | CHECKED & SET |
| Safety Cribs | ALL CLEAR |

Pre-Taxi Checklist Complete

"Clear to remove wheel chocks!" called the pilot. It was a strange-looking craft that taxied away from parking at the northeast corner of Newark International Airport on that cold winter's day. Even the most ardent of plane watchers were quick to admit they had never seen anything quite like this bird. It had no wings and one offset glassy eye—surely, it wouldn't fly!

With no aerodynamic pretense and oblivious to all such flighty comment, Newark's 1935-model B-51 "Art Deco" rolled resolutely onto the taxiway ... sideways. Observed from a distance by airport fence-huggers and by several air traffic controllers through binoculars, it was a vehicle of unfamiliar design. It was a huge machine with a heavy-looking undercarriage. There were no engines to be seen, but there it was maneuvering onto the taxiway under its own power.

Accompanied by a small army of animated attendants, waving arms and exhaling bursts of white vapor from beneath plastic hats, the self-powered terminal building eventually altered its power vector and began accelerating westward along the taxiway ... lengthways. Gaining momentum, it was soon eating up asphalt at a rate of about one hundred feet every hour or so, being held straight and level by a very old pilot, boldly yanking on chains attached to his multi-wheeled undercarriage. Only he and his stalwart crew fully understood the true beauty of their westbound craft: one interior-braced 5,400-ton building section mounted on 1,100 tons of steel beams riding on 300 tons of jacks and dollies— 6,800 tons total—rolling along on 1,312 rubber tires. Occasionally, the chain-yanking pilot would raise his attention from steering duties and peer toward the northwest where new airport construction was blocking the taxiway and forcing a revision to his flight-planned route. Having for many months visualized this strange configuration he now steered toward destination, Pete Friesen was still busy *thinking it through.*

*The 280-foot main section of Building 51
rolling toward home on 1,312 rubber tires.*

They arrived in early spring. Utilizing several of his trademark, non-aerobatic, dolly routines, Pete avoided the new construction hazard and smoothly "slithered" the B-51 into its parking place. Once on its new foundation, the center body welcomed back its two wing sections for reconnection followed by two years of serious rehabilitation and detailed refurbishment. Magnificently restored, the original Newark Airport passenger terminal has been reborn. As the attractive front section of a 100,000-square-foot administration center, now appropriately designated as Airport Building One, its clean exterior lines extend smoothly to an Art Deco interior of marble floors and period design. It truly is a beautiful building, belying its age with renewed purpose. As well as housing major airport services, Building One provides office space for a large sector of the New York and New Jersey Port Authority's administrative staff. Beneath its old domed control tower, Building One's expansive foyer now reflects the nation's aviation history with plaques commemorating significant events and paying tribute to many aviation pioneers, such as Amelia Earhart.

*Building One's 400-foot front wall—Frank Loprano.*

*The original airside control tower now overlooks a sheltered patio between the two main sections of Building One—Frank Loprano.*

"I remember it well—from July to July, birthday to birthday," states Jerry Matyiko. "While many reports call it a five or six month process ... probably meaning just when the building was in motion ... Newark was a yearlong project for many of us. We had to return many times during reconstruction, removing steel and jacking the wings down one at a time. It was a logistical challenge: moving 9,600 tons almost a mile in three pieces is one thing; getting all the bits and pieces and people there and back and organizing everything on-site is another. Actually, it went pretty well and we learned a lot."

As Pete recalled: "Yes, it was my biggest project, but not necessarily the hardest one; they all have their challenges. Block Island lighthouse, for example ... it took a long time to figure out how to move the two buildings at once. Sometimes, the smaller buildings are trickier, like the livery stable in Minneapolis ... we almost lost that one; and that little creamery south of Chicago might even rate as my hardest. This Newark job didn't get nearly as much attention as Hatteras, but it was almost as challenging: we had to fit all the dollies underneath with enough room so they could still turn. We did it, and I'm really happy to have been part of it."

Although relocation of the Newark terminal did not attract media attention and public fascination to the same degree as Cape Hatteras Lighthouse, it certainly did capture attention of the engineering community and the structural-moving industry. Local and regional recognition came in the form of various awards for excellence in historical preservation and restoration design. Also, the IASM recognized the Newark project participants with an award for heaviest building ever moved on rubber-tired dollies. Although heavier buildings had been relocated elsewhere in the world—on steel wheels and railway track—this 6,800-ton air terminal section is generally regarded as the heaviest moved anywhere on pneumatic tires.

Conspicuously absent from Newark International Airport's resume of successful building relocation is any reference in the *Guinness Book of World Records*. Although moving the 13.6-million-pound center section or the 19.2 million pounds of the entire 1935 Art Deco passenger terminal might well qualify for a world record, its movers have declined to make any such formal request. "Well, they say Guinness is good for you," said Pete Friesen with a smile, "but surely nobody needs more than four at a time. We had enough and didn't ask for any more."

# 19

## Lynden

During the 1980s, Edith and Pete Friesen were living in Downers Grove, near the West Chicago office of AMC. Having previously survived bankruptcy in western Canada and then acquired the structural-moving division of Belding Engineering in the early 1970s, Pete had relocated hundreds of buildings in northeastern Illinois, including a fire station in Highland Park, a jewelry store in Joliet, and the Widow Clarke house in Chicago. In 1980, Mr. Mover's experience and innovative technique were instrumental in his relocation of a fragile, century-old livery stable for historic preservation in Minneapolis, Minnesota. Five years later, Pete agreed to be project consultant for a six-block relocation of the historic Fairmount Hotel in San Antonio, Texas.

After almost forty years in the house-moving business, Pete and Edith had been discussing their desire to sell the company and return to western Canada. Unfortunately, business turned a bit sour during the next few years: among other things, "hard-luck" steel beams and a "haunted house" pushed Pete and his company into dire financial straits. Fortunately, Pete met a promising young house mover, Dell Davis, who soon acquired ownership of AMC. While Pete agreed to remain project consultant for this new Dell-Mar Corporation, he and Edith packed up and moved west in May 1989.

Although their intended destination was Abbotsford, British Columbia, near their original family farmstead in the lower Fraser Valley, the U.S. Internal Revenue Service (IRS) had other ideas. Insisting that Pete Friesen owed them thousands of dollars, the IRS would not allow the couple to move north across the border. After weeks of delay, the IRS finally discovered the problem and admitted to its own mistake. The Friesens were given a green light to live where they wanted. However, by this time, Edith and Pete had found a lovely home in a small city just south of the border, and in that state's hundredth anniversary, the Friesens moved to Lynden, Washington. "We liked it a lot," Pete recalled. "Lynden is a small, clean city in a thriving agricultural district … just like across the border and only about twenty miles from our old farm in Yarrow. Besides the cozy house, Lynden has a low crime rate and lots of churches in a community full of farmers."

Founded in 1871, Lynden is less than twenty miles southeast of is its only sister city—Langley, British Columbia. Way back in 1948, Pete began his structural-moving career in Langley when he and Arthur Dyck, using a few rudimentary tools and infinite imagination, learned how to jack up a house and move it off a difficult property. Although in a different country than originally planned, Edith and Pete were on familiar terrain and close to many friends and relatives, including some of their children. Nevertheless, settling into their new home was an intermittent procedure for Pete the structural-moving consultant, who often flew out of nearby Bellingham or Seattle to project commitments in the eastern states. During the first few years in Lynden, Pete worked with Dell Davis to help move hundreds of buildings in and around Chicago and Detroit, including one complete shopping center, one heritage mansion, and a challenging old creamery.

In the early 1990s, Jerry Matyiko invited Pete to consult for a major relocation project on the east coast. Pete accepted the invitation and soon found himself part of a very professional team—Expert House Movers, International Chimney Corporation, and Friesen Consulting—that completed nine major relocation projects in as many years. Beginning in 1992 with the planning for Southeast Light on Block Island, the Three Houseketeers moved tall lighthouses, school gymnasiums, monster chimneys, and classic old theaters. In 1999, they collaborated on the "Move of Century" by relocating Cape Hatteras Lighthouse. They began the new century by moving Newark Liberty International Airport's original passenger terminal three-quarters of a mile on 1,312 rubber tires.

Pete Friesen's long career as a professional house mover was nothing short of amazing. Never having apprenticed under anyone else or been tutored after buying his first miniscule operation, Pete was allowed free range of imagination and mechanical aptitude. Ever since lifting the wooden grain shed from his bruised working partner in 1948, Pete had seen job safety as his foremost concern. His self-designed wide-flange crib-jacks and his commitment to a 3:1 height-to-base safety ratio were initial steps in his lifelong process of discovery and invention. Without being trained otherwise, Pete could recognize the potential for raising a building with hydraulic pressure. Without knowing any better, he simply designed the first known unified hydraulic jacking system—a device that got bigger and better with time.

He may not have attempted it again or recommended it to anyone else, but Pete's first house move, up the steep and twisting Sumas Mountain Road, filled him with ideas and questions about building weight distribution and centers of gravity. Subsequently, he developed and shared a method for mathematically calculating these all-important factors that so strongly influence selection of equipment and technique. Forty years after this first challenging move, Mr. Mover became well acquainted with computers and soon designed software for calculating building weights and finding centers of gravity. Appropriate for structures of any size or design, these computer aids were made immediately available to everyone in the industry. Fifteen years before buying his computer, Pete had introduced his hydraulic three-zone loading principle to rails and rollers (roll-tracks and creeper-dollies) while moving a building heavier than any he had previously attempted. The following year, he successfully moved an even heavier building while initiating use of the three-point principle with rubber-tired dollies. Soon thereafter, Pete's three-zone method became an accepted industry-wide standard, and it is still used for major building relocations in North America.

Soon after returning to Lynden following the 2001 Newark air-terminal move, Pete received a telephone call from his old friend Dell Davis, who had also moved west to Washington State several years prior. Now working with Lindsay Moving and Rigging of Seattle, Dell informed Pete about a relocation project being considered by that company. The job wasn't humungous, but it would be tricky. Not way over on the east coast, it was only one state away in the town of Preston in the southeast corner of Idaho … assuming preservation-minded people there could raise enough money to move a certain registered heritage building to safety.

The building in question was the Oneida Stake Academy, a three-story sandstone and masonry schoolhouse built between 1890 and 1895 by the Church of Jesus Christ of Latter-day Saints (LDS). Long serving as one of the finest education centers in the area, the academy had been sold to the Preston School District in 1922, when the church decided to get out of the public education system. This Romanesque structure with an octagonal bell tower became Preston High School, and over the decades, students have filled that tower with their signatures. In the 1940s, the growing community built a larger high school on adjacent property, hiding the ornate face of the academy and relegating it to annex status. In 2003, to make room for a very necessary addition to the newer high school, the Oneida Stake Academy was scheduled for demolition unless it could be relocated. "Sure thing, Dell," said Pete. "If you guys land the contract, I'd be happy to consult on the project."

This academy in Preston is one of thirty-four such educational centers built by the LDS in the western United States, Canada, and Mexico around the turn of the twentieth century. Recognizing it as one of the few still standing as well as the alma mater of two of the LDS Church's presidents, the Mormon Historic Sites Foundation (MHSF) of Salt Lake City began a concentrated fundraising campaign to save it. With help from a Preston-based volunteer group, Friends of the Academy, the MHSF went looking for the necessary $1.2 million needed to move the historic structure into a nearby park. Thanks to substantial last-minute private donations, just hours before a demolition contract was about to be signed, the MHSF awarded a contract to Lindsay Moving and Rigging for relocation. Sure enough, eighty-one-year-old Pete Friesen's career in the structural-moving industry was still alive and well: within weeks of the agreement, he joined project foreman Dell Davis on the job in Preston. "I was astounded by the beauty of it," recalled Pete. "We looked the old building over and made careful measurements. When we headed off to do our calculations, the school officials and the fundraisers seemed very relieved to hear us say we were confident about being able to move it."

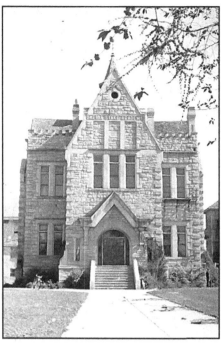

*A 1939 photograph of the Oneida Stake Academy—OSA Foundation.*

Measuring 60' by 80' and composed primarily of concrete and sandstone, the Oneida Stake Academy and its prescribed network of supporting steel beams was expected to weigh in the neighborhood of 1,700 tons. According to the project foreman and his consultant, the move would need fewer than fifty heavy-duty jacks and fifty standard-size transport dollies. Work began on August 18, 2003. However, as with most century-old structures, there were a few anomalies and unforeseen delays. In this case, it was barely surprising for Dell and Pete to discover the academy's two-foot-thick walls were not solid stone; instead, similar to many others of their age, these walls contained tons of unconsolidated stone rubble encased between two vertical plates of stone masonry. Therefore, to provide the necessary degree of strength, all walls on the lower two floors of the building were filled with concrete grout pumped through holes drilled in their masonry exteriors. Once the grout had stabilized the building, the moving crew could continue using their four-foot diamond-tipped power saw to sever the building from its foundation.

Through openings carved into the walls went three twenty-four-inch-deep main load beams inserted on the structure's long axis. Above and horizontally perpendicular to the main beams came twenty-one pieces of cross-steel, each piece being one fourteen-inch-deep beam. On a carefully arranged network of crib piles, in accordance with the consultant's three-zone loading system, the crew placed fifty inverted fifty-ton hydraulic jacks beneath the main load beams. To lock the steel support network in place and further stabilize the 108-year-old masonry walls, four thirty-six-inch-deep strong-back beams were secured around the base of the building. Mounted on the rear-wall strong-back, a nineteen-circuit jacking machine supplied unified hydraulic pressure to thirty-eight jacks through a splitter manifold. The jacking machine's common-pressure outlets supplied twelve additional helper jacks that were integrated into the consultant's three-zone system. Lifting easily on fourteen-inch jack cycles, the building was soon high enough to accept dollies underneath.

Working within and around the carefully planned network of crib piles, dolly wranglers wrestled forty-one transport dollies into place beneath the load. Across the nine rows of dolly-mounted jack rams came nine fourteen-inch-deep rocker beams to unify each row. Twenty-three of the dollies were self-propelled units responsible for horizontal movement; in customary fashion, they were evenly distributed and located near the formation's perimeter. Energized by hydraulic fluid from an auxiliary pump, these powered dollies would pull the revered academy to its new home while helping support its considerable weight. Before motoring off its old lot, however, the building required a rotation of ninety degrees around its vertical axis. Adding pressure to a lengthy relocation process, the supporting steel matrix recently assembled beneath the old academy now extended to within a few inches of the newer high school's main structure; the academy's fragile stonework was only fifteen feet away. It was now early in December, and snow showers were in the forecast.

On the evening of December 10, a small crowd of supporters and doubters gathered to witness the moving crew's attempt to rotate 1,650 tons of steel and masonry through ninety degrees without contacting the adjacent school building. To improve traction on the slippery ground, sheets of plywood were placed beneath the angled tires of the powered dollies. Crack! Snap! Crack! Workers and spectators alike were shocked by harsh and discouraging sounds. Fortunately, the cause of the noise was quickly identified to be the cold plywood unmercifully stressed by the immense weight moving across it. Mild applause and shouts of joy accompanied Oneida Stake Academy as it rotated flawlessly and headed toward the nearby street. There, at curbside, the huge load remained motionless for five days while city officials finalized arrangements to fully occupy two city streets for several days of transit.

During this break in the action, Pete had an opportunity to speak to an assembly of Preston High School students. As usual, Pete's talk was warm and friendly. In fact, his presentation was so well received, he was invited back for an encore performance that included numerous parents and teachers. After sharing information about his own life and about how he goes about the business of relocating buildings, he provided detailed information about the process for moving the Oneida Stake Academy while celebrating how preservation through relocation allows vintage buildings to offer many more years of productive use. Always wanting to inspire young people who might find themselves in desperate circumstances as he once was, Pete included ample references to his visualization techniques while urging his audience to persevere, to look on the bright side, and to never give up. Recounting several "impossible" situations he had overcome, the octogenarian house mover reminded the young students that real life is about learning from serious challenges, and not about celebrating easy victories. In closing, he recited one of his favorite verses:

> When the road is rough and the going gets tough,
> Think it through—oh yes, please do!
> And when you've done all you can to visualize,
> Then go to the Maker of earth and skies.
> Ask Him to be your guide and you will surely
> Be in for a smoother ride.

The forecasted high winds and snow flurries arrived just in time to accompany the historic academy for the most difficult portion of its journey. From its temporary parking spot, a two-foot drop in elevation led onto a steeply crowned roadway where forward progress was to begin with another ninety-degree building rotation. Facing difficult terrain and slippery surfaces, the moving crew was more than a little challenged to keep the building on an even keel while completing their mandatory maneuvers. "It was tricky!" Pete recalled. "Using the full fourteen-inch stroke on our dolly-jacks, we needed an additional six inches of cribbing at the front and eighteen inches of cribbing at the back end ... from one corner of the building to another, there was a total ground variation of more than three feet. At one point, we had to engage the dolly brakes to control the speed of the load ... later, we had to chain some of the dolly axles to the main beams so they would stay straight on the icy backside of the [road] crown. It was awkward sometimes, but we made it."

Weighing a total of 1,650 tons or 3.3 millions pounds, the fragile load was finally centered on the crowned pavement, where the movers had a much easier time with it. Using the trusty "come-along and chains" steering technique, they guided their self-propelled academy-in-motion slowly up the street and around a tight ninety-degree corner before ushering it another few blocks to its new home. During this phase, many local residents who were without electrical power because of the building-in-transit chose to line their streets and cheer for early completion of the project. While confronting uncooperative dollies and less-than-perfect weather conditions, Mr. Mover was occasionally humored and inspired by the voices of student spectators: "Think it through! Visualize! Don't forget to *derch denche* it, Mr. Friesen!"

Late in the afternoon of December 18, 2003, the 108-year-old Oneida Stake Academy was gracefully parked at its new Benson Park home. Sitting on a new nine-foot-deep foundation and restored by funds raised through the Oneida Stake Academy Foundation of Preston and the MHSF, the sandstone schoolhouse of 1895 was being returned to service as a community center and tourist information office. "It's funny," says Pete Friesen, "I've learned to like a lot of old buildings while moving them, but there's something special about this one. It's always fun solving unforeseen problems and moving a historic building, especially when it happens like this one ... without so much as a crack in century-old construction. It's always satisfying to help preserve an old school ... along with all the care and attention that went into building it."

*The Oneida Stake Academy moving crew of 2003—OSA Foundation.*

This heartwarming adventure did not signal the end of Pete Friesen's structural-moving career—in fact, far from it, for as well as continuing to consult on particularly difficult moving projects, he also maintained his reputation as a freethinking machinery inventor. In 2006, he and Dell Davis designed a new transport dolly for use by the structural moving industry. Although it would retain the size and strength of existing dollies, their new hydraulically powered unit would also operate in a reverse direction while having two electronically steerable axles. It's difficult to imagine a better dolly.

Understandably, the dolly idea had materialized while Pete's mind was wrestling with the multitudes of tire angles under the Gem, Shubert, and Newark buildings. Of course, when Pete first shared it with manufacturers and engineers, they pooh-poohed the idea, claiming it couldn't be done … it was impossible. However, such comment was of no concern to the self-taught house mover who had learned to pirouette, sashay, and slither large buildings into place forty years after designing his first unified hydraulic jacking machine. Pete Friesen and Dell Davis put several of their prototype dollies into service and received excellent reviews from users.

Recognized as an entertaining speaker with more availability because of his recent mini-retirement, Pete received more and more invitations to address schools, service groups, and professional organizations. While enjoying these public opportunities, he was also being encouraged by friends and associates to reach a wider audience through a book or a film about his experiences. Although appreciating the value of these media for recording his industry's achievements and for spreading a motivational message, Pete was not particularly excited by the prospect. "I'm not a writer. I'm not a filmmaker. I am not a real storyteller or a real engineer. I am just a building mover! I may have been blessed with a good memory and a good imagination, but I have nothing new to say. Besides, any success I have enjoyed came because of the great creator Lord and with help from my friends and fellow house movers."

Although known as a very determined and sometimes stubborn man, Pete Friesen has long embraced the values of truth and understanding. Having been within seconds of suicide as an oppressed youngster, he knows it is never too late for change. Having survived a broad spectrum of desperate circumstance in his lifetime, he knows the world always has room for encouraging words. Completed and released in 2007, the motion picture *Pete: Moving Man Made Mountains* presented an overview of his life experience while chronicling many of his structural-moving achievements.

As shown in the film, the hearts of Edith and Pete Friesen were deeply scoured by sorrow with loss of their two eldest children, Peter and Paul. In somewhat obscure circumstances, they died four years apart in the late 1990s; both were around fifty years of age. Sadly, the dark world of drug use was involved in both instances. Remembered as fun-loving and cooperative children who loved people and pets, they were deeply missed by siblings Jon, Eric, and Joy as well as by their parents. Naturally, Pete searched the past for clues regarding his fatherly role and the loss of his sons: "We were a close-knit family until the early 1960s when my house-moving business started really taking off. As well as work-related pressures, I was heavily involved with church work and helping establish a school [university] ... I think I was sitting on nine different boards at the time. Then I got committed to moving houses up the Canadian coast and then starting a new business building them. After going broke and being alone in northern BC, my work took me to the States, and our family was really spread out. By then, the oldest boys were twenty and pretty much on their own … I wasn't around much when they were teenagers."

Parenting is an imperfect science, and self-realization is a lifelong mission. In his prime, Pete was riding a wave of historic proportion while taking himself and his industry into unknown territory. It was exciting! Presumably, as do many young men, he felt pushed to prove himself; given his early childhood experience, he may have been extremely motivated to exceed his father's oft-stated judgment and perceived low expectations of him. In any case, while being enlightened by life-threatening situations, Pete Friesen threw off the mantle of mediocrity and energetically followed his instincts—his human *being*—by forever walking through the doors of opportunity. Unconfined by many of the parameters defining "normal," Pete allowed his mind free wander while never giving up on difficult problems or challenging deeds. As well as exploring his own imagination and pushing the limits of his own physical ability, Pete helped create an association of professional colleagues before becoming part of a relocation team dedicated to doing the impossible.

Pete Friesen summarized his career very simply: "Yes, the most rewarding and satisfying thing was being able to relocate those large heritage buildings that all the experts claimed were impossible to move. But if I had it to do all over again, I would find a way to spend more time with my family … especially when the kids are growing up." While enjoying the presence of his children, grandchildren, nieces, and nephews later in life, Mr. Mover also found comfort in seeing young people benefit from the community centers he helped preserve and seeing others graduate from schools he has helped create and relocate.

Living in Lynden was wonderful for Edith and Pete. Close to many old friends and several family members, they enjoyed the small city's serenity; Pete also appreciated the quality and proximity of a local golf course. Nevertheless, for the first time in decades, Mr. Mover was home more than he was away. While Edith attacked the daily crossword puzzle, Pete was on the telephone or at his computer—there were dollies to produce and a book to write!

*From their home in Lynden, Washington, Edith and Pete Friesen send
best wishes for a joyous Christmas and for happiness in the new year of 2008.*

Indeed, Pete's story is worth telling. Researching the details and probing his past makes it obvious that Pete Friesen was in a class by himself. Very few people have challenged themselves to the extent he did. While discovering how to manage his first house-move, he recognized the need for safety and better tools; at twenty-six years of age, Pete designed and manufactured the original wide-flanged screw jack with a threaded ram also projecting downwards between crib blocks. A few years later, Pete designed and manufactured the original quick-change hydraulic crib jack with a polished ram-piston within an actuating cylinder that could be positioned vertically through the wide-flange base while capable of being locked in any one of numerous available positions. As far as can be determined, no one else on the continent was manufacturing these gizmos, and no one else in his vicinity was hooking them up to hydraulic hoses at the time. Pete's design and manufacture of a unified hydraulic jacking unit to activate dozens of these jacks at the same time and rate took his profession to a new plateau. The jacking machine continues to speak for itself.

By forty years of age, Pete was managing a house-moving company in a small corner of North America, in the southwest corner of

British Columbia, where population and development were modest by metropolitan standards. Nevertheless, through perseverance and commitment as well as by generous assistance from his jacking machine, his company became known for completing four hundred successful jobs in one year. Modern Building Movers also had the distinction of moving fourteen houses in one day with help from another Pete-style invention. When the option of moving prefabricated houses by ocean-going barge presented itself, Pete, in customary fashion, walked through the door of opportunity. Soon after entering another phase, he designed and manufactured a one-of-a-kind house-moving trailer with extendable outrigger arms and jacks, enabling the on-loading and off-loading of ten buildings within a two-hour window governed by tidal conditions. The design of this unique and functional tool probably grew from his experience with related equipment and from seeing similar inventions at work in other industries. Nevertheless, Pete's mobile house-moving apparatus was regarded as the first of its kind on Canada's west coast, and it might yet be the only one.

Pete Friesen did not invent prefabricated housing. Although his manual assembly line might be considered more of a creation than an invention, his 1966 house-building factory was probably the first—and maybe the only one—to produce forty-eight living units per day with only fifty-seven employees. Pushed by sudden expansion of his house-building enterprise, Pete was far more absorbed in matters of design and production than he was in issues relating to dollars or documents. There would be time to deal with administrative details later; meanwhile, he was committed to manufacturing and shipping four thousand living units off to Montreal. Unfortunately, political interference can destroy very efficient operations anywhere.

Rescued from bankruptcy by a fortuitous telephone invitation, Pete then surfaced in Chicago where he carried a wealth of practical experience into an industry on the verge of explosive growth. Although derivatives of his jacking machine invention were being widely used, Pete's empirically obtained theories and methods were still rare within the structural-moving industry. Once proven in the field, Pete's original-to-him 3:1 height-to-base safety ratio became an accepted industry standard. His original, mathematical procedures for determining building weights and locating their centers of gravity were not the only ones of their kind; however, they were among the best, and they were easy to use. Pete being Pete, they were widely shared.

Pete did not invent three-point loading; it had been in use since time immemorial and had been instinctively employed by almost every house mover for decades. However, he has been credited as being most probably the first mover in North America to refine the principle and to apply it with hydraulic systems for relocating buildings on rubber-tired dollies as well as on rails and rollers. While performing thousands of routine house moves, Pete also risked everything by accepting projects regarded by others as "impossible" moves. As a result, he became accustomed to handling older, larger, and more fragile structures, often of historic or architectural significance.

Motivated by trust in God and faith in himself, Pete was unafraid to attempt very challenging projects; as a result, he was often forced to come up with new equipment and/or new procedures to avoid dismal failures or calamity. The boxed-beam roll-tracks, shoe beams, and inverted jacks of the fire station in Highland Park were seen as novel ideas. If not a first-time procedure, the gravity-induced, downhill slide of one heritage building toward another in Minneapolis was certainly an exciting experience. Thank goodness for pneumatic brakes and toggled come-along steering.

Pete's faith, trust, intuition, and innate mechanical aptitude seemed to carry him through ... for the most part. Interestingly, every one of his initial, envelope-pushing moves came within inches of career-ending catastrophe. The Highland Park fire station came within a crescent wrench of a four-foot freefall; Liebermann's jewelry store almost took a nosedive through a concrete sidewalk; the Widow Clarke house came within a dangling loader of a twenty-seven-foot flight; the Brown-Ryan Livery Stable was one brake handle away from taking out two buildings, twenty jobs, and millions of dollars; the Fairmount Hotel was one man's honest confession away from a totally ugly collapse. "Golly, gee whiz!" (or some such thing) we might all exclaim in unison. Ironically, after surviving all these dramatic near-misses, Pete Friesen's company seems to have been nickel-and-dimed out of business by a couple of ornery fifty-foot beams with a bad reputation. This little story within a story seems beyond easy comprehension and any attempted explanation. Who knows?

Life changed measurably for Pete when he sold his established company to become a freelance consultant. Once freed of company ownership and its paper-pushing, he could explore the limits of structural-moving capabilities without distraction. The project consultant could focus totally on the one important task at hand without being unduly concerned about workforce, administration, or finances. He was free to let his imagination wander through the project from beginning to end; he was allowed to invent new tools or new ideas to get around old problems; he was invited to share his envelope-pushing possibilities. He was a happy man doing something he loved doing. Along the way, Pete's mathematical formulae became computer programs for finding building weights and centers of gravity.

During fifteen years consulting on very challenging projects, Pete extended his industry's limits beyond what almost everyone thought possible. Amazingly, these huge and unprecedented moves produced not even one of the dramatic, near-miss incidents he had previously experienced. Impressive for their size alone, many of these later building moves inspired innovation and invention. If nothing else, most of them incited a novel approach in dealing with unfamiliar circumstances. The three disparate sections of the Southeast Lighthouse moved as one unit in a three-legged, zig-zag pattern on roll-tracks. Highland Light swayed into position on bent roll-tracks. The towering chimney in State College rotated into position on sliding plates. Negotiating barely consolidated terrain, the Gem Theatre pirouetted into alignment on a multitude of dollies. Similarly, the Shubert Theater sashayed home on dollies arcing between surface obstructions and a subterranean trap. Cape Hatteras Lighthouse made it to safety because of the consultant's inspiration of subdividing his loading zones into cells. The Newark Airport passenger terminal slithered home, around an imposing construction site, while having its cross-steel beams and main beams in atypical reversed order. The elderly collection of sandstone known as Oneida Stake Academy maintained alignment and traction on icy, crowned streets by having its dolly struts chained to its main beams underneath. Of course, there were jack failures and other hiccups in some of these complex procedures, but all of them were completed successfully without damage to the building or to its movers.

As summarized by some of his colleagues, many of the ultra-heavy, complicated relocations of the late twentieth century would never have happened without the vision and dedication of Pete Friesen. Reviewing the outstanding accomplishments of this man who moved more than four thousand buildings in his career, it is sometimes easy to forget where he came from. Considering the conditions that surrounded his birthplace, his life was a surprise. It's a long way from eighth-grade dropout to the Opal award, especially with career changes and bankruptcy interruptions enroute. Filled with investigation and discovery, challenge and realization, Pete's life led him far beyond the strict parameters of his early upbringing. Following his own motto, he has walked through countless doors of opportunity and done many things beyond the dreams of many people. Although he made mistakes, he never gave up. He consistently made the very best of every situation and learned valuable lessons where few have dared to go. Blessed with faith and understanding, Pete Friesen was always philosophical about hard knocks and fresh starts. Many people were encouraged by his straightforward manner and warmed by his love and compassion. He may not have been a perfect person, but Pete Friesen was perfectly human.

*Pete being interviewed during film production in 2004—Gary Fiegehen.*

Pete had this to say: "Since retiring, I have done a lot of thinking about the past eighty some years, and in the big picture, I am just a little pip-squeak. Although I have enjoyed more success than my father ever said I would, it's not because I am smarter than he thought. I've just been pushed and pulled and sometimes kicked ... in different directions. For example, when I was kicked out of the Mennonite Brethren Church, I went to another church where I met another house mover who wanted to sell his business that came complete with government contracts ... and I bought it. Later, when BC Hydro called to see if I could use their surplus office trailers, I just happened to be looking for dormitories for the junior college we were trying to get started. My whole life has been like that. Oh, how great God is!"

Being a devout Mennonite who recognized Jesus as his savior, Pete Friesen considered life on earth to be adventurous education. He regarded challenges and failures as learning experiences, opportunities to better know one's true being and to help prepare for the mysteries ahead. He did not hold his spiritual ideals higher than anyone else's, and he did not criticize the beliefs of others. Along with his gentle manner and trustworthy demeanor, Pete carried a warm smile and a twinkle in his eye. While his dedication to the matter of the moment could be frightening as well as commendable, his sense of humor was infectious. Although Pete downplayed his brainpower and sometimes professed to have been bounced around by life, a more objective view suggests he used his mind to investigate whatever doors opened to him. Faith in his creator brought Pete belief in his own creativity along with trust in his worldly path.

While it would require someone closer to accurately comment on his spiritual journey, it is obvious Pete Friesen had human dimensions far beyond his acknowledged ability to solve mechanical puzzles. Inside his cozy home, which is heavily adorned with pictures and plaques celebrating engineering success throughout North America, it is difficult to see Pete as an infant in the violent uncertainty of revolutionary Russia. Many of us can only imagine his family's experience of a narrow escape before abrupt introduction to a new land, to a strange language, and to a different way of living. Raised on the Depression-era prairies and receiving limited formal education, Pete soon launched himself into an unknown world of demanding technical expertise. While we can visualize much of his journey, we cannot truly appreciate the magnitude and frequency of the numerous challenges he faced. Lo and behold, Pete passed through one new door of opportunity after another. He pursued his God-given talents, and he never gave up! Of course, the majority of vocational awards around Edith and Pete's home in Lynden have derived from Pete's participation in significant mega-moves of the previous fifteen years. Ironically, all these super-major projects—Block Island to Cape Hatteras and beyond—occurred after Pete had already "retired" from his forty-year structural-moving career. However, while living a lifetime of moving experience, Pete always treasured memories from his trail-breaking days of an earlier era.

Back in February 1986, at the fourth annual convention of the IASM in Portland, Oregon, the IASM Awards Committee presented Pete Friesen with a lifetime achievement award. Of all the world records and symbols of success received during his career, Pete treasured this plaque more than any other. "It is an honor to be recognized by my fellow house movers in this way," stated Pete with emotion. "This award is very precious to me."

*To Pete Friesen who spent a lifetime doing the impossible*
*And made it possible for others to do likewise*

—*Gary Fiegehen.*

# Epilogue

It was a pleasure working with Pete Friesen and an honor sharing his story. This two-year process was inspirational and highly informative: as well as getting to know Pete, I learned a lot about house moving and something about the world we live in. I also learned a thing or two about myself. Throughout, Pete was actively involved, probing his memory and scouring his files, questioning old colleagues and providing new contacts. Along the way, it soon became apparent that Peter Dietrich Friesen moved many people as well as many buildings in his lifetime. While always expressing appreciation and hearty encouragement, he reviewed and improved every page of every draft chapter. Three weeks after approving the last chapter of his life's story, Mr. Mover himself moved on, passing peacefully from this worldly realm while comforted by his wife, Edith, and their children, Jon, Eric, and Joy. May their great loss be less painful in knowing so many others were touched by Pete's presence and blessed by his spirit.

———— Acknowledgments ————

This book-writing journey was made most enjoyable by Edith and Pete Friesen whose hospitality and candor made it a true labor of love. I am thankful for their willingness to handle myriad telephone messages at almost any time of day and receive unexpected visitors at any time of year. I am very grateful to Pete for answering hundreds of questions via countless phone calls and e-mail messages while reading and rereading every draft of every chapter produced. Along the way, his unswerving commitment led him into deep recesses of his memory and into some pretty "dusty" old computer files. Thank you, Pete. Throughout the process, his enthusiastic personal assistant, Cheri McKay, ably organized our vast collection of related information and contributed useful editorial input while facilitating our communication. Thank you, Cheri. The project first got underway when filmmaker William L. Stewart introduced me to Pete Friesen and introduced Pete to the idea of my writing his story. Thank you, Bill. Most notably, this written work greatly benefits from the encouragement and editorial services offered by the writer's loving companion. Thank you, Susan.

My thanks are extended to many people throughout North America who helped with telling this story. Pete's nephew, Tom Friesen, got it underway in fine style by sharing his excellent essay on early family history. Also, Pete's first cousin Cornelius "Neil" Heinrichs contributed significantly to the accuracy of that early material. Pete's Bible-school buddy and Canadian Army colleague Henry Warkentien provided information about his lifelong friendship with him. Having fortunately survived their first two relocation projects together, Arthur Dyck was able to provide insights into the early days of moving houses with Pete.

Now a retired anthropologist from the University of Alberta, Rod Wilson gave us colorful and enthusiastic impressions of life among the house movers while he was a student employee during the 1950s.

For Pete's subsequent career in the United States, we are deeply grateful to his longtime friend and structural-moving colleague Carl Tuxill, who provided a collection of technical details regarding numerous building moves over a three-decade time span.

In Highland Park, thanks go to Julia Johnas at the public library and to Kathy Leable at the historical society. Alan Wax, Chief of the Highland Park Fire Department, provided important details while directing research toward a history of the fire department written by a retired member. Thank you, Thomas O'Donovan. Also of great help was Charlotte Landsman, Manager of Youth Services in Highland Park.

In nearby Joliet, great thanks go out to Art Liebermann and his family of jewelers who so generously shared details while taking time to review written accounts. Former city engineer John Mezera and Heather Bigeck at the Joliet Historical Museum also helped fill in some blanks for that local saga.

In Chicago, Meg Givhan and Tim Samuelson of that city's cultural affairs department answered important questions and provided accurate directions for further research. Edward M. Maldonado, Curator of the Clarke House Museum, helped with valuable information about that project while restoration architect Wilbert Hasbrouck kindly offered details about the building and about the person who moved it.

In Minneapolis, I am deeply indebted to personnel of various city departments for their help in recounting the livery stable project. Special thanks go to Ann Calvert at Community Planning and Economic Development, to Eileen Kilpatrick at the Parks and Recreation Board, and to Richard Victor of the Housing and Redevelopment Authority. Our second chapter in Minneapolis, for the Shubert Theater project, also found keen interest among city agencies. My heartfelt thanks are extended to information specialist Sarah Parker of Creative Communications, to Jackie Cherryhomes, former President of Minneapolis City Council; to Kimberley Motes and Sarah Thompson, Directors of the new Minnesota Shubert Center; and to L. Kelley Lindquist, President of Artspace.

Down south in San Antonio, my thanks are directed to Lani Fulgencio at the Fairmount Hotel for helpful information about the building's history and its current owner. Sincere thanks also go to Beth Standifird of the San Antonio Conservation Society, who provided the basics while directing me to a published book, *Saving San Antonio: The Precarious Preservation of a Heritage*, which contained answers to most of my questions. Many thanks to the Conservation Society and to the book's author, Lewis Fisher, for permitting liberal use of excerpts and quotations from such excellent work.

More architectural preservationist than house mover, Bill Lee of Missouri is responsible for kicking off the chapter about the IASM, which also received helpful information from mover James Drake of Texas and from insurance-man Dave Pizur of Wisconsin. My sincere thanks is hereby extended to the two heroes of IASM formation, James Kabrick of Indiana and Allen Cansler of Georgia, who took time to share their stories and to review the chapter drafts. Thank you, gentlemen—may your organization live long and happy!

As Pete's career evolved to another phase, Delmar "Dell" Davis gave us great insights into his family of house movers and into his working relationship with Pete while describing their five years of intense activity. Pete's one-time secretary and long-time friend Karen Snyder warmly offered helpful and timely perspective. Also contributing to the Illinois portion of this segment were Joy Donahue of River Forest Public Library and Judy K. Herder of the Frankfort Area Historical Society.

Working on America's east coast, Pete's consulting career brought him into close working relationships with other movers and project-related engineers who willingly shared information pertinent to our story. First and foremost among them is Jerry Matyiko of Expert House Movers who, usually from a cell phone under a building somewhere, always graciously filled in the blanks with correct details about many projects while bringing me up to date with industry developments and his broadly based family business within it. George Gardner, Chief Engineer of ICC, also worked closely alongside Pete and volunteered information as well as time to review written drafts. Thank you, Houseketeers—well done!

Special thanks go out to ICC for encouraging the book project and for supplying a great deal of information. Among ICC staff members who helped, engineers Valerie Dumont, Mark Prible, and Joe Jakubik were able to offer considerable information about Pete and their mutual projects.

For his sincere contribution to this book project, Resident Engineer James A. Morocco at New England District of the U.S. Army Corps of Engineers deserves a big thank you. Similarly appreciated is Larry Rosenberg, its Chief of Public Affairs, who provided numerous details about several major relocations within their domain.

Over on Block Island, thanks go directly to Dr. Gerald Abbott, President of Block Island Historical Society and Southeast Light Foundation; having been instrumental in seeing the lighthouse preserved, Dr. Abbott donated information and words to this written account. Sincere thanks also go the organization's Executive Director Lisa Nolan for helping with details and directions. Up on Cape Cod, my thanks go to Gordon Russell of Truro Historical Society, to Francene Webster of Highland Museum and Lighthouse Corporation; and to Shirley Sabin of Nauset Light Preservation Society.

In Detroit, a warm thank you is extended to Mr. Charles Forbes who reviewed a written account of the relocation project administered by Forbes Management Group; his comments were most helpful. Also helpful were the Gem-Century Theatres' House Manager Steve Nesbitt and its Public Relations Director Scott Meyers. Thanks also go to Tina Granzo and her inspired *History of Detroit* Web site.

For valuable information about relocation of Cape Hatteras Lighthouse in North Carolina, I am indebted to Kevin Duffus of Looking Glass Productions in Raleigh for sharing his well-researched material regarding original lighthouse construction. Thanks also to photographer Mike Booher and author Lin Ezell for their excellent book on the subject, *Out of Harm's Way: Moving America's Lighthouse*. Another on-site participant, David Fischetti of DCF Engineering contributed valuable information about the process. Also supplying valuable engineering input were the "sensor guy" Jerry Stockbridge and the "pressure engineer" Bill Jahns. Special thanks go to the unnamed park rangers who delivered oodles of minutiae over the telephone.

Up the coast in New Jersey, Steve Lang of Prismatic Development Corporation helped with the passenger terminal move at Newark

Liberty International Airport and also helped with information for this written story. Frank Loprano, Chief of Aeronautical Operations at the airport, is also thanked for his contribution.

Way out west in Preston, Idaho, Necia Seamons of the Oneida Stake Academy Foundation is congratulated for her community's successful effort to save a heritage building and is warmly thanked for her enthusiastic contribution to this book.

One factor leaving this writer astonished is the not-too-distant-past scenario of researching a nonfiction book project without aid of the World Wide Web. As well as liberal use of Google, Wikipedia, Dictionary.com, and Mapquest, this project required hundreds of visits to scores of other Web sites around cyber-America, including government agencies, municipalities, libraries, museums, corporations, associations, organizations, and foundations referenced above. Then there were all the related sites pertaining to history, science, geography, and the like. To gather and organize sufficient information without Web service is almost unthinkable, and my hat is doffed to all book writers who have gone before.

My sincere thanks are extended to Rob Clark for creating this book's cover design and for coaxing its older photographs back into printable condition. Last but far from least, my heartfelt thanks go out to all the dedicated people at iUniverse for transforming my ramblings into a cohesive story and for publishing it in high-quality, tasteful format. I remain responsible for its errors and omissions.

PER, April 2009